HOW DO YOU FIGHT BACK?

The insurance industry has taken over the nation's healthcare system. **Your rights as a patient** depend on you. Insurance is now trying to take over the justice system –fight back. Their tools are high-paid lobbyists, misinformation, scare tactics, and outright lies.

You need the accurate statistics. As many as 100,000 people are killed each year by hospital error. When you, a loved one or a friend is a victim, will the justice system be there for you? Will you also be victimized by the insurance propaganda machine and your own lack of knowledge?

You will learn how to protect yourself from the few bad doctors and hospitals and how to fight the insurance companies. Their profits and CEO bonuses are accumulated from your premium dollars, at the expense of your welfare.

Your health costs and health insurance premiums go up, not from "frivolous lawsuits" or a "lawsuit crisis," but from bad insurance company investments. The government wants to arbitrarily limit a patient's rights, and you will again be the victim of insurance company propaganda.

FACT: Malpractice premiums comprise less than one percent of total health care costs

FACT: Malpractice victim payouts have been stable and flat since the mid-1980's

FACT: Insurers admit that caps, where

enacted, have not brought down premiums

FACT: Insurance business practices are the cause of high malpractice premiums

FACT: For every 8 incidents of medical malpractice, only one claim is filed

FACT: Jury verdicts are consistent with doctors assessments of the medical record.

FACT: Doctors' premiums have gone up in states where jury verdicts are limited by law

McDonald's never paid anyone millions of dollars for a coffee spill. If you believe they did, you are a victim of the tunnel vision that the insurance industry, and its paid lobbyists, have inflicted on the public in **an effort to make YOU want to limit your own rights.**

ABOUT THE AUTHOR–Michael Townes Watson
Author of four books and numerous articles on law, law and medicine, and mediation practices; Founding director of Tarrant County Hospice Society; Former Adjunct Professor--Medical Malpractice Law--Texas Wesleyan University School of Law; Certified in Civil Trial Law by the Texas Board of Legal Specialization; Mediator for plaintiff and defense lawyers for the resolution of medical cases; Expert witness in legal malpractice cases; Frequent lecturer on a variety of topics in legal seminars; Magna Cum Laude graduate of University of Texas School of Law (1976); Instructor of "Legal Research, Writing and the Court System" to Fulbright Scholars (1975); Licensed to practice in Texas and New York; Previously a trial lawyer in Texas for twenty-five years; Member of the following professional and honorary

associations: American Board of Trial Advocates (two terms on National Board of Directors); Texas Chapter of American Board of Trial Advocates (Secretary-Treasurer 1998-2002); President of the Tarrant County Trial Lawyers Association (1995); Board of Directors of Texas Trial Lawyers Association (1994-2002); Texas Bar Foundation; Tarrant County Bar Foundation; Founding member of Fort Worth Children's Society;

America's Tunnel Vision
How Insurance Companies' Propaganda Is Corrupting Medicine and Law

by MICHAEL TOWNES WATSON

Horatio Press
New York, New York

Printed by BooksJustBooks.com

Attention associations, public interest groups, consumer
organizations, bar associations or conferences: Take 30% off
and use this book or our other titles as premiums, gifts,
fundraisers or promotional material:

Horatio Press
New York, New York

Cover art by Webtonica

Dedication

More thanks than I can possibly express go to my family: My wonderful wife Becky, who has put up with my crazy work schedule and my transformation from a lawyer to a writer; my two amazing and challenging children, Peyton and Tristan, who are not only the best reasons to work, but also the best reasons to play.

Thanks also to the following four lawyers who have, for me, been mentors, challengers and models of professionalism: Judge William S. Sessions, Lawton Gambill, Jim Barlow, and Terry Gardner. Without the examples and unique talents of each of you, my trek in the law would never have taken me where I have been.

Also to the reader, who wants to know more about the system of justice that allows you to have an equal footing with those who would otherwise take advantage of you. That system can continue to be the great equalizer between you and the powerful.

Thanks to all of you,

Mike

CONTENTS

Preface

There are many divergent views about the system of justice that makes decisions regarding the law pertaining to our health care. Despite that divergence, one thing that everyone should be able to agree upon is that our health and our lives are irreplaceable commodities. Most of us would do anything and everything within us to avoid constant pain, the anguish of infirmity and immobility, or the horror of crippling disability. We have a health care system whose purpose is to deliver the necessary care to avoid these injuries, and many people would make great concessions in an effort to preserve access to affordable, quality healthcare. It is becoming increasingly apparent that a majority of people in this country perceive that the use of the justice system to judge the healthcare system may endanger their very ability to receive the benefits of that system. Those people then become susceptible to the argument that the justice system should be sacrificed. That road is a dangerous one, but I will show that the forces are now in place to travel that road. I will show you how we will all be to blame, and will all pay the consequences, if we allow the justice system to be sacrificed, all in the name of a fix.

The health insurance companies have already taken over your healthcare. When was the last time that you went to the hospital or doctors office and they asked you about your health before asking you about your insurance coverage? Now insurance companies are trying to insulate themselves and those same doctors and hospitals from liability when you are hurt or killed as a result of the failure of that healthcare system. They already save money by controlling the delivery of your care, and they now want to save money by not compensating you if that care ultimately harms you. The way they are trying to do this is to leave you powerless to fight back if the healthcare system harms you and your loved ones, insulating themselves and their clients (the doctors and hospitals) from the justice system that everyone else lives by.

Although I have expressed some of my own views on matters in this book, most of the views stated are revealed through objective studies, quotes or paraphrases of various news or periodical articles, or book material. My major imprint on this book is this: if you are going to take a position on the validity of a proposal, it is incumbent upon you to know the reason for the proposal, the motivation of those making the proposal, the effect the proposal will have, and the facts, both in support of and in opposition to the proposal. It is only through that knowledge that our democracy can work properly, and can truly represent the will of the majority, while respecting the critical rights of the minority.

The people of our unique and intriguing country are always mystified by the results of the confluence of the medical and legal systems. The details leading to those results are usually far more complex than the public ever knows. There are several reasons why the public is spared the details: the media, the public's attention span, the self-interest of the people in the conflict, politics, and everyone's differing views of the ideal situation.

When there are clashes between competing interests in society, it is always helpful to go back to our nation's founders to see how they handled such clashes. Their ideals, like those of all thinking people who have made significant and lasting contributions to our nation, were firm and rooted. Despite that, none of our founders could have predicted the details of the nation's future trek, any more than we can now predict the specific course of our nation over the next two centuries. We are, like they, all the same in one respect—we do not surrender lightly our lives, our liberties, our dreams or our happiness. If those are in jeopardy, Americans now, just as then, are perfectly capable of recognizing it and arresting it without some demagogue issuing a call to arms. We are a homogenous mass in the sense that we share a heritage that elevates virtue over vice, action over hollow words, compassion over insensitivity, and the little guy over the idle privileged. We do not need a reason to be proud above the mere fact that we are all Americans, and that most of us got where we got in this world by doing it ourselves, on our own plan, with our own gumption.

Since the beginning of time, when there are actual or potential struggles over cherished values, the law has been created for the benefit or protection of a particular group of people in that struggle. That struggle is always against a real or perceived threat from another group or groups. The frailties and imperfections of men and women require legal rules for that struggle. When one person's idea of morality and good conflicts with that of another person, laws must define what will rule. The laws necessarily become more complicated when there are more diverse groups, more numerous and worthy values, and more sophisticated methods of attack.

Between the time that Moses brought down from the mountain the ten simple commandments that constituted all of "the law," and the time that James Madison, Alexander Hamilton and the other drafters of the *Constitution* set out to draft a guide for government more than two thousand years later, we had come a long way toward understanding those human frailties and imperfections. However, during that same span of time, our society's complexities became infinitely more abundant. One could easily say that our complexities have increased even more in the past two centuries than in those previous two millennia, and the complexities necessarily have increased the need for interpretation of the law, judges, and yes, for lawyers. Does that mean that we are subject to tyranny of the lawyers and the courts, as some suggest? Or could it be that our system of democracy, albeit imperfect, has done its job of mirroring the changes in society; thus, the job of balancing the various competing interest in the struggle has also become more complex?

When the *Constitution* was being circulated among the states for ratification, there were those who had a vested interest in preserving the Articles of Confederation in effect at the time, because it empowered those who were not land owners and thrived on a decentralized government. Those whose interests were more served by those Articles cried "tyranny" in all their circles, when the delegates to the Philadelphia Convention of 1789 created the *Constitution*. The *Constitution* was threatening to some because they believed that the vested landed and other economic interests had lied about their purpose, which had been expressed as simply to make some modest additions and alterations to the Articles of Confederation. History has taught us that the nation would not have survived but for the "tyranny" practiced by those delegates to the Philadelphia Convention. One reason we have survived is that the genius of the framers was to implement a scheme to protect not only economic interests, but also liberty and personal freedom, the very tenets upon which we had fought against the mother country.

Similarly, there are those who now say that our laws are being fostered, administered, and created by lawyer and judge tyrants whose will is only to create a system to perpetuate their own superiority and power. Such an argument is made by former judge, later journalist, and now commentator, Catherine Crier, in her book *The Case Against the Lawyers*. Her arguments are mirrored by many commentators, journalists, corporate interests, and others who fear the results that come from the third branch of that constitutional government–the judiciary. They base their arguments on that same fear of their 18th century predecessors–fear of losing economic power.

So, who are these supposed judicial and legal tyrants who put their trust in twelve fair and impartial peers, just like you, who hear evidence admitted in a tribunal pursuant to equally applied and logical rules? Do these tyrants not advocate the freedom of speech and press for all citizens? Do these tyrants not live by a system that guarantees due process of law to all people regardless of the color of their skin, their religion, or their sex? Do these tyrants not have and cherish the same values, families, fears and freedoms that you have?

If any of us in America wishes to seek out and defuse tyranny, we should study the history of our laws and learn of tyranny's source. It is not in one group of men or women, in one sex, or in one or several occupations, religions, races, or set of beliefs. If it is bound to exist, it is created by the concentration of wealth, power, and influence in a segment of society whose rules are either nonexistent or so hidden that they never see the light of public scrutiny. The CEO's and centers of corporate wealth of yesterday and today will become the despots of tomorrow if we do not find and implement the rules to curb the already known and sure to-bediscovered abuses. That is not to say that corporations, bigness, and money are bad. We have all seen the advances in technology, science, and humanity that are made possible by dedicated human beings supported by corporate largesse, and fostered by our creative and individualistic capitalism. What we don't always see, until it is too late, is the tragedy and needless suffering inflicted by decisions made only for profit, without regard for the betterment of, or injury to, mankind. When our government becomes rife with people of self-interest, and there is intermarriage between the systems of government and the largest of our commercial enterprises, there exists a danger of tyranny beyond any that has ever been conceived in the world's history. Neither the *Constitution*, nor the natural order preserved by it, was meant to be bought.

The hate for courts and lawyers in general, and trial lawyers in particular, has been the subject of increased comment in the media and public commentary. The thesis of much of the comment is that judges and lawyers have some co-ordinated agenda to harm or disrupt society, all for their own pecuniary gain. The Terry Schiavo case, known to many, demonstrated two things: first, the contempt that some have for the workings of the courts and, second, the attitude that "moral values" should be left to the majority, not to this third branch of government. Even though the courts in Florida had rendered their final conclusions, the "majority" in Congress implemented a special legislative directive compelling more litigation in the federal courts, only to obtain the same result. The majority leader in the Senate, a physician, made his diagnosis that Ms. Schiavo was cognizant of her surroundings, based upon his review of a videotape, contrary to the studied and objective testimony of numerous expert neurologists who had examined her. Once the federal court system had affirmed the Florida courts' results, our majority leader in the House of Representatives proclaimed that the people responsible for the death of Terry Schiavo would "pay" for the outcome of that case. That comment was later retracted with a feeble and inadequate apology, but it represented the sentiment of many who believe that the courts are not the best arbiters of our moral tests. Upon the death of Ms. Schiavo, all were forced by her autopsy to conclude that the courts were right after all, but neither of our esteemed Congressional leaders could force himself to recognize the coequality, much less the integrity, of the judiciary. The courts' detractors failed to recognize the depth and quality of the work done by the court system. These detractors argued with legitimate judicial conclusions because they failed to educate themselves about the evidence or procedures that led to the conclusions. Such failures have become commonplace among those who quarrel with legal results.

I was a trial lawyer until four years ago. I handled mostly medical malpractice cases. I no longer do that for a living. I now teach, serve as a mediator for assistance in resolution of disputes, work by appointment of courts on behalf of minors, and work as an expert witness on legal malpractice cases. I still deal with trial lawyers on an everyday basis. I know that trial lawyers are not bad per se; nor are they good per se, and it would seem hollow to argue either proposition about trial lawyers or any other profession as a generality. They are often in the public eye since they work in the court system advocating a certain outcome in specific cases. I recognize that there are many trial lawyers who could use a really good cleaning up with a lot of elbow grease. I will speak to what I think about those who practice in my former occupation, about what they can and should do to change their image, which a lot of my former brethren will not like to hear. I do know, however, that in my twenty-nine years of practicing law, I have come across far more trial lawyers for whom I have respect than for whom I do not.

A number of trial lawyers have some quirks that predominate in their personalities, which sometimes makes them not a very lovable sort. Does that make them all the greedy, scum-sucking loathsome bottom feeders that they are often portrayed? They are just people, imperfect in many more ways than they ever would want to admit, which is no different from people in any other profession–doctors, engineers, accountants, priests, or teachers. For the most part, they got through law school by paying their own way; they have studied and worked hard; they usually find it hard to give their families the time and emotion that they should, or they wait until too late to recognize that failure; and they take themselves far too seriously. Those are some things that they can work on. However, since judicial decision-making is, and always has been, accomplished primarily through an adversarial system, most lawyers who work in that adversarial system find that they are unable to back down from action when they believe it is necessary. To ask them to do otherwise is to deny their Constitutionally-placed role in the system that our founders intentionally created, after themselves enduring hardship, death, deprivation of liberty, and tyranny.

If we choose for our legal system to function without lawyers, you can count on a return to the chains of tyranny which our forefathers fought so hard to unbind. Would any thinking person, with only the most superficial knowledge of history, make the choice to deprive ourselves of the benefits of the knowledge from our struggles? Far more than one book could be written to demonstrate the good of our legal system in our American history. I have given some thought to what I believe were some of the more important of those struggles and the role that lawyers have played, and a very few are briefly portrayed in this book. Although there are many more examples I could use, and certainly many more that I know even nothing about, I hope that these have some interest and value in demonstrating why I am proud to call myself a lawyer. I hope that I can engender such pride in others who read this, and even perhaps spawn an interest for a youngster like the one my father spawned in me. Even if I cannot do that, and you are one who still hates lawyers, that will be fine with me, so long as you do not choose to scrap the framework of the Seventh Amendment to the *Constitution*, granting to every American the right to have a jury of his peers decide legal conflicts over personal lives.

I cannot pinpoint the time that I decided to become a lawyer. I cannot say for sure that it was just because my father and his father were lawyers, since every time may father talked about being a lawyer he simultaneously tried to nudge me in a different direction and suggested alternate paths for me. I cannot say that I saw some inherent evil or imbalance in our society that I felt needed correcting, because I believe that our society does rather well for itself, all of our history considering. I cannot even say that I thought it would make me rich, since it did not do so for my father, my grandfather or my great-grandfather, and it has not done so for me.

What I can say is that, while being a lawyer and trying to be also a student of our history, I have come to believe that the vast majority of Americans have always done their best, and continue to do their best, to shoulder their responsibilities as citizens.

The cynics who bash lawyers now claim that lawyers have somehow destroyed the meaning and intent of the *Constitution*, and that the trial lawyers benefit at the expense of the total welfare. I say that these cynics fail to understand the homogeneity of our great people, the history of our struggles, and the proper balance that was so tediously and perfectly crafted by our founders in Philadelphia more than two centuries ago. Not for one moment do I believe that any group of Americans would sit idly by while any other group or combination of groups becomes tyrants and manipulate others into submission. That is just not the nature of Americans.

Since I am no longer a trial lawyer, I have no vested interest in what some would call the "trial lawyer agenda." We lawyers have become the brunt of jokes, the recipients of criticism, and the "castoffs" in society. But you should not read this preface thinking that I am going to spend this book talking about what great people trial lawyers are and how they all do what they do for benevolent or altruistic motives, because that is not the truth and I do not pretend that it is. While the criticism of trial lawyers is excessive, much of it they have brought upon themselves, and I even count myself among that group. I will point out in this book how I think that has happened and what they can do to change it. I cringe when I see a TV ad with a braggart trial lawyer who claims to obtain bags of money for his injured client. I want to shrink from sight when I hear of a lawsuit claiming that restaurants are responsible for parents' choices about the food their children eat. I shuddered when I first heard the news reports about the "McDonald's coffee case," since it sounded like another of the stories of ridiculous results of juries that you often hear about. I thought that until I heard the true facts. But I, like most Americans, want to be sure I know the facts of every situation, not the puff or propaganda of one special interest of the other, all of whom can easily make a claim and spread it over the internet or in the media without regard to truth, as so often is the case. I hope that my one consistent message in this book is that we should all be students of any political or legal position we take. If we do not study the facts, we cannot stand on a soap box.

What I have always tried to do, and what I believe most lawyers try to do in their practice, is give their clients, their fellow lawyers, and the justice system the respect each deserves. I have chosen this career path, not because it is just an occupation, but because people in my life gave me the inspiration to do it. But, that justice system is at the mercy of the misinformation that distorts, corrupts and may even destroy the system. If we will have the patience to use our God-given energy and intelligence to listen, understand and scrutinize, then only one conclusion can be legitimately reached–our system of justice, however imperfect, is the best in the world, even with all its blemishes. Most of those who criticize it are the very ones who will later turn to it when they need it. It has given us the ability to check the power and influence of those

who would overbear and overpower us. That was
the purpose of the Bill of Rights and specifically the
purpose of Seventh Amendment guaranteeing the
right to trial by jury. The justification and rationale
for that amendment are no less compelling today
than they were 215 years ago. Perhaps its need is
even more real now, when there are more ways that
power has learned to corrupt, more means of
achieving that power, and more people upon whom
that power can exert its influence.

CHAPTER ONE

LAW AND MORALS IN A DEMOCRACY

"the right of trial by jury shall be preserved, and no fact tried by a jury, shall be otherwise reexamined in any Court of the United States"
United States Constitution

"You have Glaucoma–you are going blind in at least one eye, and likely both." This news from Dixon Klein's first visit to the glaucoma specialist in April of 1988 was worse than he could have expected. On the way to that appointment he could only think how bizarre it was that he, just twenty-seven years old, was having to see a glaucoma specialist. Wasn't glaucoma supposed to be for the elderly, not those in the prime of their life? How could he tell Lana the news he heard from his new specialist? He could not bring himself to pick up his phone and call her. But Lana deserved to know it. She had been so supportive and loving, during the hard times of earlier years, working to put him through school, after they had so carefully planned everything since the time that they were high school sweethearts. His Master's degree in electronic engineering was to be their security. Along with his charm, intellect and dedication, the degree had already landed him a top engineering position with Lockheed-Martin, the largest manufacturer of fighting aircraft in the world.

Five years later, in 1993, after his lawsuit was over and the dust had settled on his legal matter, the prediction from the glaucoma specialist proved to be accurate--his vision was virtually gone. The blinding chemical treatments had kept him from playing ball with Matthew, whose toddlers' years had been a literal blur to Dixon. Lana was no longer a stay-athome mom, raising Matthew and Chelsea, their daughter who was only two weeks old when Dixon had learned of his glaucoma. The worries for the future still lingered. Would he be able to lead Chelsea down the wedding aisle? What would his future treatment be? What would he have to do to prevent further damage, or could further damage even be prevented? All of the nightmares had still not ripened into reality, as he suffered from a slowly progressing blindness.

Dixon's glaucoma story began when he went to an optometrist (let's call him Dr. Lye) at a national chain optical in 1987, for a checkup after he noticed a slight change in his vision. Dr. Lye assured him then that everything was fine, only a slight increase in the marginal amount of nearsightedness he had for several years. Dr. Lye's crucial failure, however, was that he did not perform a simple test with a device known as a "tonometer," which would have detected the elevated fluid pressure within his eyeball, a cardinal sign of the beginning stages of glaucoma. Lye gave his customary instructions to a man of Dixon's age–follow up in one year. Ten months after Dr. Lye's exam, Dixon went to a different optometrist for another exam; this exam was very similar to the exam done by Dr. Lye, different only in that a tonometer was used this time. The result? Severely increased intra-ocular pressure, the hallmark that had gone undetected for at least a year. The lack of the test by Dr. Lye, which takes thirty seconds and costs nothing to administer, was all that separated Dixon from the life he had originally chosen. Because of the failure of Dr. Lye to do that test, the chance to reverse the advancing pressure was lost, and even with the best of treatment, Dixon would begin to notice that the periphery of his visual fields would diminish–leaving him with a severe tunnel vision, decreasing to a pinpoint, and eventually to nothing.

Dixon had never been involved in a lawsuit. Becoming involved in a lawsuit was the farthest thing from his mind the day he learned of his impending blindness. Like most Americans, he had never thought that he would find himself in a position like this. What he wondered was how Dr. Lye could have made such a terrible mistake. The answer to that question would only come through the lawsuit that he later brought. Since Dixon was not one to just accept his fate without inquiry, he took action to salvage the necessary evidence to prove Dr. Lye's failure. Had Dixon not acted in his own behalf, he very likely would never have been able to prove that Dr. Lye had neglected his job, and more important, that he had lied about it.

Cases Against Doctors–What is "Right versus Wrong?"

Dixon's case, in many senses, is like most that are filed. The case never made the national news. It never even made the local newspaper. It was not a sensational case that grabs the media interest of some. It is, like thousands of medical negligence cases around this country every year, just another statistic in the mass of material that the insurance companies utilize to calculate their risks and profits when determining premiums. It is not the McDonald's coffee case that everyone talks about on the radio talk shows when they want to bash a trial lawyer or give an example of the "lawsuit lottery." (The truth of that case later). Dixon Klein's case is, however, one that demonstrates what lawyers and people involved in medical negligence cases go through in the real world, not the fantasy world portrayed for some journalistic fanfare or political talking point. He is just a normal, everyday, hard-working, intelligent, family man. It turns out that his biggest mistake in life was putting his trust in an individual masquerading as a caring professional who, instead, turned out to be an incompetent, lying, thug. What we can never truly know is the number of times medical negligence kills or maims people, and the negligence goes undetected, with no claim and no lawsuit. Many studies have stated that, more often than not, patients never know there was malpractice and never bring claims.

Dixon Klein's case lends itself to a discussion about what has now become the attempted spoliation of the legal system by the insurance companies, corporate interests and their political machinery at work. That machinery may gradually topple the balance that the law should struggle to maintain–a moral balance wherein the little guy who gets hurt has the power to stand toe-to-toe with the big guy. Although the people of that machinery would like for you to think that the little guy can bring it down on a whim, the facts demonstrate otherwise. The way that the powerful now attempt to disrupt that balance is to engage in a campaign to deceive the public about the jury system. They try to destroy the jury system by misleading the public to the conclusion that the jury system is not in the public's interest, and that the public is being harmed by that system.

In any democracy, the voters will decide the moral balance by their vote, and that vote will ultimately determine the rules by which society operates. Those rules, or laws, are made to preserve what is deemed by the majority to be right, proper and fair. But who is to decide when certain rights of the minority have been trampled by the majority will? There are multitudes of different interests competing for their own laws and protection. One of the most common competitions, historically, has been between those with substantial financial capability and those with more limited assets. If large monied or property interests have the vote, then they can easily dominate the will of the lesser monied interests, who will be subject to power of the wealthier. At the other extreme, if the voting power of the poor and middle income people overwhelm the voting power of the more affluent, then the opposite is true and the laws will ultimately favor the less affluent.

The design of the *Constitution*, as revealed in its reading and as further revealed in the writings of the time, was to empower every segment of society by implementing a scheme which minimized the opportunity for absolute power, and maximized the potential for checks on that power. Details of specific periods of our history and certain events of the development of our law demonstrate society's attempts to strike that delicate balance of power. Obviously no one book can even begin to touch upon all such periods or events. The central thesis portrayed by historical events is this: although we as Americans are genuinely proud of our individualism, our toughness, our creativity, our heroes and our pioneers, we are in danger of becoming lazy enough to lose the benefit of our heritage–we might allow our society's laws, and the struggle for balance, to be corrupted by large conglomerate and corporate interests. The more complex our society has become, and the more crowded and metropolitan our population, the more autonomy we have become willing to surrender to those who purport to have the knowledge, expertise, money, and power to "get things done." We have become complacent in the job of protecting our liberties, and have allowed the complex decisions of our future to be controlled by either the corporate interests, or by government which is ever more being controlled by those corporate interests. We are in danger of allowing our development as a nation to be controlled by those politicians, lawyers and bureaucrats who are beholden to the corporate world. They have become the manipulators, and the depositories of power.

The author's outlook

Since you have invested enough of your time to read this far, and have either gone to the trouble of borrowing this book or have spent your own hard-earned money on it, I believe that I owe you the courtesy of telling you enough about myself so that you can judge me, my purpose, my intentions, and my credibility. As stated in the preface, I was a trial lawyer for 25 years. I quit trying cases about four years ago, after having handled mostly medical malpractice cases for the last ten years of my trial practice. I no longer have any vested interest in who is right or wrong in any debate between trial lawyers and any other segment of society. For the past four years I have done a number of different things. I have taught Medical Malpractice Law as a law professor at Texas Wesleyan University School of Law; I have served as a mediator for the resolution of medical malpractice and other cases, being hired by agreement of lawyers on both sides of the cases I work on; I have worked as a court-appointed guardian for children who have cases to be resolved in the court system; I have written and published a book on Texas Civil Evidence; and I have helped my wife and daughter start a small business.

As a mediator, I see and understand that there are cases brought by plaintiffs that have questionable merits. I also see that there are cases that have questionable defenses posed by the defendants. Mediators are chosen by agreement of the parties, and a mediator must have the reputation for fairness, objectivity and honesty. I have attempted, in writing this book, to have that same approach. I do not, by any means, believe that doctors are bad people, any more than I believe that about lawyers. My brother is an internal medicine doctor, and whenever I discussed my past clients' cases with him, he and I usually agreed about the negligence of the doctors involved. I do admit, however, that I have a deep-seated fear and distrust of most insurance companies. I believe that, for the most part, they have prospered, and wish to continue to prosper, from the medical malpractice system, far beyond what is fair and reasonable to both their insureds (the doctors) and the patients. You will see, in this book, my dislike for some insurance companies and their practices. I will not deny that.

I have never been a plaintiff in any lawsuit, despite two occasions in my life where either I or one of my family members has been severely impacted by medical mishap. Since we can now count our blessings every day, we chose to avoid the emotional and stressful medical malpractice litigation system that I know only too well.

Money–Does it control Policy?

As wealth is more and more concentrated in powerful hands, and that wealth becomes more and more influential in government decision-making, the true control of the law rests in the hands of the legal and political advisors to the corporate interests, their lobbyists, and the insiders that have become institutionalized in their positions. When it comes time for an election, the money pours in. Then the accounting ledgers are the first things to be consulted when deciding the propriety of potential legislation or administrative pronouncements.

Economics is, and always has been, a major force behind political thinking and decision-making. This is nothing new. In his book, *An Economic Interpretation of the American Constitution,* first written in 1913, Dr. Charles E. Beard described the forces that led to the writing of our *Constitution*. He succinctly, with significant historical detail, demonstrated that our framers were, in the most important portions of their deliberations, more influenced by their pocketbooks than any other factors. It was not until *The Federalist Papers* were written, and the Bill of Rights was appended to the *Constitution*, that anyone gave much thought to the concept that our personal liberties needed specific protection to insure that they would not be compromised by the form of government that was being devised.

One of our current journalists, Chris Matthews, host of "Hardball" on MSNBC, has written a book which I believe hones in on some of Americans' most important values and beliefs. I refer to his book, *American, Beyond Our Grandest Notions*, because I believe it does a lot to capture the true nature of Americans. He uses our history, our art, and our movies to paint the picture of what we are–a nation of people who will not be pushed around by our foreign enemies, but who are also reluctant to push others around. I want to take his thesis one step farther–that what we stand for should be applied equally within our borders as without. None of us want to be pushed around even by other Americans, and we will fight to prevent it. All we need to do is to be astute and energetic enough to obtain all of the facts, so that we won't be victimized by our own lack of knowledge.

Although this book is not about religion, it is

about morality and the spirituality that I believe is within most Americans. It is about how some use the term "moral values" to influence a result which is directly contrary to our truly most important moral value–the intrinsic and inherent value and worth of a human life. When one writes about anything that is happening in this country today, it is difficult to do so without taking some inspiration from the events of September 11, 2001. I refer to that date, not to exploit the horrible fate met by our countrymen on that date, but to demonstrate this point: the men and women who gave their lives trying to save others did not have time to stop and ponder their place in society or their economic or social caste, as they climbed into the burning towers. Letting their natural instincts, patriotism and humanism take over, they assisted and rescued millionaire accountants and stock traders, as well as hourly wage employees, janitors, and everyone in between, even carrying down to safety one woman who was unable to descend seventy floors of stairs in her wheelchair.

Our historical struggles for Liberty

Most people would not dispute that the most epic struggle of our country between its formation and the present day was the period from 1860 to 1870, when we went through the division of America into two separate nations, followed by reunification and the subsequent struggle to heal the wounds created by the Civil War. The lawyer that led us through the darkest days of that strain was a country lawyer, with little formal education, who started his career as a trial lawyer with a gift for capturing the essence of our spirit and morality with but a few well-chosen words. His belief was that every individual in this country should be treated equally, even those individuals who believed that every individual should not be treated equally. That moral conviction was often spoken by him, proclaiming that it was derived from his belief in a supreme being, a being who gave Lincoln a spiritual compass for both his public and private lives. Both before and during his presidency, he applied and practiced this belief, to the point that he was assassinated for it. One of our nation's greatest losses is that we never learned what he would have done with the rest of his presidency and his life thereafter.

America's heroes are not her corporate types whose decisions are made, or at least influenced, by the bottom line of profits and personal bonuses, nor are they the personal injury trial lawyers who look for the one big case or a bunch of little ones. Our heroes have always been the little guys whose motivation is something other than personal gain, notoriety or influence–the people who act upon a moral and spiritual compass. When Louis Brandeis, one of our country's most admired and influential lawyers and Supreme Court justices, began to rise in prominence and notoriety, he did so only because he sought just the opposite of prominence and notoriety. He sought to obtain balance on behalf of the little guy and middle class against large corporate corruption and monopoly-seeking conglomerates. Without asking for it, he was given by the nation and his admirers, the name "the people's attorney." From the time of his college years he was known to have a keen intellect, and was highly recruited to represent many of the large then-forming corporate interests. He chose, however, much to his financial detriment, to fight against their tendency to take over politics, create monopolistic power, and infringe upon the economic freedom of their employees and the public. This fight did not end when he was confirmed as a United States Supreme Court justice, a position he never pursued, reluctantly accepted, yet embraced with just as much dedication as any cause for which he had ever stood. While on the Court, his record was one of steadfast devotion to the belief that monopolistic and economic power and influence over the laws and lawmaking was not good for our democracy. He never believed that the corporate bottom line should dictate the direction that we take. That belief was not one that came about from some prejudice or affinity that Brandeis had for the masses, or from some populist distaste for money that he did not have. Throughout his legal career, he was known for studying every detail of every picture from every angle, so that no fact or argument went unnoticed or unconsidered. His conclusions were always made with thorough analysis and unbiased thought. His operating conviction was a single one--that morality came from within every human being, rather than from a collection of individuals gathered for the sole purpose of furthering a business venture or economic enterprise.

Thomas Jefferson, a lawyer, and author of the Declaration of Independence, wrote in his *Summary View of the Rights of British America,* that the English immigrants who first inhabited America were possessed of a right which nature granted to all men—"establishing new societies, under such laws and regulations as to them shall seem most likely to promote happiness." He was one of the first to articulate that happiness was something that people had a right to expect, and that government should foster it. Americans, he believed, were entitled to establish these laws, because: "America was conquered, and her settlements made, and firmly established, at the expence (sic)of individuals, and not of the British public. Their own blood was spilt on acquiring lands for their settlement, their own fortunes expended in making that settlement effectual; for themselves they fought, for themselves they conquered, and for themselves alone they have right to hold."

Jefferson went on to observe, in his oft-stated list of grievances against the crown, that the economic gain of the trading companies of the mother country should not be supreme over the human inalienable right to self-government. Great Britain had maintained that America should be grateful to it because, after all, the mother country had come to America's assistance in war against the

French and Indians. Jefferson responded that England had given assistance to other countries when it was commercially advantageous for it to do so, but that fact did not give England the right to control individuals in those countries. Such assistance, he said, had been given "to other allied states, with whom they carry on a commercial intercourse; yet these states never supposed, that by calling in her aid, they thereby submitted themselves to her sovereignty." That steadfast belief in individual liberty was the main reason that we fought Nazism and Communism nearly two hundred years after Jefferson.

Money, power and influence in corporate hands give great opportunity for good things. It goes without saying that the money provided for corporate interests in modern day medicine often provide great benefit to our people. We need the new drugs, new products, new treatments and new discoveries which they produce. Does that fact, any more than England's assistance to the colonies it established for trading purposes, entitle the corporations to control our individual destiny or pursuit of happiness? Are we becoming so disinterested and indifferent that we, in the interest of accepting such benefits from corporate America, relinquish our individual safety, security, health and freedom? I do not think that we have become so complacent. We have simply become too busy and too easily influenced that we do not take the time to study or understand the true facts. We allow the very interests who seek to benefit from our complacency to be the ones to convince us to be complacent. Their most often used tool is to redirect public animosities. They convince us that exercising those liberties prevents our enjoyment of the fruits of the economy and corporate activity. They, like the colonists' mother country, try to convince us of their benevolence so that they can continue to profit from us. Should we accept the new products that kill, the new drugs that cripple, and doctors who maim, all in the name of progress and creativity? Should we immunize one segment of society from being responsible for the harm they do, simply because they have provided us some benefits? Shouldn't society, through its laws, discourage irresponsible conduct that hurts us? When individuals are hurt by such conduct, shouldn't we provide a mechanism to compensate those who are harmed, and spread the cost of that compensation among those who have received the benefits?

Where Do Money, History and Right take us?

In our society's striving to balance the competing interests of each of its components, the laws are necessarily influenced by the lawyers representing those interests. Countless newspaper columns and editorials, magazine articles, books, cartoons and jokes have been created and fueled by the notion that these lawyers are not only unnecessary, but undesirable, and a drain on our nation's resources. The most common application of the notion in the past few years has been the derision of trial lawyers. Bottom dwellers, sharks, greedy, rich and without any guiding moral principle, according to some.

The elements of our legal system go back many centuries. Reading the history of that system reveals that nothing is new in the criticism of lawyers. Throughout that history there are references to that criticism. Even Abraham Lincoln, a figure whom no one today could critique about his morals or character, made references in his letters to the fact that his opinions might be less than well-received since they came from a trial lawyer.

The actions that come into criticism most today are the actions for some damage or injury to persons. These types of actions have been authorized in courts of law for centuries, not only in democracies, but in common law and even non-common law countries all around the world. The argument now against such cases is that they are burdens to our legal system and to our economy, that they earn far too much money for injured individuals and their lawyers, and actions need to be implemented to curtail such cases, all for the betterment of society. An analysis of the statistics about such cases and their results, from factual rather than rhetorical sources, demonstrates that, in fact, the arguments against such cases are unfounded. Those cases are actually less common per capita than they have been in the last several decades, and the amounts of money actually received by injured victims and their lawyers, adjusted for inflation, are on the decline.

The thesis of much of the current comment is that trial lawyers have some co-ordinated agenda to harm or disrupt society, all for their own pecuniary gain. Whether or not that thesis is true, harm or disruption may be the ultimate effect if we do not recognize that some changes must be made. If those changes are not made willingly and with some attention to common sense, then undesirable and unjust changes will be imposed, after a huge waste of time, energy and money, resulting in injustice to you.

Why is our public discourse replete with arguments for "tort reform" limiting the rights of people to seek redress through the legal system? The answer lies in two things: first, the propaganda of the insurance industry; second, the small number of trial lawyers whose conduct enables the argument. The insurance and corporate interests profit from a curtailment of the individual rights of the victim. These are the large corporate manufacturers of consumer products, tobacco, pharmaceutical products and medical devices, and the insurance companies, who have a vested interest in limiting their financial exposure resulting from their negligence and irresponsible behavior. It is like Great Britain and the colonies all over again. They say, "We give you these nice new things and yet you treat us like the enemy!" Now when you get hurt by the corporate conduct, they say "How dare you sue us and hurt us, after accepting the benefits of all we have given you!" The catch is that they have profited by the billions for their benevolence, and now want to leave all of us holding the bag.

But the second reason that we have calls for tort reform is this list of notables: those of the trial lawyers who are self-promoting, yellow-page advertising, big-talkers who seek cameras and publicity, wanting only to brag about their highest jury awards. They are more than an eyesore to those of us who have some pride in our profession. Those of the class-action lawyers who seek only to line their pockets because of what they claim is some injustice, while their clients get a check for seventy-five cents. Those of the lawyers who file a volume of car wreck cases, hoping that a few will "hit." Those of the lawyers who pursue cases even after they learn those cases lack merit, just to extract a settlement and pocket a fee. Those of the "big-guy wannabees" who do not properly evaluate their cases early, only to discover later that they have wasted the time, energy, emotions and money of everyone. These types do exist, although in far fewer numbers than the good, conscientious lawyers. That small number of lawyers, like the small number of doctors who kill and maim, are central to a deterioration of the public confidence in the jury system and enablers of abuse of the legal system. Ironically, they may be the reapers of their own demise.

It has become simple for the corporations and the insurance companies to sell this idea of limiting the rights of the victims. It has become easy because they make it sound like the consumer will be the ones to pay for "skyrocketing jury awards" and "frivolous lawsuits." The truth of the matter is that these words are a scare tactic designed to perpetuate the unchallenged and limitless profits from the products or services that we think are always safe, but are really not. I will give you the details so that you can judge for yourself about whether the courts are being used solely to line the pockets of trial lawyers, or whether the corporations, their insurance companies and their lawyers are trying to change the system so that they can grease the moneymaking machine without being required to answer for the consequences of their conduct.

It turns out that the insurance companies do not always tell us the truth about what goes on in a lawsuit. It also turns out that the trial lawyers will sometimes use the system to their own advantage, without weighing the resulting costs to society. The insurance companies   blame the "exorbitant" litigation expense on the plaintiffs and their lawyers, not owning up to their own lawyers' abuses.

Who judges the corporations?

Corporations are no more than a collection of individuals, all with their human limitations and frailties. A common frailty of those individuals is to cower to the ultimate purpose of the corporation itself-- to limit its own liability and to make money. When these individuals get together for this purpose and in this environment, the purpose of the game is to win, to climb to the top. The top, ironically, is always the bottom line–the largest bottom line that can be achieved. What better evidence than the recent financial ruin of the shareholders affected by the collapse of Tyco, Worldcom and Enron?

An interesting study that is far too esoteric for this book, and perhaps more appropriate for the philosophers, is how normal human beings, usually with no evil motive or intent, can have their imperfections so magnified when they gather together for the purpose of profit. It was human beings who knew of, but so callously ignored, the fatalities they would cause while designing fireball Ford Pinto gas tanks that would explode upon rear impact. It was human beings who proceeded to mass produce super-absorbent tampons while knowing the all-too-real risk of their potential for causing women's death from toxic shock. It was human beings who designed Firestone tires and hastily slapped them on Ford Explorers that would then rollover and kill hundreds of people. It was human beings who occupied the offices of accountants, corporate lawyers, and management of Enron and Tyco when they conveniently overlooked the misleading information that was put in shareholder reports–the reports relied upon my thousands of families who saw their retirement savings mutilated. So what is the common thread? It is the fact that they all had gathered for a purpose. The purpose was to make a profit for their companies. That purpose, in its own pernicious way, becomes malignant and pervasive. When it does, it grows as rapidly and insidiously as the most invasive and advancing cancer. I will not attempt to explain why this happens. I will show you how it affects you when it does happen.

The three branches of our government were all created for a specific purpose by the framers who so carefully considered the balancing of society's competing interests. We all know from our junior high and high school civics and government classes that the laws are created by our legislative branch, that they are carried out by our executive branch, and that they are interpreted by the judicial branch. Each of these is to act as a check on the other, so that no one of them becomes the absolute arbiter of the law. As our legal system developed, there was soon born the concept of judicial review. In its simplest terms, that means that the judicial branch has the authority to review the actions of the other two branches to ascertain that the fundamental authority of the *Constitution* has not been somehow overreached or defeated. This is the most marvelous example of our framers' wisdom. As was observed earlier, the more complex and populated our country has become, the harder it is to properly balance the competing moral interests of American society. The framers made the judicial branch the one that was not elected, and thus ultimately not answerable to the whims of money. The only thing that the judiciary is answerable to is the *Constitution*. The judicial branch is the only branch that allows real people to participate directly in the process of decision-making. The jury is the ultimate finder of the facts in any dispute before the courts. In both of the other two branches the people who speak or decide either have to raise money to be elected, or they work for someone who has to raise money to be elected. In the final analysis, where does the money come from? It comes from those who can afford to give it. It comes from those who are interested in the outcome of the election and the laws that will be passed after the election. Those interests then spend more money on the lobbyists who fill the halls of Congress or the state legislatures after the election. In the judicial branch, the final arbiter of the facts is a group of people who are not beholden to anyone, who come randomly from all walks of life, who none of the participants have spoken to before nor will they ever again. They hear evidence that is presented by rules that apply equally to all sides of the conflict. The conflict is one that is adversarial, guaranteeing that all issues appropriate for the decision will be presented, and that all arguments will be made.

That the justice system has some flaws is undeniable. It, too, is a system comprised of people. The people who make up the system determine whether and how that system functions. Any student of history, philosophy, religion or civics instinctively knows that people have their imperfections, so a system dependent upon them will always have its imperfections. What any system of government must do is determine the steps that are necessary to minimize the imperfections, to allow the most fair and reasonable results to flow from that system. I will suggest some things that I consider beneficial and appropriate to accomplish that end.

What I will not suggest, and what I think I can convincingly demonstrate to be unnecessary and in fact destructive of our liberties, is the wholesale destruction of the jury system. That right is one that is guaranteed by the Seventh Amendment to our *Constitution*, and it was put there for a reason. That reason was centuries old even before there was such a thing as the *Constitution*, and it exists today more than ever–the right of every person to have important issues in a legal dispute to be resolved by people beholden to no one, controlled by no one, and people who cannot be penalized or chastised for the results obtained.

      The results obtained by the jury system are not, in every case, correct. Who among us was not outraged by the jury's verdict of guilty rendered against Tom Robinson, and his lawyer, Atticus Finch, in *To Kill a Mockingbird*? Although a fictional work, it was based upon true beliefs, actions, biases and emotions of the time. What percentage of our nation's people were cynical over the outcome of the O.J. Simpson criminal trial? Every day across America, one-half of all the people hearing a jury verdict is aghast, and sometimes in disbelief, at the result. My clients and I have been on the receiving end of what I thought to be right and fair from a jury, and many times I have had the opposite fortune. But every time I know that, as a whole, the system works and it is the best system we could have. I say that not just because it is the system we have, but because it is tried, tested, and fair. There is no other society in the history of mankind that has ever been able to devise anything nearly as good, much less any better.

Is there a problem with majority rule?

One of the best-known, oft-quoted and most well-respected political news columnists in our history, Walter Lippmann, wrote in 1955 of the crucial decisions facing thoughtful citizens of the 20th century. He urged us to take a lively, responsible interest in our government to preserve our liberties and defend ourselves against totalitarianism in his short, but compelling work, *The Public Philosophy*. Mr. Lippman, according to the contemporaneous *Newsweek* review of his book, believed that men will continue to be free, only if they elect officials who cannot be bribed, appeased or intimidated by private groups, but who will govern "according to the public philosophy, or those principles of unselfish behavior which formed the basis of the *U.S. Constitution*." I believe that such advice is even more meaningful at the beginning of the 21st century. Government, he said, must assert a public interest against private inclination and against what is easy and popular. If a government is to do its duty, he states, it must often swim against the tides of private feeling. This is true because, as the question was posed at the beginning of this chapter, who is to decide when the rights of the minority have been trampled upon by majority will? Lippman points out that successful democratic politicians may advance only so far as they placate, appease, bribe, seduce, bamboozle, or otherwise manipulate the demanding and threatening elements in their constituencies. Their decisive consideration is not whether a proposition is good or moral, but whether it is popular. Then the politicians become pressed and harassed by the agents of organized interests to the point that the executive and legislative departments, with their civil servants and technicians, have lost the power to decide matters according to the public good and purpose. Mass opinion should not be used to transform the legislatures of democratic states from defenders of personal rights into boss-ridden oligarchies.

So beware, the popularity of a thought or idea that serves your advantage today may well result in it becoming a rule of law. Tomorrow, you might not be the one to make the rules; or even more ironic, your popular rules may easily turn to your disadvantage. Do you support the rule of popular will when in the minority, as you do when in the majority? Do we give away our rights under natural law when we are relegated to the minority, or is there something that preserves these inviolate to all people, as was said by Thomas Jefferson and repeated by Abraham Lincoln ninety years later? Have we regressed farther since Lincoln than we progressed between Jefferson and Lincoln? I do not think that we have, and I do not think that we, as a unified people, could stomach ourselves if we did. The answer must be that we have to take a hard look at ourselves and determine what is important to the survival of the meaning of the phrase "justice for all."

Assuming that most would agree that justice

for all is a worthy goal, then how do we best come close to achieving that goal? Realizing that it would be impossible to write one book and answer that question for all purposes, let's limit the question to one issue-- how do we achieve it for the purpose of compensating those persons, or their families, wrongfully injured or killed by medical error. That question is a common one today. We know that grave mistakes are made in medical treatment. Jessica Santillan, a teenage girl died at Duke University Medical Center Hospital as a result of receiving an incompatible heart and lung, because of clerical error. Surgical instruments are left in people's bodies with alarming frequency. If such needless and avoidable errors can occur at such highly-regarded institutions, it is almost incomprehensible how many such errors occur every day at those hundreds of thousands of medical providers of lesser quality. The National Institutes of Health did a comprehensive study in 2000 and determined that somewhere between 48,000 and 98,000 people are killed each year by needless and preventable medical error in hospitals. That number does not even include people who are killed by medical error outside of hospitals, nor those who are severely maimed. Yet, although we think nothing of spending hundreds of billions of dollars to *prevent the loss* of even one life to an act of terrorism, many of our politicians, prodded by the insurance companies, want to limit *compensation for the same loss* of a medical negligence victim to $250,000?

Do we do away with lawyers who handle such cases for wrongfully injured people? I suppose that there are some who would take that position, although not even the staunchest proponents of tort reform (the insurance companies) would be in favor of that, because, you see, there would then be nothing for them to insure against, and thus, no premiums to be charged and thus, no money for them to make. So, even they would not argue for either doing away with the lawyers, or doing away with any system to compensate wrongfully injured people. But the trial lawyers would not suffer long—we could all find other work. The real victims are those who have lost what Jefferson and Lincoln sought to protect for all people. Those victims have lost, for no compensation, their right to happiness and to pursuit of the lives they have chosen for themselves, just like Dixon Klein lost when his optometrist failed to perform a simple test.

Should we simply get rid of doctors, hospitals and nurses that make serious mistakes and kill or maim their patients. That would be a wonderful accomplishment, but any system that we now have or ever would have to handle the problem must recognize that people, and the institutions that function solely as a result of the efforts of human beings, will err. So, efforts aimed toward that error could only succeed in reducing it, not eliminating it. We know that we must still be ultimately required to compensate those whose suffering cannot be avoided through error reduction.

It seems only reasonable to suggest that we attempt to find a system, or combination of systems, that accomplish three things that, without question, all of us should want: (1) lessen the prevalence of medical errors (2) provide an avenue for compensation, without undue reward or "lottery" windfall, for those who are injured by medical negligence (3) place the ultimate cost of such compensation on those whose conduct is the most reckless. To do this we must rid the insurance companies of the notion that their bad investment decisions should be rewarded by either soaking the doctors for more premium dollars or further robbing the innocently injured victim of his day in court. We must also disabuse people of the notion that all bad medical outcomes should result in a payment by someone.

In order to find the right system, we need to know how the current system works, or doesn't work. We need to know more than just that the insurance companies claim that there is a "crisis" because their profits are not high enough unless the malpractice premiums are dramatically increased. We need to understand that the elderly and children will be the first to be wronged by a system that limits "non-economic" damages. We need to find the causes of frivolous lawsuits and frivolous defenses, so that we can lessen the costs attributable to those frivolities. We need to reward the good doctors and hospitals with recognition in the form of lesser malpractice premiums; and to foster the disclosure of serious medical error so that action may be taken to prevent it.

If we do not do these things, we will be left with two unacceptable choices–(1) relegating crippled and brain-damaged victims of medical negligence to monetary recoveries for their life of suffering that would not even pay for one week of salary of an Enron executive or our president's four years at prep school, or (2) allowing insurance companies to reap profits from good and caring doctors and hospitals in such huge sums that these health care providers will no longer be able to afford to render the type of care that the system should seek to obtain.

We cannot afford to allow the corporate interests and their political maneuvering to afflict the voting public with tunnel vision –failing to have the full ability to see that when they or their loved ones need the jury system to redress a serious medical error with devastating and life-altering personal consequences, there will be no such system left. Nor can we let a person like Dixon Klein go uncompensated for a grievous and incomprehensible error that led to the destruction of the life that he was trying to build for himself. Through the truth of his case and other truths, I will show you the full field of vision about how the insurance companies use all of their money and power to paint a picture, all to the detriment of the people that they are supposed to serve, and all to the detriment of the system which they use to make their own profits. Then I will show you how we can prevent the damage from those who use the system to line their own pockets, while clamoring that they are only protecting their clients' interests. These are the ones who raise the cost of medical malpractice insurance and the increase in the cost of medical care.

So whose side should you be on? There really is only one side—the side that promotes good quality, safe healthcare, at a reasonable cost, in a system that allows for reasonable compensation when an innocent patient is harmed by negligence (albeit well-intentioned). If you are hurt by a doctor who, while driving home from the hospital, runs a stoplight because he was not paying attention, it should not matter that he was well-intentioned and did not mean to hurt you. You should still be compensated. If you lose the use of your limbs in that accident, your recovery of damages should not be limited by some arbitrary amount, based on the argument that a high award would raise the doctor's insurance premium. No one would stand for such an argument. Why, then, should the doctor's malpractice insurance company be allowed to limit your damages if he unintentionally, but negligently, operates on you, causing the same injury, before he leaves the hospital?

Through your new understanding of the system and how we got where we are, you will come to see the full picture. It is a far different picture than the one portrayed by the insurance companies and their beholden politicians through the publicity which they have so pervasively promoted. Once you finish this book and discover the true facts, if you let them succeed in their endeavor, you will have only yourself, and others like you, to blame.

The truth of Dixon Klein's case is that the case was finally settled, after three years of litigation, for an amount which was the same amount that Dixon would have accepted before the case was even filed. During those three years there were dozens of depositions taken, multiple hearings required for Dixon's lawyers to obtain information they were entitled to, and several hundred thousands of dollars spent by the insurance companies on lawyers. The insurance companies even fired one lawyer (who had a conflict of interest that he knew about from the beginning, but accepted the case anyway) and hired three more. There were two daylong and expensive mediation sessions, requested by the defendants, resulting in not one single offer of money to Dixon and his family. After multiple unnecessary hearings and file boxes full of paper that filled half a room, the case was finally settled on a Friday afternoon before the next Monday on which it was to go to trial. What happened after that, for the next three years, was that the two insurance companies who hired the lawyers to fight against the plaintiff, fought each other, both claiming that they should get some of their lawyers' fees, expenses and payments back from the other. The ultimate result was that hundreds of thousands of dollars were spent on the defense to get a result that should have occurred without all of the frivolity. Only two things were learned in the process. First, that the defendant optometrist, Dr. Lye, lied when he testified that he performed the routine glaucoma test on Dixon; and second, that someone in Dr. Lye's office altered the records to cover that lie. So, whom do you think was at fault for causing all of the litigation expense in Dixon's case? Whose litigation course was frivolous? Was it Dixon, who did nothing more than try to get compensation for the loss of his vision, caused by the reckless failure to perform a fundamental, easily administered exam? Or was it the insurance companies for the optometrists, who used every obstructionist technique known to the lawyers, finally settling on the courthouse steps, then litigating against each other for another three years? The answer is clear.

Ignorance of the law

The judicial system in The Terry Schiavo case made a factual and legal decision about the intentions that she had expressed. Despite Congressional intervention, no federal court was willing to override, no matter how conservative, "moral value" oriented, or "err-on-the-side-of-life" that federal court may have been. Each of the federal courts that considered the Schiavo case after the enabling legislation was overwhelmingly Republican and conservative and presumably "value of life" and "moral values" inclined. What we learned from that was that most of the public is not familiar with what goes on in specific cases, and that we should not judge based upon a quick review. Our courts are an integral and equal part of the process of interpreting and assuring the implementation of rights of the people. That process should not be destroyed by the voices of those who simply do not like the results of a particular case, unless those voices emanate from people informed, educated, and knowledgeable about what has gone on in the process.

That is the purpose of this book–to inform those who would like to know how the legal system works when the subject is whether a person should receive compensation from being injured by medical error. I am convinced that those who will listen to the facts will believe that our civil justice system should not be controlled by some legislative decree about the worth of a life. The old worn-out expression "ignorance of the law is no excuse" should be amended to state "ignorance of what happens in the law is no excuse." Conscientious, knowledgeable, attentive jurors are the best equipped to render decisions on the quality of life and credibility of people who have been the victims of medical error. Who is better placed than they to make those decisions?

CHAPTER TWO

CIVIL LAWSUITS-- THE MYTHS VERSUS THE FACTS

"The liability system makes persons who injure others aware of their actions, and provides incentives for them to act appropriately."
President's Bush's Council of Economic Advisors, *Who Pays for Tort Liability Claims? An Economic Analysis of the U.S. TortLiability System*, April 2002.

The jury system that serves as the cornerstone of the civil justice system has come under severe attack increasingly in the past several decades. How do we know the true facts about the civil justice system and how it operates? Should we believe the trial lawyers, who claim that they are only interested in the rights of their clients (all while some of those lawyers spend more and more advertising dollars boasting of their success)? Should we believe the medical malpractice insurance companies who tell the doctors and the public that they really just want fairness? Or does the truth lie somewhere in between?

Most people believe that suits for personal injuries, including automobile suits, product liability suits, and medical malpractice suits, are on the rise, and that juries have gone crazy awarding huge amounts of money to people who claim to be injured. The true facts demonstrate just the opposite–the actual number of lawsuits for personal injuries has declined, while the number of suits by businesses suing each other has substantially increased.

An editorial in the *Houston Post*, written by law professor Richard Alderman, of the University of Houston Law School, touched on the subject of the debate over civil lawsuits and lawyers, stating that whenever a new election cycle approaches, the trial-lawyer bashing begins anew. That bashing is what was going on when insurance companies blamed trial lawyers for everything from the shortage of doctors to the high cost of insurance. Insurance companies promised lower rates for doctors (which have not occurred even now more than two years after medical malpractice recoveries have been limited by the legislature). Professor Alderson argued, "Whether you have been defrauded by a stock broker, ripped off by a used-car dealer, injured as the result of a careless doctor, lost a parent to nursing home negligence or had medical problems because of a drug that didn't work as promised, trial lawyers are your only hope for compensation."

Are the culprits doctors or lawyers?

Are the lawyers or the doctors to blame for the state of our medical malpractice system? If you believe that there is some problem with the system, then the real answer to this question is that it is not just one group, but it is both. If there is a problem withe the system, it is the fault of the worst of each of professions. It is not the civil justice system that is somehow the problem. I confess, as does Professor Alderson, that some lawyers are overzealous in the pursuit of a defendant, and some juries act out of malice or revenge instead of justice, but such cases are the exception, not the rule. Nor is it always something inherently bad in the nature of health care delivery that brings about the lawsuits that occur. There are bad apples in both professions, even though the majority of both professions seek to do what is right. We should not throw out all to punish the few.

Some basic facts crush the notion that malpractice lawsuits are causing a crisis according to the National Practitioner Data Bank, which was created in September 1990 by the federal government to track malpractice judgments and settlements against physicians. The National Practitioner Data Bank, authorized by Congress and established by the Department of Health and Human Services, has collected nationwide information "relating to the professional competence and conduct of physicians, dentists and other health care practitioners" since September 1990. All insurers or health care providers paying medical malpractice judgments or settlements are required to report to the NPDB the amount of the payouts as well as information about the health care providers on whose behalf the payouts were made:

1. The number of payouts has increased by less than 1 percent since 1994. In 1994, the number of medical malpractice payouts made by physicians in the U.S. was 15,166. In 2003, the number of payouts was 15,295 – an increase of only 129 payouts or 0.85 percent.

2. From 2001 to 2003, the number of malpractice payouts declined by 8.4 percent. In 2001, the beginning of the medical malpractice "crisis," the number of total medical malpractice payouts nationally was 16,690. By 2003, that number had *fallen* to 15,295, a drop of 1,395.

The number of medical malpractice payouts per 100 doctors has declined 11 percent from 1994 to 2003. In 1994, there were 15,166 malpractice payouts made by physicians in the U.S., according to the NPDB, which represented 2.46 payouts per 100 doctors. In 2003, there were 15,295 payouts, which represented 2.19 payouts per 100 doctors.

Population-adjusted medical malpractice case filings declined between 1992 and 2001. In the 17 states reporting figures to the Court Statistics Project, medical malpractice filings per 100,000 population have decreased by 1 percent. While there has been a gradual increase in the medical malpractice caseload it has not kept pace with the increase in population.

Communication is key

Some physician groups, believing that better doctor communication skills will minimize the number of lawsuits, state that we should teach doctors to be more communicative with their patients, rather than find ways to restrict jury awards. Dr. Angelo Georges, President of the Federation of State Medical Boards, established a policy whereby all medical students nationwide will have to pay an extra $950 so trained actors can test their ability to communicate with their patients — a move that medical officials believe will cut down on medical malpractice lawsuits. All students, before they start their residency program, will have to travel to one of about five testing sites nationwide to take the clinical portion of their United States Medical Licensing Examination, which already tests their medical knowledge. Representatives of that group told West Virginia Board of Medicine members that they want to weed out bad doctors before they get their licenses —— not years later, when it costs money to revoke the license of an inadequately trained doctor.

"You have some book-smart people who really don't have any communication skills," said Dr. Georges. "If this is developed and not watered down, it'll be wonderful." Good doctors need good communication skills. A few doctors account for most medical malpractice lawsuits, said Lisa Robin, the federation's assistant vice president of leadership and legislative services. Doctors who don"t have good communication skills make up a majority of the cases, she added. A study in West Virginia (a state some politicians used to argue that doctors there needed relief from malpractice suits) found that 40 doctors in West Virginia were responsible for more than a quarter of the $534 million in verdicts and settlements reported to the state medical board from 1993 to 2000.

The test proposed by Dr. Georges is expected to prevent 300 to 800 doctors nationwide from getting their licenses each year. Other students may also fail the test, but get more training and eventually pass. The test will mirror a doctor's normal clinical day. The student will have about 15 minutes each to examine 10 patients–actors who've been trained to mimic a variety of illnesses. The students will be scored on their ability to form a rapport with the patient, their ability to correctly diagnose the problem, if they learn relevant medical history, among other items.

Are there other ways that changes in the health care delivery system would help matters, rather than changing juries or the civil justice system? What about reducing medication errors in hospitals? Would that also cut down on malpractice claims? An average of 195,000 people in the U.S.

died due to potentially preventable, in-hospital medical errors in each of the years 2000, 2001 and 2002, according to "Patient Safety in American Hospitals," a study released by HealthGrades, July 2004. The Health Grades study reviewed three years of Medicare data covering *all* its enrollees' hospital discharges in *all* 50 states. This Medicare population represents about 45 percent of all hospital admissions in the country. In an article appearing in the *Wall Street Journal* in November of 2003, it was reported that a study by US Pharmacopeia, a nonprofit group of pharmacists and other health care professionals that monitor medication errors, revealed that hospitals continue to make a large number of medication errors despite efforts to cut down on those mistakes. So, if a medication error occurs in a hospital and a patient is injured as a result, is that the fault of the civil justice system, or is that a problem that the civil justice system should be allowed to judge?

Does the blame lie elsewhere?

Most states currently do not place limits on the amount of damages that a jury may award to an injured victim of malpractice. That system we will call the majority system. Other states do place limits, and it is the position of many politicians, insurance companies, and almost all doctors and hospitals, that limitation should be the rule everywhere. A system limiting the amounts that juries may award we will call the minority system.

The major outcry for reform of medical malpractice cases in states using the majority system is the result of complaints by doctors that the malpractice premiums they have to pay are too high, and that they are being run out of business as a result of the exorbitant costs. If we closely examine what has happened, however, we see that even in states where there have been caps placed on the amounts that plaintiffs can recover in medical malpractice cases, the insurance companies have not reduced their premiums that they require the doctors to pay.

The rate of increase in medical malpractice premiums is less than the rate of medical inflation overall: an average of 6.7% between 1990 and 2001, according to the *Journal of Health Affairs*. It's also worth noting that, nationwide, malpractice payouts by physicians and their insurers were $4.5 billion in 2001--less than 1% of the country's overall healthcare costs of $1.4 trillion. They have risen slowly, if steadily, since 1996, when the total was $3.5 billion. Meanwhile, some states are finding that a small percentage of physicians accounts for the majority of big malpractice verdicts--which would indicate that the problem is a few bad doctors, not greedy tort lawyers. Officials in Nevada, which adopted a $350,000 cap last year, discovered that only two doctors were to blame for $14 million of the $22 million in claims awarded in one recent year. Both are still practicing. Malpractice premiums are not taking a larger piece of their already minuscule proportion; and only a small number of doctors–the worst ones–are the worst offenders. So, is there a problem? If so, is it the lawyers and injured patients causing it? The answer is a clear "NO."

None of the insurance companies that write medical malpractice policies in the state of Texas reduced their premiums in the first two years since the passage of 2003 legislation that capped non-economic damages at $250,000. In fact, now that reform has been in effect for more than two years, rates are higher than they have ever been in the past. One must logically conclude, then, that something else must be the cause of the high premiums that the insurance companies are charging doctors for malpractice insurance. Reducing the amount of money that people recover has not done the job. Other indicators of this are discussed in later chapters, showing that placing caps on damages does not help insurance premiums.

If medical malpractice and personal injury lawsuits are not on the rise and are not causing problems for the civil justice system, then why do we keep hearing about the crowded court dockets and the so-called "rash" of lawsuits? One thing that we do know is that the legal "reforms" advocated in Congress only cut off the rights of consumers injured or killed by faulty products or medical error. However, the "reforms" do nothing to curb the truly ridiculous lawsuits filed each year by businesses against each other. Here are some of the facts and figures on those types of cases:

•• Business cases account for 47% of all punitive damage awards. In contrast, only 4.4% and 2% of punitive damage awards are due to product liability and medical malpractice cases respectively (Rand Institute for Civil Justice, 1996).

•• Businesses suing each other over contracts comprised nearly half of all federal court cases filed between 1985 and 1991 (The Wall Street Journal, 12/93).

•• Contract and property cases - most involving business - comprise more than 1/3 of all civil cases in state courts; by comparison, only 0.21% of all civil cases were product liability claims (National Center for State Courts, 1995).

Businesses are the true kings of frivolous lawsuits. If anyone wants to find examples of waste of judicial resources and unnecessary legal expenses, one need only look at some of the cases that businesses have been involved in:

•• In 1998, Kellogg Co. sued Exxon Corp., claiming that Exxon's "whimsical tiger" logo, which had been in existence for more than 30 years, would confuse consumers who associate the tiger logo with Kellogg's Frosted Flakes mascot, "Tony the Tiger." A federal judge in Memphis threw out the suit, saying that Kellogg was "grossly remiss in failing to assert its rights" sooner. This didn't stop Kellogg, which further clogged the courts by appealing the verdict to the Sixth U.S. Circuit Court of Appeals in Cincinnati. In its brief, Kellogg argued that the Exxon tiger, like Tony, "walks or runs on his two hind legs and acts in a friendly manner."

●● In 1998, Enterprise Rent-A-Car filed lawsuits against Rent-A-Wreck of America (a tiny rental company) and Hertz Corp. and threatened to file lawsuits against several other car-rental companies who use the phrase "pick you up," claiming that "We'll pick you up" is Enterprise's slogan. While those suits were pending, Advantage Rent-a-Car countersued Enterprise, claiming that Advantage had used the phrase "We'll pick you up" long before Enterprise did. Enterprise argued in its lawsuits that the phrase means more than "We'll give you a ride"; it means "We'll pick up your spirits." Competitors said that there was no other way to say "We'll give you a ride." Enterprise attorney Rudolph Telscher said that "We'll decide in the courtroom who is correct here."

●● In November 1995, Hormel Foods, the maker of the luncheon meat SPAM, sued Jim Henson Productions to stop the creator of the Muppets from calling a character in a new movie Spa'am, claiming that the character was unclean and grotesque and would call into question the purity and quality of its meats. A federal court rejected Hormel's claims, and Hormel also lost on appeal.

●● Mattel, Inc., the maker of Barbie, is waging an

aggressive trademark war against unsanctioned use of the Barbie name, attacking the founders of the "Barbie Makes a Wish" weekend that raises money for critically ill children; artist Paul Hansen, sued for $1.2 billion for making $2,000 from the sale of his Exorcist Barbie, Tonya Harding Barbie, and Drag Queen Barbie; and Mike Grove, who distributes Sizzler toy cars to sick and dying children. Mattel made almost $4 billion in annual sales in 1996, but has filed copyright and trademark infringement suits against all three toy enthusiasts.

●● Coca-Cola, the producer of Minute Maid orange juice, sued Procter & Gamble charging that ads for Citrus Hill Select "falsely" claimed that the juice was made from the "heart" of the orange.

●● In 1989 Walt Disney Company used a lawsuit to force a public apology from the Academy of Motion Picture Arts and Sciences for an "unflattering" representation of Snow White in the opening sequence of the 1989 Academy Awards ceremony.

●● In 1980 the manufacturers of Haagen-Daz ice cream, in a suit against Frusen Gladje, tried to lay claim to the concept of premium ice cream with a "Scandinavian flair."

Is it any wonder that businesses and corporate entities complain about lawyers and lawsuits? But the source of their frustration is not, and their anger about the system should not be directed at, the consumers of products and healthcare. One of the tools used by the propaganda machine that tries to vilify lawyers and personal injury lawsuits, is to make up crazy and unbelievable stories about suits that never really existed. Have you heard the one about Little League baseball threatened by lawsuits? The story goes that Little League Baseball's very existence and the ballparks where Little Leaguers play, are nearly a thing of the past because of suits over injuries to the kids playing. How about the claim that a huge part of the Girl Scouts budget is dependent upon cookie sales to cover liability costs? Have you heard that Firefighters can't do their job out of fear of a lawsuit? These are just some of the myths corporate and insurance industry-backed legal "reform" groups are cynically exploiting. But careful scrutiny of the facts reveals a very different picture.

The claim that Little League is unduly burdened by lawsuits is unfounded. A search of the Lexis/Nexis database (a database that reports all civil suits over the entire country) reveals only two cases in which people who filed tort or injury suits against Little League were compensated for injuries. Both cases were settled out of court. The search exposed two other lawsuits against Little League -- neither of which was a tort claim. One was in 1992, when a wheelchair-bound judge who coached a Little League team filed suit against the organization after he was barred from the field. Little League claimed that the wheelchair constituted a hazard to players. The outcome of this case was not available. In the second case, a girl who wanted to play Little League baseball claimed that a policy of excluding girls was unconstitutional. After the suit was filed, Little League publicly stated that it would immediately permit girls to register for its programs.

Whoever is responsible for perpetuating the ludicrous claim that the Girl Scouts must sell thousands upon thousands of boxes of cookies just to pay liability insurance is wrong. The Girl Scouts have repeatedly denied they are burdened by lawsuits and even demanded that ads asserting otherwise be stopped. After a Member of Congress invoked the Girl Scouts name in trumpeting "legal reform" in 1995, Sandra Jordan of the Washington, D.C., area Girl Scouts said such statements were misleading and the Scouts had no position on such legislation.

Firefighters afraid to save lives because of liability fears? Don't tell that to the Texas State Association of Fire Fighters, which in 1995 denounced this lie as a "disservice." Firefighters acting within the scope of their job are generally immune from lawsuits -- it's only egregious actions outside this scope, such as failing to rescue or committing a non-duty violation, that are and should be cause for alarm. More significant are the examples of firefighters exercising their legal right to hold accountable manufacturers and other wrongdoers that endanger their lives: (A). A Texas firefighter died of injuries he received while fighting a fire when the high pressure hose on his air pack melted, releasing large amounts of air which not only intensified the fire, but also prevented him from using the air pack, forcing him to breathe toxic fumes. (B). A California firefighter suffered brain damage when a defective gas mask malfunctioned. The manufacturer knew of the defect, but failed to advise the fire department or its distributor.

Could it be that the malpractice insurance companies are not shooting straight with their insured doctors about what is raising the malpractice premiums? In December of 2002, the National Law Journal reported that a jury in Santa Monica, California found that medical malpractice insurers "knowingly" misrepresented the benefits of their policies. That jury slapped Norcal Mutual Insurance Company with a $156 million dollar compensatory damage award for "fast-talking" 700 doctors into buying malpractice policies. Before the jury could discuss punitive damages, plaintiffs and the insurance company settled for an undisclosed amount.

Horror stories used to make an illogical point

A widely circulated e-mail from the sponsors of tort reform legislation contains some horror stories about alleged abuses of the civil justice system. Here is one of the stories: "A man sets his Winnebago motor home on cruise control and gets up to make a cup of coffee in the moving vehicle. It crashes. He sues the manufacturer for failing to tell him to stay in the driver's seat. A jury awards him $1.75 million and a new motor home, and the company changes its handbook." There's a simple reason this story sounds unbelievable. **IT'S PHONY. THE CASE NEVER HAPPENED**. It's fabricated and so are six other "lawsuits" summarized in the same e-mail, which has been widely circulated in various forms on the Internet over the last few years. The 2002 version of the e-mail contains the FOLLOWING **FALSE** INFORMATION:

"January 2000: Kathleen Robertson of Austin Texas was awarded $780,000.00 by a jury of her peers after breaking her ankle tripping over her son who was misbehaving in the store.

June 1998: A 19-year old Carl Truman of Los Angeles won $74,000.00 and medical expenses when his neighbor ran his hand over while Truman was trying to steal the neighbor's car.

October 1998: A Terrence Dickson of Bristol Pennsylvania received one half million dollars in mental anguish damages after he was forced to spend eight days in a garage after robbing the house."

The e-mail goes on to list a variety of other "DREAMT-UP" cases. This e-mail is false, according to Snopes.com, a widely respected Web site dedicated to rooting out urban and Internet myths. According to Snopes.com, "all of the entries in the list are fabrications - a search for news stories about each of these cases failed to turn up anything, as did a search for each law case." Snopes.com's analysis of this phony e-mail also mentions that "some versions bear the following footer, although many omit it."

PLEASE ASSIST OUR LAW OFFICES IN A TORT REFORM PROGRAM. WE ARE ATTEMPTING TO PUT A STOP TO THESE INSANE JURY AWARDS BY SENDING THIS E-MAIL OUT TO THE PUBLIC IN THE HOPES OF SWAYING PUBLIC OPINION. PLEASE FORWARD IT TO EVERY EMAIL ADDRESS YOU KNOW.

> Mary R. Hogelmen, Esq. Law Offices of Hogelmen, Hogelmen, and Thomas; Dayton Ohio

As Snopes.com points out, "[t]here is no law firm of Hogelmen, Hogelmen, and Thomas in Dayton, Ohio, as a call to directory assistance quickly confirmed. This detail was included to give the mailing credibility in the eyes of those who received it - if a law firm had pulled this list together to build grassroots support for its tort reform program, then it went without saying a pack of lawyers had properly researched each item and were guaranteeing the information provided. But of course this detail was as false as everything else in the e-mail."

Unfortunately, the seven cases in the e-mail aren't the only fake lawsuits in circulation. An earlier version of the e-mail included another phony case about an alleged plaintiff suing over her poodle that she accidentally microwaved. Phony lawsuits are a common occurrence on the Internet and even in mainstream newspaper articles. They all share one characteristic - no citation to a source. So where do these cases come from? All indications are that they're part of a massive campaign by corporate America and its allies to propagandize for tort "reform" - limits on the legal rights of individuals to hold corporate wrongdoers accountable for causing death and injury. Another common strategy is to cite outrageous cases without disclosing the fact that they were dismissed by a judge shortly after being filed. As Snopes.com notes, such dismissals prove that America's civil-justice system works and that there are adequate safeguards against baseless cases. But big business interests don't want working Americans to understand that.

Corporate lobby groups like the U.S. Chamber of Commerce - which has launched a multimillion-dollar advertising war against trial lawyers - intentionally mislead the public in an attempt to convince Americans that our legal system is broken and needs fixing. They want Americans to distrust their fellow citizens who serve on juries - our friends, relatives, neighbors and coworkers. That is the underlying sadness that infects all of the tort reform efforts–they try to turn the citizens of this country against our peers. These peers are the ones who take their time from work, from their families, and from their other enjoyable pursuits, usually for a few bucks a day, to assist in a system that most of them truly believe in.

The truth is that businesses are the biggest users and abusers of the legal system. According to the American Bar Association, the number of contract cases (in which businesses often initiate the lawsuit) filed in state courts in 2000 was 50 percent higher than the number of injury cases by individuals. In addition, the number of product liability lawsuits by consumers against businesses declined about 20 percent between 1996 and 2000, the ABA says.

A report by two national consumer groups found that corporate America is hypocritical when it comes to our legal system - seeking to destroy individual rights while "maintaining unfettered access to our nation's courts as their own private playground." The report found that "American businesses often file anti-competitive litigation, designed to intimidate or harass."

Even major print journalism gets into the act of exaggerating and misstating the facts. In a sweeping attack on the civil justice system, *Newsweek* magazine, in one of its 2004 editions, does little more than incite unwarranted fears of doctors, teachers and ordinary people about the legal system. Because Newsweek refused to provide any documentation, supporters of the civil justice system prepared a factual refutation. The following are confirmed instances in which Newsweek chose to report "Myths" rather than

70

"Facts."

1.   "In Kentucky, a mother sued her daughter's school after the girl had performed oral sex on a boy during a school bus ride returning from a marching-band contest. The woman blamed poor adult supervision, saying her daughter had been forced."(p. 49).   The **truth**– According to an article in the *Lexington Herald Leader*, the girl was suspended by the school principal for ten days for having consensual sex on a school bus. When the mother appealed the ruling, the board of Education ruled that the act was forced and the girl had been sexually assaulted. But the Board then suspended her for two days for not promptly reporting the assault. The mother's suit demanded that the Board set up a training program for its employees about how to deal with sexual assault.

2.   "In California recently, a couple won a $70 million judgment against Stanford University Hospital and two other healthcare centers for failing to prevent their child from becoming disabled by a rare birth condition." (p. 47) While Newsweek reported the verdict at $70 million, the present value of the award was $8.3 million ($6.3 for medical expenses, $1.8 for lost wages, $250,000 for non-economic damages), meaning the verdict required the

insurer to set aside a total of $8 million to cover the out-of-pocket costs of the injury to the child.

The **truth**: The victim in this case is a young boy who had a genetic disease that was proven to have not been properly diagnosed at birth by the hospital and the boy's pediatricians. The failure of the diagnosis, not the condition itself, was what resulted in permanent brain damage and a need for lifetime care.

3.   The cover of Newsweek features three people who claim to have changed their ways due to the fear of lawsuits:

> Ryan Warner canceled his softball tournament. The Rev. Ron Singleton never hugs people. Dr. Sandra R. Scott is constantly berated by patients threatening to sue her.

> The **truth**: Ryan Warner (the softball organizer), Dr. Sandra Scott (the emergency room doctor), and the Reverend Ron Singleton (the minister) have never been sued. Warner enjoys immunity from suit. Under the Volunteer Protection Act of 1997, volunteers for nonprofit organizations or government programs around the country -- even those dealing with children - cannot

be held responsible for their negligence. As for Singleton, no cause of action for clergy malpractice (i.e.: negligent counseling) exists in South Carolina. Furthermore, state courts which have considered this theory of liability, have universally rejected claims for clergy malpractice.

4. "Parents sue McDonald's...... Convicted sex offender threatens to sue police for failing to find him...... Cheerleader's parents threaten to sue school...... They sue local governments when struck by lightning on city golf courses...... They sue ministers for failing to prevent suicides...... They sue their Little League Coaches."......

The **truth** is: McDonald's obesity cases were dismissed...... The sex offender could not find a lawyer willing to take his case and never filed suit...... The Cheerleader's parents never filed suit...... The lightning strike case was lost at every level due to governmental immunity. ...... Every state court that has considered the question of Clergy malpractice has rejected these claims...... Under the Volunteer Protection Act of 1997, volunteers for nonprofit organizations, including Little League, cannot be held responsible for their negligence.

5. "[T]he litigation explosion of the past 30 years may be leveling off (though one study shows a sharp recent uptick)."(p. 45).

The **truth**: There is no "litigation explosion" in personal injury cases. Litigation is down and awards are steady. A recent analysis from the National Center for State Courts found that since 1992: personal injury tort filings have declined by 9%; automobile tort filings, which make up the majority of all tort claims, have fallen by 14%; and medical malpractice filings per 100,000 population have fallen by 1%. The same holds true in federal courts. Federal civil filings are down, and so is the percentage of civil filings that are personal injury cases.

6. "The cost to society cannot be measured just in money, though the bill is enormous, an estimated $200 billion a year, more than half of it for legal fees and costs that could be used to hire more police or firefighters or teachers." (p. 45).

The **truth**: Tillinghast Towers Perrin's $205 billion estimate, paid for by the insurance companies and tort "reform" groups, is the cost of the entire property/casualty insurance industry. The "legal fees and costs" include plaintiff and defense attorney fees, insurance industry salaries, overhead, and investments. Nowhere in its report does Tillinghast suggest that $100 billion can be cut anywhere. The estimate also includes non-tort claims, like property damage caused by a storm, and almost 40% of the claimed $200 billion goes to insurance industry overhead.

7. "According to one estimate, doctors waste $50 billion to $100 billion on 'defensive medicine' to prove that they left no stone unturned, no test untried, no medication unprescribed, no specialist unconsulted."(p. 49).

The **truth**: In its study of the causes of rising health care costs, the Congressional Budget Office took the position that "defensive medicine is probably not a major factor in the costs of medical care." Another study found that statistics used to determine these costs are "suspect because physicians have a direct financial incentive to overstate their costs." Even with the use of suspect figures, the costs of "defensive medicine" are, at most, 1/6 to 1/3 of what Newsweek claims.

8. "[T]housands of lawsuits by people who hurt themselves at playgrounds." (p. 44).

The **truth**: in 1991, the Consumer Product Safety Commission (CPSC) issued its "Handbook for Public Playground Safety," which has become "the state-of-the-art source for accident claims." According to independent researchers in this area, "Concerns of legal liability arising from failure to meet the recommended guidelines of the CPSC have lead to a widespread upgrading of playgrounds in schools, public parks, and day-care centers." In many situations, insurers have played a large role in forcing compliance with CPSC standards and other safety changes. All of these changes make playgrounds safer for children.

9. "In Penobscot County, Maine, authorities hunted for a convicted sex offender wanted on felony charges for three days after he disappeared into the snowy woods. When the suspect was finally tracked down, he had frostbite and lost two toes. Incredibly, police say, the man threatened to sue the police for not catching him sooner. He couldn't find a lawyer, but his sheer chutzpah did not surprise Penobscot County Sheriff Glenn Ross. 'We're always facing lawsuits,' says Ross. 'It's on our minds all the time.'" (p. 50).

The **truth**: the basic facts of the story are true - the man was wanted for a probation violation in Florida, Maine cops got a tip that he was in the state, attempted to interrogate him and he turned and ran. "Harvey Taylor has not filed a suit in Maine or Florida, because since most lawyers refuse to take cases without merit, no lawyer has agreed to help him.

10. "And when patients do sue, their malpractice allegations are unfounded in as many as 80 percent of the cases, other studies suggest; insurance companies pay to settle the vast majority of claims anyway, rather than risk a big hit." (p. 48).

The **truth**: There is no evidence that 80% of malpractice claims are unfounded. Professor Neil Vidmar of Duke University, author of *Medical Malpractice and the American Jury*, states that "In interviews with liability insurers that I undertook, the most consistent theme from them was: 'We do not settle frivolous cases!' . . . [Insurers'] policy on frivolous cases is based on the belief that if they ever begin to settle cases just to make them go away, their credibility will be destroyed and this will encourage more litigation."

Power to decide life or death, but too dumb for you and me

The Newsweek article mentions almost nothing about the critical benefits of our civil justice system. Society benefits in countless ways as a result of lawsuits: they prevent future injuries by removing dangerous products and practices from the marketplace and spurring safety innovation; they educate the public about unnecessary and unacceptable risks associated with some products and services through disclosure of facts discovered during trial; and they provide authoritative judicial forums for the ethical growth of law. The power and authority of juries represent an important counterweight to the dominance of organized moneyed interests elsewhere in our government. Newsweek ignored all of this in its article. It also ignored observations by doctors like Dr. Wayne Cohen, who in 1995 was medical director of Bronx Municipal Hospital, who said, "The city was spending so much money defending obstetrics suits, they just made a decision that it would be cheaper to hire people who knew what they were doing." (Dean Baquet and Jane Fritsch, "New York's Public Hospitals Fail, and Babies Are the Victims," *New York Times*, March 5, 1995.) The Newsweek article calls juries overly sympathetic, emotional, and unable to handle complex issues, but close observers of the jury system, including judges, believe the opposite. Why is it that the justice system trusts juries to sentence people to death in criminal cases, but does not trust juries to determine monetary awards in civil cases? Isn't life more precious than money? Who better to determine the value of loss than your friends, family members, neighbors and co-workers?

Next.......A Cup of Coffee for a fish tale

All of my maternal uncles were architects, who lived in Tyler, Texas. In the summer when my family would visit them, I would spend time with my uncles going about their daily routine. Their day usually began at the little drug store lunch counter at local shopping center less than a block from their office, where they would meet business associates for a cup of coffee. When they would greet their buddies, the greeting was one intended to start a conversation about anything newsworthy that any of them had to report. The greeting was "cup of coffee for a tale?" Everyone knew that to mean, "what's going on with you?" or "anything newsworthy?" That was back in the late 1950's and early 1960's. Nowadays, that conversation would be done via e-mail, cell phone, or maybe still even over coffee, but the purpose is the same–to pass on information, news, items of human interest, or just idle talk.

Often idle talk these days is focused on the justice system. Anyone who ever talks about the place of the jury in our civil justice system has, no doubt, heard about the "McDonald's Coffee Case." That is the real mother of "cup of coffee for a tale," only it was all a fish tale. Stella Liebeck of Albuquerque, New Mexico, was in the passenger seat of her grandson's car when she was severely burned by McDonald's coffee in February 1992. Liebeck ordered coffee that was served in a Styrofoam cup at the drive-through window of a local McDonald's. What most people do not know, and what the propaganda machine does not want most people to know, is the rest of the story. After receiving the order, the grandson pulled his car forward (as requested by the Mcdonald's employee) and stopped momentarily so that Liebeck could add cream and sugar to her coffee. (Critics of civil justice, who have pounced on this case, often charge that Liebeck was driving the car or that the vehicle was in motion when she spilled the coffee; neither is true.) Liebeck placed the cup between her knees and attempted to remove the plastic lid from the cup. As she removed the lid, the entire contents of the cup spilled into her lap.

The sweat pants Liebeck was wearing absorbed the coffee and held it next to her skin. A vascular surgeon determined that Liebeck suffered full thickness burns (or third-degree burns) over 6 percent of her body, including her inner thighs, perineum, buttocks, and genital and groin areas. She was hospitalized for eight days, during which time she underwent skin grafting, where old skin was ripped from her and replaced by healthy skin removed from other parts of her body. She also received debridement treatments, where the raw skin is repeatedly washed with a sterile saline solution. Any physician or nurse who treats such burns will tell you that burns, and their treatment, are some of the most painful medical problems and treatments that a person can encounter. Liebeck, sought to settle her claim for $20,000, but McDonald's refused.

During the investigation phase of the suit, McDonald's was forced to turn over to the plaintiff documents showing more than 700 claims by people burned by its coffee between 1982 and 1992. Some claims involved third-degree burns substantially similar to Liebeck's. This history documented McDonald's knowledge about the extent and nature of this hazard. McDonald's officials also testified that, based on a consultant's advice, it held its coffee at between 180 and 190 degrees Fahrenheit to maintain optimum taste. Other establishments sell coffee at substantially lower temperatures, and coffee served at home is generally 135 to 140 degrees.

McDonald's quality assurance manager testified that the company actively enforces a requirement that coffee be held in the pot at 185 degrees, plus or minus five degrees. He also testified that he was aware that a burn hazard exists with any food substance served at 140 degrees or above, and that McDonald's coffee, at the temperature at which it was poured into Styrofoam cups, was not fit for consumption because it would burn the mouth and throat. The quality assurance manager admitted that burns would occur, but testified that McDonald's had no intention of reducing the "holding temperature" of its coffee.

Plaintiff's expert, a scholar in thermodynamics as applied to human skin burns, testified that liquids, at 180 degrees, will cause a full thickness burn to human skin in two to seven seconds. Other testimony showed that as the temperature decreases toward 155 degrees, the extent of the burn relative to that temperature decreases exponentially. Thus, if Liebeck's spill had involved coffee at 155 degrees, the liquid would have cooled and given her time to avoid a serious burn. McDonald's asserted that customers buy coffee on their way to work or home, intending to consume it there. However, the company's own research showed that customers intend to consume the coffee immediately while driving, and those were a large group of consumers whose business they targeted.

McDonald's also argued that consumers know coffee is hot and that its customers want it that way. The company admitted its customers were unaware that they could suffer third-degree burns from the coffee and that a statement on the side of the cup was not a "warning" but a "reminder" since the location of the writing would not warn customers of the hazard.

The jury awarded Liebeck $200,000 in compensatory damages. This amount was reduced to $160,000 because the jury found Liebeck 20 percent at fault in the spill. The jury also awarded Liebeck $2.7 million in punitive damages, which equals about two days of McDonald's coffee sales. Post-verdict investigation found that the temperature of coffee at the local Albuquerque McDonald's had dropped to 158 degrees Fahrenheit.

McDonald's lawyers argued that there should have been no award of punitive damage. The trial judge, a conservative Republican, reduced the punitive award to $480,000 -- or three times compensatory damages -- even though he called McDonald's conduct reckless, callous and willful. Subsequent to the reduction of the verdict, the parties entered a post-verdict settlement.

Who defines Frivolous?

The law generally defines a frivolous lawsuit as "presenting no debatable question to the court." But there is certainly no debate for corporate defendants and their lobbyists. They simply don't like getting caught when they harm people. Much like convicted prisoners who contend that there are no guilty people in jail, some corporate defendants don't ever seem willing to admit their guilt, no matter what the evidence. Instead of listening to the complaints of those who are held accountable for their misbehavior, let's take a closer look at statistics and unbiased studies that give us the facts, not the excuses:

There is not an avalanche of frivolous suits–

I. Richard Turbin, of the American Bar Association's Tort and Insurance Practice section, a group which includes plaintiff and defense lawyers, publicly stated that the **rate of federal lawsuits per capita has not changed since 1790.** Mr. Turbin also noted that plaintiffs have steadily won 30 to 40 percent of cases and that the size of awards has increased due to natural inflation only.

II. According to a Department of Justice study published in August 2000, overall, plaintiffs in the country's 75 largest counties won slightly fewer tort jury trials in 1996 (the last year for which numbers are available) than in 1992. Half of plaintiff winners in tort jury trials won $57,000 or more in 1992; in 1996 half of plaintiff winners won only $30,000 or more, *a significant drop in those amounts awarded.*

III. *When given, awards are generally small.* The DOJ study said $30,500 was the median final award received by plaintiffs in the study. This includes both compensatory and punitive damages. (Compensatory awards are given to restore the plaintiff to the condition he/she occupied before the injury. Punitive damages are awarded to punish a defendant who commits a willful or malicious act)

IV. The Legal System Knows How to Deal With Truly Frivolous Lawsuits, and Does:

A. Our 225-year-old legal system has multiple *procedural safeguards to ensure defendants' rights.* The contingency fee system keeps attorneys from taking baseless cases. A certain amount and quality of evidence must be present for any case to proceed. Judges monitor filings at every step, and can dismiss a case at any almost time. Attorneys can be punished and, in some cases, may have to pay money penalties if they bring frivolous suits to court, or otherwise abuse the process.

B. *The civil justice system works.* Only wrongdoer defendants are punished despite the excuses guilty defendants give their shareholders for paying plaintiffs. ("We just settled to avoid court costs" is the battle cry of the guilty. Why pay a settlement if you can get the case dismissed and pay nothing?)

The cry for relief by the corporate guys

So, now that we know that the true facts have been obscured, that the propaganda is inaccurate, and that the "malpractice crisis" is not a crisis at all, what do you see going on around you? You will recall the indescribably terrible tsunami in the Pacific. Shortly after that, President Bush sent his brother, Florida Governor Jeb Bush, to the area to survey the damage and determine in what ways we could help. While Jeb was there, the President was here still at it, declaring that Congress, "Needs to pass real medical liability reform this year." At an event and speech in Illinois, filling the bleachers behind Bush with people in white lab coats, Bush declared that large jury damage awards as compensation for malpractice claims are driving up the rates of malpractice premiums so high that doctors are being forced to shut up shop. Those nasty trial lawyers, at it again, trying to take away your health care! But, here are the true numbers about malpractice suits: sixty-one percent of lawsuits brought alleging malpractice are dropped or dismissed, so the doctors win. (And don't forget, where lawsuits are shown to be frivolous, the plaintiff can be ordered to pay the legal bills of the defense.) Thirty-two percent of such cases are settled.

This quest for medical liability reform became part of Bush's stock speech, insisting that the "Constant risk of being hit by a massive jury award" is driving doctors to settle cases "Even when they know they have done nothing wrong." Except, for that judgment to hold true, those doctors have to assess the case against them and decide that their behavior was worse than 61% of other malpractice lawsuits, since their conduct has to be worse than all those dismissed cases to put them in danger of this huge jury payout.

Clearly, what is more likely is that the doctors know that they would lose money by going to court because they are in fact liable for some awful mistake that rises to the clear definition of malpractice applied by our judicial system. This leaves only seven percent of all malpractice cases that ever make it to trial at all, and the doctors win eighty percent of the time!

In only seven percent of the cases actually filed do the physicians charged with harming their patients actually believe that the plaintiff cannot prove that they failed to provide reasonable medical services. (Didn't you know? The injured—or dead— patient has the burden of convincing a jury that the doctor failed to act competently.) This means that out of all malpractice suits, only 1.3% result in a jury granting the plaintiff one of their dreaded awards. Yet even after the jury sets an award amount, there are still factors that can bring the award figure down. First, the judge in the case has discretion to decrease the amount of damages assessed, just like in the McDonald's coffee case. Second, the plaintiff and defending doctor can also negotiate the award, as the doctor decreases the amount paid to the plaintiff in exchange for not seeking an appeal attempting to reverse the decision (all the while delaying payment). All these factors combine to make the average jury award, as reported to the National Practitioner Data Bank (which receives all malpractice settlement and court award information by federal law), $235,000. That would be less, for those of you keeping track at home, than Bush's proposed cap.

So whom does this "medical liability reform" protect? The insurance companies would like you to believe that the rising insurance premiums are punishing all doctors, but this is simply not the case. Insurance premiums have indeed been rising, but at a demonstrably lower rate than individual health insurance premiums, at least one percent lower in increase per year since 1997. And, despite insurance operatives insisting that malpractice insurance has skyrocketed in the last decade or so (to correspond with the rise in trial litigation), recent rates of increase have been roughly the same, or even less, than the average increase in rates since the 1970s.

Doctors spend more on the rent for their office buildings than they do on malpractice insurance—but you don't see anyone angrily insisting that the real estate market be brought to heel. So who, again, is protected by the "medical liability reform?" With even the average malpractice jury award (which, again, is only granted in 1.3% of all cases brought alleging malpractice), under the proposed cap on jury awards, this means the people that will truly benefit from such a cap are those few and far between upon whom doctors have truly committed a ghastly act of malpractice.

Limits on damages would protect the doctor who mistakenly amputated both breasts of Linda McDougal, a cancer-free woman, for example, or those whose shoddy paperwork resulted in the brain death of a child. Is this really who Bush, Congress and the insurance companies want to protect? Is this really what Congress should be spending its time on? Other insurance companies and their politicians have an identical agenda for products liability tort lawsuits. Remember the Ford Pinto, which when struck from the rear in an auto collision, exploded in a fireball incinerating the occupants, even in a minor impact? Ford Motor Company knew that their gas tank design would cause such horrible, needless deaths, yet fought each lawsuit, settling with desperate plaintiffs only on their promise to keep the result a secret, until some crusading injured consumer decided to force the issue by insisting on a trial. How about the Ford Explorer (or "Flipper") of a few years past?

When you hear about all of the ills that trial lawyers cause, consider the following:

1.   The Kansas woman who died from Toxic

Shock Syndrome after using the company's super-absorbent tampons. After the verdict, Playtex strengthened its warnings on other products about the association between tampons and TSS.*O'Gilvie v. International Playtex, Inc.*, 609 F. Supp. 817 (D. Kan. 1985), *rev'd*, 821 F.2d 1438 (10th Cir. 1987), *cert. denied*, 108 S.Ct. 2014 (1988).

2.   Overpriced prescription drugs are driving up the cost of health care for everyone. The pharmaceutical company SmithKline manufactures the antidepressant drug Paxil, which in 1999 grossed more than $1.4 billion in sales. When other companies sought approval from the FDA to market a less costly, safe and generic version of the drug, SmithKline wrongly filed patent challenges to delay any generic from reaching the market—keeping a monopoly, and keeping prices artificially high for patients. The judge even applauded "the high caliber of plaintiffs' counsels' work in this case." *Nichols v. SmithKline Beecham Corp //The Stop and Shop Supermarket Co. v. SmithKline Beecham Corp.*

3. Airco, Inc., the world's largest manufacturer of anesthesia equipment, marketed an artificial breathing machine that assisted patient breathing during surgery, caused oxygen deprivation and brain damage. A punitive damage award was upheld on appeal in 1982, after which the manufacturer voluntarily issued a medical device alert under auspices of the Food and Drug Administration. Further, the defendant doctors testified at trial that they would never use the ventilator in the same way

again. *Airco, Inc. v. Simmons First National Bank*, 638 S.W.2d 660 (Ark. 1982).

4. A 27-year-old woman suffered a severe pelvic infection requiring a hysterectomy after wearing an IUD for several years. After the surgery, the woman's marriage disintegrated and she divorced. She must take synthetic hormones that increase her risk of developing endometrial cancer. Evidence established that the manufacturer had known its IUD was associated with a high rate of pelvic disease and septic abortion, that it had misled doctors about the device's safety, and that it had dropped or concealed studies on the device when the results were unfavorable. See, e.g., *Tetuan v. A.H. Robins Co.*, 738 P.2d 1210 (Kan. 1987).

5. After a man's liver was destroyed by a toxic reaction when he took Tylenol and drank wine, the Food and Drug Administration announced that all pain relievers containing acetaminophen, including Tylenol, would bear warning labels. Pharmacologists have known about the link between Tylenol, alcohol and liver damage since the late 1970s. The man, who required an emergency liver transplant, was awarded compensatory and punitive damages by a jury. Steve Bates and Charles W. Hall, "Tylenol Verdict Puts Spotlight on Drug Labels," *Washington Post*, October 22, 1994, at A1.

6. In 1983, a 13-month-old baby was found hanged to death on the headboard of a crib made by Bassett Furniture. The girl's head was caught in a cutout

between the top corner post and a blanket roll, lifting her feet off the mattress. All of the cribs were later recalled. *Crusan v. Bassett Furniture Co.*, Cal., Sacramento Super. Ct., June 11, 1986.

7. A manufacturer of children's pajamas, the fabric of which was 100 percent untreated cotton flannelette, stopped making the highly flammable garment after a Minnesota jury ordered the company to pay compensatory and punitive damages to a 4-year-old girl who had been badly burned when her pajama top caught fire. A company official acknowledged that flannelette was not treated with flame-retardant chemicals because of costs, even though the court noted that such treatment would have been economically feasible. *Gryc v. Dayton Hudson Corp.*, 297 N.W.2d 727 (Minn. 1980), cert. denied, 101 S. Ct. 320 (1980).

8. Four days after a St. Louis (Mo.) Circuit Court jury returned a $78 million punitive damages award against Domino's Pizza, the world's largest pizza delivery company dropped its fast-delivery policy. Domino's promise of delivery within 30 minutes encouraged company drivers to speed and drive negligently or recklessly. From 1984 to 1986, a late-arriving pizza was left at no cost to the customer. Since 1986, customers have been given $3 off their orders. In announcing the policy change, Domino's President Thomas Monaghan said the jury verdict had persuaded the company to rescind its 30-minute promise. "That was certainly the thing that put us over the edge," he explained, adding that there

"continues to be a perception, a perception that I believe is not supported by the facts, that the guarantee is unsafe. We got that message loud and clear." The St. Louis jury ruled for Jean Kinder, who suffered head and spinal injuries when a Domino's delivery driver ran a red light and hit her car broadside in 1989. Kinder and her daughter were headed to a bowling alley to try out her daughter's new ball, a Christmas present, when the accident occurred.*Kinder v. Hively Corp.*, Mo., St. Louis County Cir. Ct., No. 902-01235 (verdict Dec. 17, 1993).

Jury verdicts ring loud and clear with corporations

All of these defendant corporations in the above cases, their insurance companies, and all manufacturers of dangerous products call the trial lawyers evil and greedy, but these evil people are tired of having to make safe products because trial lawyers take them to task - this reduces profit margins. They are relying upon Bush and the new Republican majority in Congress to make sure that you will just sit by and watch, or even that you will join the fray to punish innocent victims and trial lawyers. They're just trying to make their rich friends even richer, and to help you, the American Public. Into your graves.

This is not a book that is either pro or con to either political party; Nor is this a book about conservative versus liberal. It is not about doctor versus lawyer. My brother is a doctor, and quite a good one, who believes, by the way, that if he is negligent and harms someone, his insurance company should pay for his conduct, just like his car insurance would if he negligently harmed someone while driving his vehicle. This book is about trying to find the right ways to keep good people from being hurt by bad conduct, regardless of whom the good person is and regardless of the source of the bad conduct. I am sure that there are Republicans who are not in the pockets of the insurance companies, and I am sure there are Democrats who take their share of corporate dollars in contributions.

The things that we now know about the debate are that (1) the "facts" used to support the arguments for limits on medical liability are not true; (2) the people who will be the worst hurt will be the ones to further suffer under any plan for limitation of liability and (3) IT WILL BE THE CHILDREN, THE ELDERLY, AND THE STAY AT HOME PARENTS WHO HAVE NO PROVABLE CLAIM OF ECONOMIC LOSS, that will be harmed if Congress places caps or limits on non-economic damages.

What are damages awarded for?

The central point of most of the plans for limitation of liability is a limit on the amount of damages that a jury will be allowed for certain types of damages. These damages, in almost every plan before Congress, are what is known as "non-economic" damages. The legislation now before Congress, strongly urged by President Bush, is to "cap" non-economic damages in medical malpractice suits at the total sum of $250,000. This is the identical plan that was passed in Texas at the behest of Governor Rick Perry, Bush's former Lieutenant Governor. Under the Texas and Congressional Plan, this means that a person, no matter how badly injured and no matter how egregious the conduct of the physician, could not be awarded more than $250,000 by a jury for the non-economic damages.

"Economic damages" take two forms. First, the amount of income that an injured person has lost and will lose as a result of his injury. Second, amounts of money that the injured person has been caused to expend for his or her own care and treatment resulting from the injury. The first type is generically called "lost wages" and the second type "medical expenses." It is important to note that, most commonly, a person who goes to a doctor for medical care already has some ailment, disease or infirmity. If that patient is further injured as a result of the malpractice of the physician, the patient can only recover for lost wages and medical expenses that the patient would not otherwise have incurred. A negligent doctor is required to pay only for the results of his negligence, not for all things that may be wrong with the patient. As a good example to demonstrate this, let's say that a construction worker hurts his back on the job, and requires surgery to remedy the injury. He goes to the hospital, has the surgery, and does well, except for the fact that one of the operating room nurses leaves inside the wound a "sponge," which is really a small cloth or gauze used for soaking up extra blood or other fluids. Since it is the job of the surgical nurse to count these items and remove them before the surgeon closes, the patient may have a legal claim against the nurse and the hospital for whom the nurse works. Another surgery will be required to remove the sponge. The patient will have a legal claim for wages he loses as a result of the extra time off from work for the second surgery. He will have a legal claim for the extra cost of the second surgery. He does not have a claim for the cost of the initial surgery nor for the time he loses from work for that surgery. Let's further assume that the patient does not recover well from the back surgery, but still has some pain and physical limitations on his movement or his capabilities. He has no claim against the sponge-leaving nurse for those damages, since those were not the result of leaving the sponge behind. Nor does he have a claim against the surgeon for his limitations, unless there was something that the surgeon did wrong that caused this pain and physical limitations.

The law is very precise in what is allowed to a patient in a legal action against a health care provider. He cannot recover legally for pre-existing conditions, or any treatment complication unless he can prove, through the competent testimony of a qualified expert physician, that the condition or complication was caused by the doctor's negligence.

Now that we know the specific and limited types of economic damages may be legally recovered, it is easier to define "non-economic" damages. These are the types of damages that result from the negligent treatment of a health care provider, but do not result in specific dollar expenditures by the patient. Although different states have different characterizations for these, they generally include "pain," "mental anguish," "loss of companionship," "disfigurement," and "physical impairment." An injured person, if he has been hurt in these ways, may recover an amount to compensate for this injury. The key term there is "compensate." Although it is difficult to put a price on these damages, the purpose of a jury finding these damages is to compensate for the injuries to the patient–it is not to punish the wrongdoer. The law does not allow for damages intended to punish negligent conduct. These types of damages are called "punitive" damages, and are only allowed when the conduct of the wrongdoer is so egregious as to rise near to the level of "intent." In all jurisdictions in this country, in order for punitive damages to be awarded, a jury must find that the wrongdoer caused an injury even though he knew of a specific, substantial risk of harm, and proceeded with his conduct with knowledge that such harm was likely to occur. Each state has precise definitions of such conduct, and the words used to describe it vary from state to state, but the type of conduct which will allow an award of punitive damages if far more nefarious than mere "negligence."

Why pick on non-economic damages?

Most of the states that have limited damages have limited either punitive damages, noneconomic damages or both. Limitations on punitive damages are more common, and have been in place, in some states, long before the proposal for limitations on non-economic damages. What has happened now is that the insurance companies have done a good job of making people confuse non-economic damages with punitive damages, and they have done a good job of making the public think that non-economic damages are out of control. But the cap on noneconomic damages is far more hurtful to the victims of malpractice, because now they cannot even recover money to compensate for their injuries. Punitive damages are very infrequently awarded, so what remains is a victimized patient without an adequate remedy.

Patients do not have a right to recover attorney's fees. They must have a contract to pay their attorney out of what they receive. So, when lost wages are awarded, the patient actually has to give away part of his earnings to receive the services of the lawyer that took on the negligent doctor or hospital. When medical expenses are awarded, one of two things occurs. If the patient has paid those himself (which is not often the case since either a PPO, HMO, Medicare or Medicaid are usually involved), he does not get back all of his money, since he had, again, to pay a lawyer a percentage of his recovery. More often, when insurance of some sort is involved, the insurer gets to keep for itself any medical expenses a jury awards for expenses that the insurer has had to pay. This is called the "right of subrogation," which means that a health insurance company who pays your medical bills is entitled to receive back from you any amount you received for medical expenses in a settlement or jury verdict.

These insurance companies are not stupid. They know that injured victims of malpractice do not often have the money to hire a lawyer and pay an hourly fee (like the insurance companies do) for the representation. They also know that the defendant and his insurance company will defend the case until the cows come home to run up the time and expense to the plaintiff's lawyer. They know that it costs tens of thousands of dollars and hundreds of attorney hours, if not thousands, to successfully prosecute a case to conclusion for the plaintiff, with a less than even chance of success, based upon all of the known statistics. So, a trial lawyer with any degree of business sense cannot take a case unless there is enough of a chance of success, and enough of a chance of some decent compensation for his time. The only real source of compensation for both the victim and his lawyer will be from the "noneconomic" damages. Otherwise, there is no sense in even bringing a suit. The lost wage damages are directly out of the victim's pocket. The medical expense damages are repaid to the medical insurer. The only thing left is the non-economic damages. Limiting those damages takes away most incentive to sue, no matter how badly the victim is hurt.

One of the best ways to demonstrate the harm and injustice in a cap on damages is a case of a severe injury to a small child. Let's say that a medication dispensation error (an all too common occurrence from reading the medical journal articles) occurs in St. Mercy Hospital, and a baby in the neonatal unit is brain-damaged. That baby will live a full life in terms of the number of years, but will never be able to walk, talk, eat, sit or stand without assistance. Custodial care and medical attention will be required constantly. That little baby has no lost earnings, since these must be proven with reasonable certainty, and there is no way to do that. That little baby will likely be on medicare or medicaid, or some other government-funded program, for the rest of its life. That child is limited to a maximum of $250,000 for the rest of life. That amount does not even account for the loss suffered by his parents, who have done nothing but wish to bring their newborn home. Since there are no lost wages to recover, and any recovery for future medical expenses will go the entity who pays the medical expenses in the future (whether it is a private HMO, PPO, or a governmental entity), the most that can be recovered is $250,000. A case like this one will likely never be brought. Where is the good to society in that? Why should the hospital or its insurance carrier go scott-free, while someone else pays for this the rest of this child's life, payment in the form of money, emotion, pain, anguish, despair and probably the ruination of the family?

It is now easier to see why non-economic damages are the target of those who would destroy the system. They know that the system will no longer exist, for all practical purposes. Good evidence of this fact comes in this form. In the Dallas-Fort Worth Metroplex, I serve as a mediator for medical malpractice cases. I always inquire of my friends on both sides of the bar, both plaintiff and defense lawyers, about what suits are being filed. I know nearly every one of those lawyers in this area, and there are usually no more than two degrees of separation between me and any lawyer in the Metroplex who does this type of work. Among all of these lawyers, and all the lawyers whom these lawyers know, I have been able to learn of only a handful of lawsuits that have been filed in the last eighteen months. This is in an area were there are over four million people—an area where there are huge corporate hospital and physician groups. The passage of the law that took effect in September of 2003 had its intended effect—not just to limit "outrageous" damages and do away with frivolous lawsuits, but to do away with this pesky thing called malpractice suits.

In the next chapter you will see some specifics of the cases that are used to paint the distorted picture. The misinformation that you have been reading in the past will be dispelled. The cases that you hear about that are ridiculous–they are not only ridiculous, they are untrue. But that does not matter to those who want you to give up your rights. If you believe that plaintiffs are reaping outrageous and unwarranted benefits from the system, you will help change the system. If, on the other hand, you do not believe that to be the case, and you understand that the propaganda is false, then, I hope that you will take action, so that the system will be there when you need it. You need to know the truth.

CHAPTER THREE

INSURANCE COMPANIES LOGIC IS ILLOGICAL

Medical malpractice filings per 100,000 population have decreased by 1 percent over the past decade. National Center for State Courts, Court Statistics Project (2003)

How to Lie With Statistics was a book that I was required to read in my senior year of high school. How boring it sounded! But the more I read the more interesting it became. Its basic theme was that anyone can use statistics to try to establish most any point, no matter how fallacious, if one simply juxtaposes the numbers and the words artfully. One amusing example from the book is a story from a supposed ancient tribe in Africa. The story goes that this tribe had a belief that it was healthy to have lice crawling all over the body. They derived this belief from the following reasoning: they only had lice when they felt good; when they were ill and running a temperature, the lice would leave their body. Consequently, having lice was healthy. The flaw–lice do not like heat. The reasoning makes perfect sense if you do not know the science behind why we have fever. All too often there is one unknown factor behind faulty logic. When there is this unknown factor, we do not know that the logic is faulty. That is why statistics are often used to prove a point that is patently untrue, but the untruth is not discovered by the reader, because one fact is missing.

The faulty logic of the reformers goes something like this: medical malpractice premiums are high; as a result, health care costs are high. People need reasonable health care costs. Therefore, we should help the doctors make their costs lower by lessening the amount that people can recover in lawsuits against doctors. Sounds reasonable, right? Several facts are left out of the equation, the most important of which is that malpractice premiums have not gone down when caps have been placed on damages. The true reason for that is that damages are not the reason for high malpractice rates. Less than one percent of health care costs result from malpractice premiums. We will talk more about those statistics in a later chapter, and we will also talk about insurance companies and their investments, and the negative effect of those bad investments on premiums.

One recent book is filled with such flaws in reasoning. I mentioned in the last chapter that Catherine Crier, in her book *The Case Against the Lawyers* made some observations that were accurate, in the portrayal of corporate dominance over the lawmaking function of our government. Ms. Crier, however, fails to recognize that it is this same corporate dominance and misrepresentation that has resulted in the trumped-up popularity of the calls for "tort reform." Her failure is due, in part, to the use of unsupported statistics and her apparent belief in the false propositions fostered and perpetuated by the same corporate interests which she says she dislikes. She has become a victim of "How to Lie With Statistics."

It is interesting that Ms. Crier blasphemes all lawyers regardless of which side or what type of work, when the predominant characteristic of lawyers is that the entire system in which they work is an adversarial one. How is it that lawyers are all so bad, when one half of them are fighting, tooth and nail, against the other half? Ms. Crier uses the same fallacious arguments and nonexistent cases that the insurance industry uses to advance its position. Further demonstration of the fallacy behind other of Ms. Crier's arguments and suppositions in particular detail later in this book, but for now I would simply point out the lack of basic logic in her major premise. She states that she believes, as I do, that money and influence in corporate behavior have corrupted the political and governmental processes, but she fails to see that plaintiff's trial lawyers, representing persons injured by that corporate behavior, are fighting against that same corporate behavior. Instead, she falls prey to the corporate party line that injured party's lawsuits are bad and we should allow corporate irresponsibility to go unpunished, undeterred, and uncompensated.

I would invite Ms. Crier to take a look at the work of Ralph Nader and Wesley J. Smith entitled No Contest, where the authors make a thorough, detailed, fact-ridden demonstration of the absolute and corruptible power of the corporate lawyers. They show how our corporate-dominated legal system and its "power lawyers" are behind the erosion of the basic rights of access to true and timely justice for ordinary Americans. Some of the facts, figures, statistics and quotes from No Contest will be used later in this book to show how Nader is right, and Crier is wrong. There is not a compendious scheme by all lawyers against the average Joe in this country. There is in fact a scheme by the corporate types against the average Joe, who is joined by the good and competent trial lawyers. (Notice I did not say that all trial lawyers are good and competent, just like all doctors are not good and competent.) The corporate-financed blitz has painted multibillion-dollar corporations as hapless victims of ordinary Americans bent on suing their way into prosperity. In fact, those corporations have caused many of the courts to become their nearly exclusive domain. The history of our legal system, and particularly our jury system, is that juries have decided questions of fact pertaining to whether one party to a lawsuit violated the legal rights of another party. That has always been the case. Now we are hearing cries that the legislators should create new laws that limit the ability of jurors to do their job. The supposed justifications for such limitations on jurors findings include a host of different hypotheses. The main two are (1)that increasing numbers of frivolous lawsuits are resulting in damage awards and/or settlements that are not fair, and (2) that jurors are finding ludicrously high monetary awards as compensation for the violation of the legal rights. The supposed result is that businesses who are the defendants, or potential defendants, in these cases are going to be run out of business, or their insurance premiums are going to be so high that the consumer of the products they make will ultimately pay the price for the juries' stupidity.

Nothing could be further from the truth. These claims were made as part of the "Contract for America" propounded by Newt Gingrich in 1994. In fact, tort claims accounted for only about five percent of all civil claims filed in state courts in 1992, according to data compiled by the nonpartisan National Center for State Courts (NCSC). National Center for State Courts, "Examining the Work of

State Courts," 1994 (1996). In addition, tort filings in state courts declined between 1989 and 1998, according to an NCSC study of tort filings in 28 states -- by 1%. This is particularly significant because more than 95 percent of all tort cases are filed in state courts and states' populations increased between 1989 and 1998. In a study of 16 states, NCSC found that the number of tort filings decreased 16% between 1996 and 1998.

The real cost of injury

Tort system costs pale in comparison to costs associated with injury. A Rand study estimated that medical spending for the treatment of injuries cost the U.S. economy nearly $154 billion in 1997 (about 20% of the nation's health care bill) and that lost work time adds another $100 billion. The National Safety Council estimates that accident costs totaled $480.5 billion in 1998. About 6,000 deaths and millions of injuries are prevented each year because of the deterrent effect of product liability, according to the Consumer Federation of America.

Compare that 480.5 billion dollar annual cost of injury to the cost of malpractice premiums that help pay for medical error. Doctors allocate 13 times more of their practice income for their own salaries than they pay in malpractice premiums. According to the federal government's Medicare program, doctors nationally spend an average of 52.5 percent of their practice incomes on their own pay, about 31 percent on such overhead expenses as office payroll and rent, and only 3.9 percent on malpractice insurance. Source: "Annual Percent Change in the Revised and Rebased Medicare Economic Index, 2004 Cost Categories and Price Measures," Centers for Medicare and Medicaid Services (CMS), Nov. 7, 2003.

Isn't that what insurance is for? It pays for injuries to those who truly get the short end of the stick. When juries speak for those victims, corporate America listens. That's why defectively designed cribs no longer strangle infants. Flammable children's pajamas have been taken off the market. Once-harmful medical devices have been redesigned. Auto fuel systems have been strengthened. Cancer-causing asbestos no longer poisons homes, schools and work places. And farm machinery has safety guards. Despite these accomplishments of the trial bar, the corporate lobby groups, like the U. S. Chamber of Commerce, which has launched a multimillion-dollar advertising war against trial lawyers - intentionally mislead the public in an attempt to convince Americans that our legal system is broken and needs fixing. They want Americans to distrust their fellow citizens who serve on juries - our friends, relatives, neighbors and coworkers.

A report by two national consumer groups found "American businesses often file anti-competitive litigation, designed to intimidate or harass." In fact, when you read most of the literature printed by the corporations, indeed even the book of Ms. Catherine Crier, you are not told of the fact that most of the lawsuits that they use as examples of "frivolous suits" are, in fact dismissed before they go anywhere, proving the fact that the system works. It is really interesting that she claims that huge contingent fees are bad because they promote abuse of the system, yet she does not explain how the "greedy" lawyer benefits by filing frivolous suits that result in no recovery, and thus, no fee.

Another characteristic shared by the anti-lawsuit corporate interests is a lack of citation to source. So where do these cases come from? All indications are that they're part of a massive campaign by corporate America and its allies to propagandize for tort "reform" - limits on the legal rights of individuals to hold corporate wrongdoers accountable for causing death and injury.

Comparative negligence accounts for the fault of plaintiffs

We hear a lot of talk about people taking responsibility for their actions. Some of that talk is about the legal system, and how it sometimes seems to let people sue even in those cases when the people suing contributed to their own injuries. Our civil justice system is all about making sure people take responsibility. Where plaintiffs' actions need to be accounted for, a legal tool called comparative negligence--which is used in some form in every state-makes sure people who sue take responsibility for their portion of fault. Here is how comparative negligence works: Say a woman is driving a down a road. She glances down to change the station on the radio, which causes her to hit the curb. The impact causes the tread of one of her defectively produced tires to peel away, and she loses control of the car, which flips over. Her spinal cord is severed. She is paralyzed, and will require constant medical care for the rest of her life. This care will eventually cost millions of dollars. Who will end up paying for those medical bills? It depends on how her courts decide who should pay when someone is hurt by a defendant's misbehavior. So if the jury found she deserved $1 million in compensation for her lifelong injuries, but also said she was 50% at fault for the accident, the court would reduce the award by $500,000 (50%) to $500,000. This way she "pays" for the portion of the accident for which she was responsible. This is exactly what happened in the famous McDonald's scalding coffee case. The jury awarded Liebeck $200,000 in compensatory damages (not the millions you have heard). This amount was reduced to $160,000 because the jury found Liebeck 20% at fault.

An interesting historical note is that the rule used to be known as the "contributory negligence" rule. That rule was in existence in most states until about forty years ago, and it provided that if the plaintiff was even one percent at fault, he would get no compensation, no matter how bad the defendant's conduct, and no matter how badly injured the plaintiff was. That is one of the law changes that the current reformers call the "liberalization" of the tort laws. Now, most states' laws provide that any plaintiff who is more than fifty percent responsible receive nothing. So if a defendant is 45 percent to blame, plaintiff gets nothing; if a plaintiff is 45 percent to blame, he gets a 45 percent reduction in his award.

"Assumption of the Risk" negates a plaintiff's recovery

A common complaint of the detractors of the jury system is that people should not be compensated when they have assumed the risk of being injured by dangerous conduct. Interestingly, Ms. Catherine Crier, in The Case Against the Lawyers, complains that the abrogation of this rule is what has caused all of the horse renters across the country to quit business because they cannot afford the liability insurance premiums. (I guess it would be too facetious of me to point out that Ms. Crier complains of the "exorbitant costs" attributable to lawsuit abuse and complains of "rich trial lawyers," yet she manages to gratuitously mention her Wyoming horse ranch and her four-acre plot of land in Westchester County, New York, one of the most prime and expensive residential sections in the entire country. When she begins to feel too disenfranchised she can retreat there and write another book). It is those in her position who seek to advance their economic interests over the personal liberties guaranteed by the Seventh Amendment.

The "assumption of the risk" rule requires that the juries be instructed by the judge that, to the extent that a plaintiff assumed the risk of injury with knowledge of the risk of his conduct, then he is unable to recover for the injury. That rule once provided a total defense to any claims against a person who negligently maintained a dangerous condition on his or her premises. Now, in many states, assumption of the risk is considered as a part of the negligence of the plaintiff, and will bring about a potential finding of comparative negligence, resulting in a reduction of the recovery. So, to say that "assumption of the risk has been abandoned" is inaccurate, and Ms. Crier knows that because she, as a former Texas trial judge, presumably knew and properly instructed the jury on the law. A plaintiff may assume the risk of some injuries. The question in a real trial, not some made-up scenario for a book, becomes what types of risk could the injured victim have known about and how much responsibility for his injury should he bear?

An example: if you are prescribed medication for extremely high blood pressure, and your doctor tells you that studies have shown a less than one percent chance of minor liver damage, should you be denied compensation from the drug manufacturer if your liver totally fails, if the manufacturer failed to disclose its knowledge of a higher rate of serious liver problems and known deaths of people from the drug? This happens to be the case with some of the actual, real drug litigation going on now, after some people went to lawyers to find out what the drug manufacturers really knew when they marketed the drugs. Most people would disagree with the total defense that the law once provided, where your "assumption of the risk of liver damage" prevented any recovery at all. The law now allows the jury to consider your knowledge and your actions in the face of that knowledge, so that your damages may be apportioned accordingly. Hardly a "giveaway" to a Plaintiff!

Asbestos Injuries

One type of case that has come under recent attack by the reform groups is claims against asbestos manufacturers. The asbestos lobby says people whose asbestos-related disease appears only on X-rays aren't sick, but medical studies have proven that this disease is all too real. Many people have become ill or have died as a result of a devastating cancer– mesothelioma-that is proven to be caused by only one thing--breathing asbestos fibers. Exposure to the fibers may only be from contact with someone who has worked around asbestos. Many times people do not know that they have been exposed for years after the contact. That's because it can take decades for symptoms of asbestos disease to appear, even though lung damage begins when the fibers are first inhaled. After cancer is diagnosed, injured people go to court to hold the company that poisoned them accountable.

The companies say they are innocent, claiming they never used asbestos in products. Unfortunately, lawyers who represent asbestos victims say this type of corporate cover-up is nothing new. They say the asbestos industry knew its product was deadly at least by the mid-1930s, but hid that fact for decades. In the meantime, millions of innocent Americans were poisoned. The information began to leak out in the 1970s, as more people became sick with cancer and other lung diseases. Because the asbestos industry chose to fight legitimate claims, workers were forced to go to court to get their medical bills paid. Their trial lawyers uncovered buried company documents. Now these same companies and their insurers are lobbying Congress to change the law on asbestos lawsuits. They say they want to fix a system that unfairly forces innocent companies to compensate people who aren't really sick or injured. The asbestos lobby says people whose asbestos-related disease appears only on X-rays aren't sick. But victims' groups say that's like saying people with HIV aren't sick because their disease can be detected only by a blood test. And they note that insurance companies have no trouble saying that supposedly "not sick" asbestos victims are "too sick" to buy life insurance. The asbestos lobby calls changing the legal system tort "reform." Victims' groups and their lawyers argue that the industry plan isn't really reform – it's special treatment for corporate wrongdoers. Equally important, the court that has heard evidence in these cases said that manufacturers had known about the dangers of inhaling asbestos as early as the 1930s and had failed to test asbestos to determine its effect on workers, even though they had a duty to do so. Since the hazards posed by asbestos were clearly foreseeable to the manufacturers, the Fifth Circuit Court of Appeals said they had a duty to adequately warn of these hazards. This they failed to do. Instead, they remained silent. The manufacturers' silence -- internal company documents more accurately depict a conscious "coverup" of the product's hazards -- put at risk about 20 million Americans who have been occupationally exposed to asbestos. Hundreds of thousands of these workers are expected to die of asbestos-induced cancer. Borel v. Fibreboard Paper Prods. Co., 493 F.2d 1076 (5th Cir. 1974), cert. denied, 419 U.S. 869 (1974).

If Congress passes this tort "reform," they say, most asbestos lawsuits would be eliminated and innocent victims would get nothing – no help with medical bills and no compensation for their injuries. That would give guilty companies a financial windfall amounting to millions or even billions in profits. The asbestos lobby also says claims by people who aren't sick are ruining innocent companies. But lawyers who represent asbestos victims say there's evidence that the companies are using the bankruptcy laws to limit their financial obligation to the people they harmed. Unlike when a family goes bankrupt, the lawyers say these huge corporations aren't literally out of money. Most return to normal business operations

– free of claims against them – in a few years. Some of the biggest asbestos companies that went bankrupt have made millions in profits in recent years.

In America, no one is supposed to be above the law. So asbestos victims are asking, if companies that poisoned millions are allowed to change the rules on asbestos, will corporate wrongdoers try the same tactic with other deadly products in the future?

Medical Malpractice Reforms

The stories that have been written in some newspapers are truly alarming, stating that doctors are leaving their practices because they can't afford to pay their medical malpractice insurance premiums. But is there really a mass exodus, as some of these news reports have portrayed? Or, have we not yet heard both sides of the story? Many of these stories have emerged in states where legislatures are considering laws to limit patient rights through medical malpractice "reform." But consumer advocates say that patients need to know that, while the word "reform" sounds positive, the results of medical malpractice "reform" laws typically mean that patients have less chance of receiving the help they will need if they are injured by a medical mistake.

In states where legislatures are the targets of these lobbying campaigns, such as Mississippi, West Virginia, and Pennsylvania, reporters have investigated the anecdotes about doctors leaving their practices and discovered they are unfounded. In Mississippi, The (Biloxi) *Sun Herald* reported, that while there continue to be claims that doctors are leaving their practices, "So far, the numbers don't bear that out." The newspaper reported that the state gained 564 doctors over the past five years, and that "[o]nly four states have grown faster in physician population: Alabama, Alaska, Arkansas and South Dakota." In West Virginia and Pennsylvania, medical and insurance lobbyists testified before state legislatures that doctors fled those states because they were forced to pay high medical malpractice insurance premiums. But a Pennsylvania state agency census and a West Virginia newspaper investigation found the opposite was true. The *Philadelphia Inquirer* reported, "[Doctors] claim huge premiums are driving many physicians out of the state, particularly high-risk specialists.... But the most recent count of doctors in the state tells a different story.... In fact, the [state agency] census of Pennsylvania doctors shows the number grew." The *West Virginia Gazette* reported, "The number of doctors in West Virginia has increased yearly, contrary to reports by the state Medical Association that doctors are fleeing the state in reaction to medical malpractice costs."

Further, Dr. Anthony Robbins, a physician who headed the state health departments of Colorado and Vermont and oversaw programs addressing recruitment and retention of rural doctors, says, "The difficulty in recruiting talented physicians to serve in rural areas is a nationwide problem.... It is a continuing problem and one that has nothing to do with changes in malpractice premiums." According to Robbins, physicians have left rural areas "for decades," and have done so "regardless of medical malpractice insurance crises and regardless of tort "reform" statues." He cites a government report on the status of the physician workforce in America when he says, "shortages in the number of rural physicians nationwide are due to... [social and professional] isolation, the lack of hospitals and medical technology, and a desire for greater affluence."

A survey by the Center for Research in Ambulatory Health Care Administration found that medical malpractice premiums are not cited by doctors as a reason to leave their practices. Instead, the survey found that spouse and family issues are the number one reason rural doctors leave their practices. What is the case in your state? You may not really know until a reporter there investigates.

A six-week study by *USA Today* finds that while some doctors in particularly vulnerable specialties, obstetrics, neurosurgery and some high-risk surgical fields face severe problems, most physicians are minimally affected by the claimed skyrocketing cost of malpractice insurance. Premiums are rising rapidly, but no more than other health care costs. They represent only a small slice of doctor's expense. Even for the hardest-hit specialists, the most sever problems are concentrated in a small handful of states.

Real people get really hurt

The truth is that there are real events that cause tremendous pain and heartache to real people. You may have heard the true stories of Jessica Santillan dying at Duke after the transplant of incompatible organs; and of Linda McDougal, the 46-year old who received an unnecessary double mastectomy because her biopsy results were erroneously confused with those of another patient, who was told she was cancer-free. These are true stories. There is a need for the jury system, and it should be free of arbitrary ridiculous limitations of a one-size fits all solution, trivializing the suffering of the victims and their families. Cases like Santillan's are not that rare: A new study in Pediatrics journal finds that medical errors occur in more than one in 10 cases involving children with complex medical problems.

The proposal to limit damages currently before Congress has also been tried in California, passed originally in 1975. Russell Kussman, a Los Angeles attorney who handles medical malpractice cases, says that if Jesse Santillan had died in California after the bungled heart-lung transplant, and not in North Carolina, her impoverished family "wouldn't have been able to find an experienced, competent malpractice lawyer to take the case, because of the $250,000 cap.

There's really no economic loss, because the child died. It's a $250,000 recovery, maximum, and a very complicated case with a lot of costs."

Readers may wonder why a case with a potential $250,000 recovery is not one that would attract a competent plaintiff's trial lawyer. The reason is very basic–the way that the defense of these cases is handled, the insurance companies pull out all stops on behalf of the hospitals and doctors, requiring thousands of hours of preparation by the plaintiff's lawyer. In addition, in complex medical cases, it is very common for there to be a requirement that the plaintiff, in order to prove the case, must hire several expert witnesses, at a normal cost of tens of thousands of dollars apiece. By the time a case is tried at the courthouse, a plaintiff's lawyer will have often paid as much as $100,000 or more out of his pocket. The potential fee for that lawyer is usually 40% or less (unless the legislature of the state has mandated a smaller percentage) of the recovery. Why would any reasonable businessman spend thousands of hours and $100,000 in order to earn a maximum fee, in the best scenario of slightly over $100,000? So, the victim is without remedy if the lawyer will not take the case. Exactly the result desired by the propaganda machine that went to work thirty years ago in California, and is still at work today.

I remember the line from George Herbert Walker Bush when he ran for vice-president in 1984, where he criticized the trial lawyers in their "penny loafers" at the Republican National Convention. In that same speech, he came up with a figure that we now hear as the "tort tax," reputed to be something like $300 billion a year. If you remember that, as I do, you were probably shocked and dismayed by the expenditure of that kind of money on lawsuits. I was, too. However, no one has ever determined why he used that figure, where it came from, or what he meant by it. The only figure that bore any resemblance whatsoever was the figure of $298 billion, which was the insurance industry's estimate for all liability payments in the whole country. It has now become part of the literature that we see floating around whenever one of the trial lawyer bashers comes out of the woodwork. Ironically, Bush the elder apparently could not convince his son not to hire a trial lawyer when Jenna was in a minor traffic accident. Her recovery became part of the $300 billion figure.

Politicians prone to misinformation

It was only two years before George Herbert Walker Bush's "penny loafer" line that Ronald Reagan started the ball rolling on the tort reform misinformation effort. President Reagan's Public Papers show that in May of 1986, at a speech before the American Tort Reform Association, he told one of his favorite anecdotes:

"In California, a man was using a public telephone booth to place a call. An alleged drink driver careened down the street, lost control of her car, and crashed into the phone booth. Now it's no surprise that the injured man sued. But you might be startled to hear whom he sued: the telephone company and associated firms."

This is one of the earliest examples of politicians using hyperbole and misinformation to take a very sad and true case and twist it to make it support an argument against the victim. The way it was posed by Reagan, it was another tale of a civil justice system gone amuck from money-grubbing trial lawyer sharks looking to line their pockets at the expense of our flag-waving corporations. The truth could not be more the opposite–the victim was Charles Bigbee, who lost his leg in the accident. He was a custodian who worked for the city of Los Angeles. The night of his injury, he was making a call in the phone booth located on a liquor store parking lot, twelve feet from a busy boulevard. He saw a speeding car, apparently coming toward the phone booth and the liquor store. He tried to flee, but could not, because the door of the booth jammed, pinning him inside like a sitting duck.

His lawyer, doing his job, learned in his investigation that twenty months prior to Bigbee's accident, the phone booth, at the identical location, had been hit by another car on the very same destructive path. The phone company erected another booth in the exact same spot, with no guardrail or other barrier, no warning to users, and with a door that did not work properly, with no regard to what had happened prior, and without considering alternatives. Bigbee could no longer walk and could not work. The driver's insurance did not even cover Bigbee's medical expenses. The trial judge dismissed the case, but the California Supreme Court said that Bigbee's case should be heard by a jury. Eleven years after the beginning of his personal version of hell, Bigbee got his case settled for an undisclosed amount. In July of 1986, after having heard of Reagan's jab at the system that saved him some personal dignity, Bigbee came to Washington to testify at a congressional hearing on tort law. He tried to meet with Reagan and discuss the case. Reagan refused, and continued to tell the same misleading story for the rest of Bigbee's life, which ended in 1994 when he was 52 years old. See, Nader and Smith, p. 273-74, supra.

Reagan did not make up the facts. He was given these facts by the tort reformers who sought to change the system that was holding them accountable for their wrongdoing. What Reagan and other politicians do wrong is they get taken in by the propaganda. Reagan was said by all who knew him to be a kind, compassionate man who would not hesitate to go out of his way to help or bring some joy to others less fortunate than he. So why would he tell such a story? We all know that Reagan loved a good story. Could it be that he was constantly barraged by a mass of misinformation? Could it be that even his powerful empathy for his fellow man was simply overwhelmed by the sheer weight of the massive campaign to pervert the system? Could it be that the strength of their numbers and their money leaves the policymaker at their mercy? It could have seemed so innocuous to Reagan to poke fun at the civil justice system. But he failed to see the harm he was doing to the system that is so necessary to our democracy, not to mention the hurt to the faceless Mr. Bigbee.

Another of Reagan's stories, as related to the College of Physicians and Surgeons, in April of 1987:

> "Last year a jury awarded a million dollars in damages. She'd claimed that a CAT scan had destroyed her psychic powers. Well [you can almost hear Reagan's 'well' as you read this], recently a new trial was ordered in that case, but the excesses of the courts have taken their toll."

Again the story is filled with hyperbole and misinformation, and leaves out all of the important facts. Judith Haimes, the thirty-three-year-old plaintiff in the case, was referred by her doctor for a CAT scan. During a prior scan, she had a severe reaction to the dye commonly used in such scans and was cautioned never to allow the dye to be injected again. Radiopaque dye is known from the medical literature to cause such reactions in a very small percentage of patients. She cautioned the radiologist before the second scan, but he replied that she was being "ridiculous." Immediately after injection of the dye, she suffered a sharp pain, followed by difficulty breathing, loss of bladder control, and began vomiting. Welts and hives appeared on various parts of her body, along with nausea, vomiting, and headaches for several days. She suffered debilitating headaches when she performed tasks involving intense concentration.

An interesting part of the case is that Ms. Haimes actually worked as a professional "psychic" and was often retained by police to assist in solving crimes. One of her claims in the lawsuit was that she no longer could do that type of work, and she did, indeed, close her business one month after the CAT scan. The trial court informed the jury that Ms. Haimes could not recover for this part of her claimed damages because she did not offer any expert testimony that the dye caused these problems. After a jury award, the trial court reversed the jury, stating that the award was excessive. In a second trial, the trial judge dismissed the case, and that dismissal was affirmed by the Supreme Court. Ms. Haimes, as is the case with many victims of malpractice who are unable to support damage claims with medical expert testimony, never received a penny from the civil justice system. See, Nader and Smith, pp.274-75.

So, Reagan's statement, and the desired implication of all such statements when they criticize cases, is that "the excesses of the courts have taken their toll." What excesses is he talking about? Whose excess was it? This lady told the doctor that he would injure her, and he dismissed her like a miserable peon, but she turned out to be right. There was no doubt that she was injured. The difficulty of sufficient proof in malpractice cases (a matter that often serves to leave injured plaintiff's uncompensated), left her without a judicial remedy. But, if you believe that the court result was right, where is your complaint? The system worked. There are probably very few trial lawyers who would have taken the case to trial if they could not bring expert witness testimony to show that the dye caused her chronic headaches. But, why should Ms. Haimes not have the right to bring her case for the injury that she could demonstrate? Is it an excess to ask a jury to listen to your complaint where there was clearly medical error? Is it an excess to expect that a professional will listen to your prior medical history and take his patient seriously when she fears being injured again? The radiologist simply dismissed her as "ridiculous!" Would he have done that if it were his mother or daughter? Was he having a bad day, cavalierly putting someone's health in jeopardy? How dare he second-guess her and her prior radiologist, who instructed her never to allow the administration of the dye! She was simply being "ridiculous" to question the superior knowledge of this physician, presumed to have the superior knowledge. After all, he was the physician, and she was only the patient.

Mr. Reagan probably did not mean harm to, nor did he bear ill will to, either of these two plaintiffs. What he and others who speak without thinking and knowing the facts actually do is to harm the system themselves. If the faith of the people in the civil justice system is ruined, then the true excesses, for which there will be no redress, will be by those who seek to dismantle that system. There will be no recompense or redress for those excesses in a court of law. The decline of the system will leave it powerless to accomplish its Constitutionally-designated task. There will be nine, not ten rights in the Bill of Rights. The Seventh Amendment will be without meaning.

One of the things that I most vividly recall from my time as a practicing trial lawyer was a doctor in my town contacting me to assist him in a case on behalf of his mother. This doctor, whose name I will not state, was one who had been a defendant in several malpractice cases. The defense lawyer who represented him in all of those cases was the person this doctor turned to when he needed help for his mother. Unfortunately for the doctor, his defense lawyer could not help him, since that lawyer worked only for defendant doctors and hospitals. Those clients would no longer retain that lawyer if he decided to represent, of all things, a plaintiff. So, this lawyer, for whom I have the utmost respect and admiration, contacted me to refer this doctor to me. I spoke on the phone to the doctor to find out about his complaint. He told me that his mother, 92 years old, believed that she got hurt slipping off of a 10" high step stool while standing for a chest x-ray at a radiology center. I asked what injury she received. He told me that he was not sure, that his wife was "handling all of that," and he would have his wife contact me. The wife did contact me to tell me that she believed that her mother-in-law, who had been in a nursing home for many years after several strokes, was "hurt." When I asked her to detail what she meant by "hurt," she told me that her mother-in-law seemed to be more senile, from the scare that she received, even though she did not actually fall, did not break any bones, did not hit her head, or receive any other direct physical injury. The mother-in-law, her son (the doctor), and his wife all wished to talk to me about filing a suit against the radiology center, since they believed that the x-ray should have been performed lying down, rather than standing up. Although this is by no means the most ridiculous call I ever received from someone wanting my services as a plaintiff's medical malpractice lawyer, my point is simply this: This doctor was and always has been one of the most outspoken on behalf of the tort reform movement, specifically the quest for medical malpractice reform. Yet, when he thought it was time for his family to avail itself of the fruit of the tree, he had no problem trying to find a ladder to reach the limb. I want to quote from a part of Chapter One of this book, which I would invite this doctor to think about if he reads this book:

So, beware, the popularity of a thought or idea that serves your advantage today may well result in it becoming a rule of law. Tomorrow, you might not be the one to make the rules; or even more ironic, your popular rules may easily turn to your disadvantage.

In The Federalist Paper #78, Alexander Hamilton was trying to let his fellow citizens of his newly-formed country know of the purposes and benefits of the proposed *Constitution*, in a way much more eloquent than I. He stated, in reference to the moderating effect of an independent judiciary:

"Considerate men of every description ought to prize whatever will fortify or beget that temper in the courts; as no man can be sure that he may not be tomorrow the victim of a spirit of injustice, by which he may be a gainer today."

The rules that we choose for our society should be rules that we would choose to apply to ourselves if we were on the other end of the debate. A doctor may some day well be a patient. An insurance agent may have a child injured. A hospital administrator's wife may be brain-damaged by a neurosurgeon. Democracy should give everyone a glimpse of justice, not just the view for those who make the rules, but for those who watch the rules being made. How many times is your eye caught by a tabloid story at the grocery store check out line, such as the ones Reagan told, the McDonald's coffee case, or other such rendition without the full facts? You then fume all the way home from the store thinking that you are victimized by the system, when the truth is that the system is victimizing you.

We all are vested in the justice system. Every person now breathing in this country is just as likely as anyone else to have fate's hand turned against them in some form or other at some point in time. When you support an idea, a thought, a proposal, a law, a reform, please be sure that you know what it is, what it will do, what it will not do, and who will be affected by it before you decide your position. Inform yourself, listen to all sides of the debate, and imagine what it would be like if it were to some day apply to you!

In the next chapter you will see some of the true and documented facts of bad things that can happen in the world of doctors and hospitals? Am I, like the insurance companies, trying to scare you into action? No, but you should know these facts and think about what can happen to you, and where you would be without the jury system to help you.

CHAPTER FOUR

THE MEDICAL SYSTEM IS NOT ERROR- FREE

"Our estimates clearly support the Institute of Medicine's contention that medical injuries are a serious epidemic confronting our health care system." *Journal of the American Medical Association*, 2003:290:1868-1874.

Remember the Dixon Klein case I told you about in Chapter One? The mistake in Dixon's care came purely from the human side, in two ways. The first was sloppiness; the second was pure lack of caring. It was simply sloppy for Dr. Lye to fail to take the extra thirty seconds necessary to do the tonometer test. The pure lack of caring is something that we will talk about later, but sloppiness leads to a lot of medical error. Even with the best of intentions on the part of doctors and nurses, sometimes sloppiness occurs, just like in Dixon's case. He just happened to be at the wrong clinic at the wrong time with the wrong doctor. We will never know how many other people dodged the bullet that hit Dixon. We do know that Dr. Lye did not do the tonometer test on Dixon at the time that Dixon was there. What is still never knowable is how many others had the same test skipped. During the course of the suit, Dr. Lye was deposed, where he sat with a room full of lawyers and a court reporter and a camera and gave sworn answers to the pertinent questions. He claimed in his sworn answers that he did the test. The basis for his claim was twofold: first, he said that he knew he did the test because he always did the test; and second, he knew he did the test because the blanks for the test results were filled in–miraculously, by the time his deposition was taken the blanks were not blank any more. There was now a number in the two blanks, one for the right eye and one for the left eye. Someone had filled in both blanks with the number "11." That was a convenient number for two reasons. First, it was easy to write a one, as opposed to a different number, and not have anyone be able to test the handwriting, since a one is a simple line, unlike other numerals. Second, eleven is a very normal and common pressure measurement for the eye. One thing that is rather odd is that virtually no one has the same pressure in both eyes, but Dr. Lye and the others in the clinic were not sophisticated enough to know that.

He, of course, could not remember

Dixon three years after the event. Dr. Lye was what is known in the medical industry as a "locum tenens," which is a way of saying that he is someone who gets hired to fill in gaps where people are needed, having no particular office or regular set of patients. Everyone else involved in the case knew that he could not have done the test, since it would have been virtually medically impossible for Dixon to have a normal pressure at that time, and then one year later have extraordinarily high pressures that were by then out of control. But the human error of Dr. Lye, which was probably no more than always being in too big a hurry, and perhaps not caring or believing that someone as young as Dixon would be struck by glaucoma, caught up with him. Rather than face up to the error, he chose the low road and lied.

One reason I have chosen the case of Dixon Klein as an example in this book is that Dixon's case would likely not have helped him one bit except for a rare stroke of fate that intervened for him. The whole case turned on the question of whether Dr. Lye had done the air puff test (known as the "tonometer"test to detect early glaucoma). Dixon, in his heart, knew it was not done, but before he even went to a lawyer he wanted to see for himself. You see, Dixon, like many others brought up in this age, did not trust lawyers. He did not want to hire a lawyer if there was any doubt in his mind about the test. So, he took it upon himself to do his own investigation. After he learned about the function of the tonometer test, he talked with his new optometrist about how the results of the test would be recorded on the exam notes, and he then went to the office of Dr. Lye. When he arrived, he asked the receptionist if he could see his records, and she retrieved them, brought them to the desk and showed them to him. In the bottom right-hand corner of the sheet, there were two little boxes marked "tono," and both of these boxes were blank. Everything else on the sheet had been filled in. When Dixon requested copies of the sheet, the receptionist went back to the office section, returning a few minutes later to tell Dixon that the records did not belong to him, so he could not see them any more or obtain copies of them, even though it was his legal right (unknown to him) to obtain copies.

Dixon, at his next visit to his new optometrist, told that doctor (let's call him Dr. Tell) the story. By pure and strange coincidence, Dr. Tell had previously been at the offices of Dr. Lye, since the owner of Dr. Lye's clinic had advertised the clinic for sale, and Dr. Tell had gone to meet with that owner. While there, Dr. Tell (who had previously discussed the whole history of the case with Dixon, including where Dixon had been, when, and what tests had or had not been done), asked the owner, purely out of curiosity (Dr. Tell knew this was the chain of opticals where Dixon had been) if he had a patient named "Dixon Klein." The owner proceeded to check the file cabinet, where he retrieved Dixon's record and showed it to Dr. Tell, who then saw that the "tono" boxes were blank. The owner of the clinic, at that time, had no reason to hide anything, not yet knowing of Dixon's plight, and there having been no claim yet made.

Everyone in the case figured out that the "tono" test had not been done by Dr. Lye. There is simply no other explanation for the facts–Dixon's "sudden" and unexplained increase in pressure, the blanks seen by Dr. Tell (who, you will recall, saw the actual record when it had no numbers filled in), and the blanks seen by Dixon on the page that the office manager refused to turn over. More telling even than these facts are those that occur later in the investigation. But for now, let's talk about errors in the medical system.

While working on this book, I was sitting with my computer on my lap and reading some e-mail, when I heard a feature on the nightly news. The report said that, Jacobi Medical Center in the Bronx, New York, owned by Health and Hospitals Corporation, had apparently failed to report pap smear results to more than 300 patients out of 19,000 tests done in 2004. The cause of the error was a procedural change that was made in December of 2003. As a result, it was later determined that, out of all the women the hospital failed to notify, thirty had abnormal pap smear results that showed some cancerous and precancerous cells. These women were to be notified, but it was already May of 2005. At the time of the announcement, it was still not known how many of those ladies will be able to become cancer-free, and how many will be significantly harmed by the error. Allen Avila, the director of the hospital, was quoted as saying that the error was inexcusable, and that some employees had already been disciplined.

Any error of this sort has the potential to harm a large number of people. It is not known how many will be harmed. Whatever the number, it is more than acceptable. As I am typing this right now, there are 300 women who do not know if they are among the 30 who have abnormal pap smears. What about the ones that go there tomorrow and next week? What about every woman who has gone for a pap smear anywhere in the past year, or will go at any time in the future, and has heard this news story? Aren't all of these people entitled to know that, if they have such a misfortune of life, that society will not have already made its judgment about the worth of their life? I feel for the people who are responsible for the error. They are all probably as sorry as any human can be for such an error. That does not bring back the past eighteen months of cancer growth for the thirty women whose abnormal results were missed! We need a system that will protect those thirty women.

We will never get rid of all of the mistakes.

People make mistakes. People are the ones that provide our care. There is no way that we can ever have a system where no one is hurt because of going to a doctor or a hospital. This does not mean that we shouldn't do all that we can to prevent error. There is really no way to determine whether doctors are more careful because of the potential for a negligence lawsuit. Some doctors do not change their conduct, for the better or the worse, out of such fear. I have personally had some doctors lie to me, even knowing my former occupation. Recently I sought help to relieve pain resulting from five prior back surgeries. I arranged to have a doctor implant a "spinal stimulator," which is an electrical device implanted into the back, with wires running into the area around the spinal nerve, to block pain signals. I was literally on the stretcher on the way to the operating room, when the surgeon who was to assist my doctor cancelled the procedure because he did not feel comfortable working with my doctor in the operating room. The reason–my doctor had never done this surgery before in his entire life!

Why did I not know that? Because **my doctor** had looked me in the eye and lied to me–he told me that he had done this surgery "countless times." Obviously, once I learned the truth, I chose a different doctor. I verified, by checking with the manufacturer of the stimulator device (who initially refused to provide me with the information) that my doctor had never performed the surgery. Even then, my doctor would not fess up, taking the position that the reason that the surgeon was not comfortable was because of "jealousy, envy, and petty hospital politics." When I requested a refund of part of the money I had prepaid for the surgery, he even fought me on that, despite the fact that he did not do the work I had paid him for. The things that still perplexes me–why would the hospital even let my doctor schedule this surgery, when he had never even done one before? Why would the device manufacturer put it into the hands of someone not properly trained? It was almost as easy as scheduling an overnight stay at the Holiday Inn.

Setting aside for the moment the question of whether malpractice cases have any deterrent effect on malpractice, let us look only at the question of what other things can be done to lessen the rate of error in the delivery of health care. Doctors cannot cure everyone. Hospitals are for the sick, and we will always have sick people. So what health care professionals do every day fits into one of two categories. It is either to make a diagnosis of disease or injury as early as possible, in order to create the best possibility for cure; or it is to take a known disease or injury and bring about the best potential outcome in the face of the circumstances. So, negligence in the delivery of health care is necessarily going to have a rather severe impact, because even without a mistake, the health care provider is already dealing with a person who is not healthy. All the more reason why the use of due care should be considered important. In other words, if we know by definition that we are dealing with human conditions that are dangerous, then we should want a system that will maximize the opportunity for being careful and "getting it right."

There are, however, several factors that have made the delivery of medical care a sometimes dangerous proposition. Doctors and hospitals increasingly are conscious of the bottom line as their time and resources are squeezed and their expectation of high income is threatened. Errors creep into the system from lack of time and division of attention. Studies prove that the medical system comes to expect that such errors, and the injuries resulting from them, are a fact of the business. Recently, *U.S. News and World Report,* (January 31, 2005), dedicated its cover story to the question of "Who Needs Doctors," and pointed out that "a growing gap separates doctors and patients." There were several related articles, all of which focused on the fact that the "bureaucracy of medicine" harried that doctors to the point that they no longer had sufficient amounts of time in their daily schedule to adequately address the patient's concerns, and obtain answers to the questions that they really needed to ask to give the best care that they could give. Interestingly, when the doctors are asked what they think the reasons are for this phenomenon, the existence of malpractice suits is not at the top of their list. The biggest concerns are the dictates of the HMO's and other healthcare insurance companies, more and more paperwork, and the declining reimbursements from insurance carriers. Regardless of the culprit for the lack of time, it is time that matters most when a doctor is trying to get to the bottom of a patient's complaints and determine the cause.

As in Dixon's case, it is the little things that get overlooked. Perhaps a doctor fails to do a test because he thinks that the risk of harm is low. Perhaps he just forgets. What matters is that sometimes the little things are what makes the difference. At some point in time, the odds are bound to catch up, and when they do, the consequences can be devastating. Unlike a case where a driver makes a "little" mistake and fails to make a complete stop at a stop sign, when a doctor makes a little mistake the results can be horrendous.

Should doctors and hospitals get special treatment and consideration?

When people get hurt, should the injured patient be just a statistic in the bottom line? When injuries occur, should the system respond by hiding the ball with a conspiracy of silence? Should the health care profession be exempt from civil liability, or should different rules apply to it, simply because doctors are harried, and they provide a valuable service to society?

In many of the larger health care institutions, the system for delivery of health care includes residents and interns who are being trained in their various fields. This is done for a twofold purpose. First, it is the best training for them, and second, it is the cheapest way for the health care to be delivered. Studies have shown that many of the residents and interns are expected to work huge numbers of hours without rest, and they often are forced to compete against one another to prove themselves qualified to get the best positions at the best institutions. These constraints on their energy and physical abilities often produce a significant increase in errors that lead to death or serious injury of the patients. The National Institutes of Health, in an exhaustive study in 1999 determined that as many as 98,000 patients are killed each year as a result of medical error in hospitals, and as many as one million are injured needlessly. The cost of health care is, in fact, skyrocketing, but the cost of medical malpractice insurance cost is not the reason. Reliable studies have shown that medical malpractice insurance premiums are only one percent of the cost of health care. In other words, only one penny out of every health care dollar goes to pay for medical malpractice insurance.

In an Associated Press article from February of 2003, it was reported that a study on medical mistakes found operating room teams around the country leave sponges, clamps and other tools inside about 1,500 patients every year, largely because of stress from emergencies or being hurried after complications discovered during surgery. Both the researchers and several other experts agree the number of such mistakes is small compared with the roughly 28 million operations a year in the United States. However, they say there is room to improve. "It shows the system works. It just doesn't work perfectly," said Verna Gibbs, a surgeon at the University of California-San Francisco who has done separate research on medical mistakes.

Dr. Sidney Wolfe, health research director of the public-interest lobby group Public Citizen, was more critical. He said the real number of lost instruments may be even higher, because hospitals are not required to report such mistakes to public agencies. He also pointed to the study's finding that surgical teams failed to count equipment before and after the operation, in keeping with standard practice, in one-third of cases where something was left behind. It tended to happen during emergencies. "It's not something that takes a lot of time," Wolfe said. "I just don't think it's excusable." The study, which was published in *The New England Journal of Medicine*, the most highly respected medical journal published, was done by researchers at Brigham and Women's Hospital and Harvard School of Public Health, both in Boston. It is the biggest and most reliable study yet on such mistakes.

In a February, 2003 story written by *Washington Post* writer, Michael Rubinkam, it was reported that Researchers at Ottawa & Harvard Medical School contacted 400 patients hospitalized at an unidentified urban teaching hospital & found that one in five patients had "adverse events" in days after they were sent home. The patients surveyed reported new or worsening symptoms resulting from the treatment they received, not from the underlying diseases for which they were hospitalized and treated. The study, which was published in *Annals of Internal Medicine*, found that most of the problems could have been prevented with better care.

The lady whom I mentioned in Chapter Two, Linda McDougal, sheds some light on how a minor error can have devastating results. She wrote of her experience for *Newsweek* magazine, in the Dec. 22, 2003 issue, where she said:

> Like most people, I never expected to be involved in a lawsuit. But then, in May 2002, two doctors switched the pathology slides of my breast biopsy with another woman's. Following my double mastectomy, the surgeon told me I didn't have cancer. What a relief! The operation had been a success. "You don't understand," the surgeon explained. "You never had cancer." And so I became involved in a lawsuit against the hospital and the people who wouldn't even own up to their error.

We will return to Linda McDougal later and see what she has to say about the jury system, but it is easy to see how quickly a "minor" error can have a devastating effect on a patient's life. One important point about the delivery of quality health care is that it ultimately makes us far more productive as a people. That is a worthy goal in and of itself. "The benefits from just lower infant mortality and better treatment of heart attacks have been sufficiently great that they alone are about equal to the entire cost increase for medical care over time," wrote economists David Cutler and Mark McClellan (later an FDA commissioner) in 2001. In a 2002 paper, Yale economist William Nordhaus argues that the value of increasing longevity over the past century could be as large as the value of growth in all other goods and services over the same period: "It would suggest that the image of a stupendously wasteful healthcare system is far off the mark." The obvious implication is that a healthcare system costing 20% of our Gross Domestic Product might actually be a good thing if the medicine is worth it -- say, an expectation of 120 years of healthy life. If that is true, then why can't we accept a rise in malpractice premiums, which are only one percent of healthcare costs, if it will help compensate for the loss of value of the hundreds of thousands of lives that are hurt by malpractice every year? If doctors and insurers argue that decreasing the cost of medical care by capping damages will help doctors make society more productive, then shouldn't victims be able to argue that their productivity to society counts as well? We allow people to be wasted by malpractice, losing their productiveness to society, but yet the insurance companies say they want to put a cap on damages to assist medicine in its quest to make society more productive? Rather an ironic argument, doesn't it seem?

Patients with unwanted medical souvenirs

In an article by journalists Karl Stark and Josh Goldstein of the *Philadelphia Inquirer* (Feb. 01, 2004), it was reported that, in the Philadelphia area alone, surgical instruments are left behind in patients after surgery at the rate of about eighty per year. They reported that a two-foot-long guidewire was left in the chest of a gentleman named Donald Gable after heart surgery. That "unwanted momento" remained in his chest, as he walked around carrying the guidewire inside his chest. An X-ray later showed it extending from his groin to his upper chest. "I was flabbergasted," said Gable, who developed a blood clot and had to be hospitalized again after the wire was removed. "That thing could have penetrated my vein, and I could have bled to death."

The authors for that article state that such mistakes occur about once in every 3,800 surgeries in Southeastern Pennsylvania, basing their conclusions on an analysis of hospital billing data. The problem has changed little in recent years, occurring on average about once a year per hospital. No one has come up with a regional estimate until now. Even a few such cases are serious because they can cause infections and perforations and lead to stinging court verdicts. The journalists also reported that a northern New Jersey woman developed a hernia and severe scarring from gauze left inside her abdomen for six months.

"These mistakes can go undetected for years if they cause no problems. Sometimes, they are found by accident," according to the authors. A Seattle cancer patient did not learn the reason for the searing pain in his stomach until he set off a metal detector at the local airport in mid-2001. The cause for alarm? A 13-inch metal instrument left inside his abdomen at the University of Washington Medical Center.

A Canadian woman set off an airport metal detector in 2002 because of a similar, ruler-length instrument left inside her abdomen. "There is absolutely no reason for these to occur," said Philadelphia lawyer Paul Lauricella, who won a case against Frankford Hospital in 1999. A 15-inch-square towel had been left in his client's abdomen for three weeks. "All you have to do [to prevent them] is be able to count."

"Surgical teams try hard to see that their lifesaving tools are safely removed," the authors of the article argue, stating that, "the main protection comes from new variations of a venerable practice: Two nurses count each item at key points during an operation."

Gauze pads that sop up blood - the most common items left behind - have been tagged with a special strip since the mid-1950s, making them stand out on X-rays. Many surgeons call for such X-rays when counts do not add up. But the system is far from foolproof. Chunliu Zhan, a physician and researcher for the federal Agency for Healthcare Research and Quality, found that this mistake occurs 2,700 times a year in the United States - a rate that closely tracks the Philadelphia region's.

Zhan found that a foreign body added four days to the average hospital stay and led to $36 million a year in added charges. More troubling, he said, about 57 people died from this mistake in 2000, the year he analyzed. Even hospitals with strong patient-safety efforts face persistent problems involving foreign bodies.

According to the article in the *Philadelphia Inquirer*, Abington Memorial Hospital, one of the leading hospitals in the state, was found responsible for leaving gauze inside a 67-year-old Philadelphia woman after a hysterectomy. Robert Wood Johnson University Hospital, an eminent teaching facility in New Brunswick, N.J., left behind a 21-inch guide wire in a patient after a lifesaving procedure. After the wire went undetected for 61 days, the patient developed an infection and died. And the Hospital of the University of Pennsylvania, whose system ranks second nationally in federal research grants, faced a suit from a New Jersey man who says doctors left in gauze for 14 months after removing part of his colon.

While medical experts have been trying to do away with this error for decades, regulators have been slow to collect cases and study them. New Jersey health authorities say they lack a comprehensive system to track medical errors and identify trends involving foreign bodies. Pennsylvania hopes to start such a system within the next year under its new patient safety authority. Yet even the main national group that assures hospitals' quality - the Joint Commission on Accreditation of Healthcare Organizations - also does not specifically collect information on foreign-body cases. "Would it have been better to include that type of event? Yeah," said Richard J. Croteau, executive director for strategic initiatives. "We'll consider expanding our definition to include that."

The National Quality Forum, a Washington nonprofit entity whose directors represent all areas of health care, lists foreign bodies as one of 27 "never" events - ones that everyone agrees should never occur in health care. "Obviously [a foreign body case] does happen, and it's going to continue until there is a concerted effort to report and publicly acknowledge and systematically try to prevent it," said Kenneth W. Kizer, the forum's executive director. Kizer, among others, is concerned about the sheer number of tools in modern operations. From 200 to 500 items can be involved in a surgery.

"When you have hundreds of different elements, maybe we need to rethink the whole thing," Kizer suggested. "That's exactly the dialogue that needs to occur." Much that is known about foreign bodies was summarized last year in the *New England Journal of Medicine.* Harvard researcher Atul A. Gawande and his colleagues found that patients faced the greatest risk when they underwent emergency surgery, such as for the bursting of a major blood vessel or a hysterectomy with uncontrolled bleeding. The authors suggest a simple explanation: Surgical teams often lacked the time to count as carefully in those cases. Unplanned changes in surgery also raised patients' risk. So did obesity. Extra girth affords more space for items to hide, the authors suggested. More than half of items were left in the abdomen and pelvis, followed by the vagina and the neck.

So, in view of the fact that we have incontrovertible evidence of the vast number of cases in which instruments of surgery are left within patients' bodies every year; and in view of the fact that healthcare providers universally agree that leaving such instruments behind is negligence, are we to excuse such events just because they are common? Do we excuse people who run stop signs and injure our citizens just because such events are more common than we like? No, we most certainly do not, and we should not just look the other way and say that the practice of medicine is somehow different, just because we think for some reason that it would be a burden on our healthcare delivery system if we hold the wrongdoers accountable. If every driver did everything he or she was supposed to do when he approached a stop sign, there would never be any accidents that result from running stop signs. If every surgeon and surgical nurse did everything that each of them was supposed to do during and after surgery, then we would not have instruments left in patients' bodies. Unfortunately, people do not always act appropriately–neither drivers nor surgeons nor scrub nurses. So we should have and we do have laws for the protection of the injured. These laws should be for the protection of _all_ of the injured.

Who defines what care should be given?

In an editorial authored by a physician in January of 2003, that physician stated a proposition with which no one could disagree–when it comes to setting the standards for delivery of healthcare, we should leave it up to the physicians, not the HMOs the PPOs or any other form of insurance or business person. The editorial argued that you get what you pay for, so managed care plans and the federal government alike figure that if they want physicians to provide high-quality care, they should reward them for it with financial bonuses. Improved quality is expected to lower utilization rates and thereby reduce health care costs. Utilization is a term that is used to describe the costs of the care delivered. Over-utilization means that the doctors order more tests and more specialist visits, and often the insurance companies penalize the doctors if they have "high" utilization rates.

The physician author also said, "This well-intended proposition may very well live up to its potential -- it sure sounds good on paper -- yet physicians are right to view it with a somewhat skeptical eye." Certainly, many physicians soon will have the chance to get a closer look. The Center for Medicare & Medicaid Services is now instituting a three-year demonstration project for groups of 200 or more physicians. It will pay groups a bonus for meeting certain quality benchmarks, as well as have them share in any savings resulting from better quality of care. [These people have the unique view that we can save money by having good healthcare, rather than skimping on quality to save a buck here and there]. The program got extra backing in October 2002, when the National Academy of Science's Institute of Medicine released a report saying the federal government should reward high-quality health care by giving financial rewards to the best doctors, hospitals, nursing homes and HMOs.

Blue Cross of California in 2003 is expanding to its PPO the pay-for-performance program it already has in its HMO. Blue Cross and five other large California plans have said they will adopt at least some of the quality criteria for rewarding physicians that have been developed by Integrated Healthcare Assn., a California-based health policy group. Other plans across the country are developing, or already have, some form of quality-based pay.

On the surface, this movement of pay for

performance seems to be an improvement over some plans' strategy of paying bonuses to physicians based on how much money they could save the plan. That structure was rightly criticized by physicians as more often intended to provide the least care rather than the right care. And pay for performance has the potential, depending on the bonus structure, to align physician and payer interests in providing the best care for the least cost.

However, when it comes to pay for performance, the question is: Who is defining quality? Any quality-pay structure that is developed without physician input is doomed, because there will be questions over whether it truly represents quality, or if it's a mask for cutting costs by cutting care. As a report on the subject by the AMA Board of Trustees noted in 2004: "Physicians and other health care professionals express serious concerns over the use of data by coalitions and health plans to make clinical practice decisions and guidelines without the input or consent of physician groups, hospitals, medical staffs and/or organized medicine. ... Such determinations can be particularly damaging if they are improperly linked to the use of economic or practice incentives for particular care regimens and disincentives for other treatment options."

Physicians discovered quality long before there was an HMO or a PPO or a Center for Medicare and Medicaid Services, which oversees quality in the government healthcare services. In their daily lives and physicians still strive to give the best care they can. But if CMS and health plans are serious about this proposition, the only credible proof of their goodwill will be if those at the front line of caring for patients have a strong voice in defining what quality is.

In an article entitled "A Free Ride for Bad Doctors," Dr. Sidney M. Wolfe, a physician, director of the Public Citizen Health Research Group, wrote about the death of Jessica Santillen, the 17-year-old who, while at Duke University Medical Center (recognized as one of the finest institutions of medical study and treatment in the world), was given a heart and lung transplant from an incompatible donor. Dr. Wolfe stated that the case has now become the latest argument in Congress against President Bush's plan to limit malpractice damage awards. With doctors in several states staging work stoppages to protest the soaring costs of premiums, the plan to put caps on pain-and-suffering payouts had been picking up steam.

Dr. Wolfe points out that, even with all the discussion of tragic cases and dollar amounts, a **major cause of the malpractice problem is ignored: the failure of state medical boards to discipline doctors.** The fact is, only a small percentage of doctors account for most of the money paid out in malpractice cases. Dr. Wolfe stated that from 1990 to 2002, just five percent of doctors were involved in 54 percent of the verdicts and settlement payouts. According to the National Practitioner Data Bank of the Department of Health and Human Services. (The data bank allows hospitals and medical boards to see the records of individual doctors but, thanks to pressure from the American Medical Association, Congress forbids it to release information to doctors or the public.) Of the 35,000 doctors with two or more payouts during that period, only 8 percent were disciplined by state medical boards. Among the 2,774 doctors who had made payments in five or more cases, only one out of six had been disciplined.

Is it any coincidence that the states least likely to discipline doctors are among those with insurance crises? Pennsylvania, where the governor had to intervene to keep doctors from going out on strike over malpractice insurance costs, has disciplined only 5 percent of the 512 doctors who had made payments in malpractice suits five or more times, the lowest percentage of any state. (Arizona, for example, has disciplined nearly half of the doctors in this category.) And while Pennsylvania has 5.3 percent of the doctors in the United States, they make up 18.5 percent of American doctors with five or more malpractice payments. One doctor there paid 24 claims between 1993 and 2001 totaling more than $8 million (one was for operating on the wrong part of the body; another was for leaving a "foreign body"in the patient) yet was never disciplined by Pennsylvania authorities. The state with the next highest over-representation of doctors with five or more payouts is West Virginia, where doctors went on strike last month. It has 0.57 percent of the country's physicians, but they make up 1.69 percent of American doctors who have had made malpractice payments five or more times. Only one-quarter of the state's doctors with five or more payouts has been disciplined by the medical board.

In New York, another state with a claimed pending malpractice crisis, the number of doctors who have had five or more malpractice payments is two and one-half times higher than would be expected from the number of doctors licensed. Yet only 15 percent of these 698 doctors have been disciplined by the state board.

Amid the uproar about malpractice premium increases, Dr. Wolfe says that there is a "deadly silence from physician's groups on the crisis of inadequate doctor discipline." The problem is not the compensation paid to injured patients, but an epidemic of medical errors. If medical boards, which are state agencies, are unwilling to seriously discipline doctors who repeatedly pay for malpractice, including revoking medical licenses from the worst offenders then legislatures must step in and change the way the boards operate. Dr. Wolfe also argues that Congress should also rethink the secrecy surrounding the practitioner data bank. While a few states release some data to the public, most Americans have no way of finding out their doctors' backgrounds. What patient would not like to discover the malpractice history of a potential doctor, especially if he is among the 2,774 in the

United States who have had five or more payouts?

Houston, we have a problem!

An Associated Press article posted on Sun, Mar. 21, 2004 in the *Houston Chronicle* stated that some doctors still find work in Houston area hospitals, despite their past habitual instances of malpractice. Officials at several area hospitals overlooked or ignored negative information about doctors disciplined by state regulators, allowing even those that have been sued for malpractice ten or more times to continue practicing, the *Chronicle* reported. The newspaper examined six years of physician disciplinary records from the Texas State Board of Medical Examiners and determined numerous instances where disciplined doctors still had hospital privileges. A few small for-profit hospitals, such as Houston Community Hospital, repeatedly accepted doctors that others have rejected. At least one hospital, Vista Medical Center in Pasadena, allowed an orthopedic surgeon to perform operations in an apparent violation of his probation, according to the state Department of Health. The surgeon has been sued for malpractice more than 60 times and was doing surgery while his license was suspended.

According to the newspaper's analysis, the 39-bed Houston Community Hospital had the highest number of disciplined doctors per bed. Seven doctors who have held privileges there have faced state discipline. One of those doctors is accused in civil suits of contributing to five patients' deaths. Another was accused of using drugs and operating on the wrong limbs, and in 2000 was hit with the largest malpractice penalty reached by a jury in Texas history - $40.6 million. (More on that verdict, which was overturned by the Texas Court of Appeals). Both doctors are now on medical board probation. That hospital's administrator explained the hospital's failures in selection of its physicians by saying that most of the disciplined doctors were screened by the hospital's previous owner, and that only three still practice there. He also said small hospitals have a hard time recruiting top doctors because the best can make a lot more money elsewhere. He explained that his doctors were good doctors who specialize in surgery that is "demanding and complex." One would wonder whether choosing the correct leg for surgery was too demanding and complex!

There are two problems which can lead to a hospital keeping bad doctors on their staff. First, losing the doctor means losing the revenue from the patients he admits there. Second, fear of lawsuits by the doctors (these are the same doctors who criticize patients for hiring lawyers), makes hospitals reluctant to revoke staff privileges. The National Practitioner Data Bank, the national clearing house for information shows hospital privilege revocation or suspension of only 54 of the state's 37,000 doctors in 2002.

It is not just the doctors who do not get disciplined. One month prior to the article about the lack of doctor discipline, the *Chronicle* published an article about the lack of punishment for hospitals. After undergoing neck surgery, a patient at Vista Medical Center in Houston, developed breathing problems while in the recovery room. For seven hours he complained of shortness of breath, but was advised by doctors and nurses to suck on ice chips. His licensed vocational nurse, who had one year of training, seemed unconcerned. Nurses did not try to contact a respiratory specialist or an on-call emergency-room physician, according to depositions of nurses on duty. One of the doctors, a Vista anesthesiologist, eventually returned a call nearly three hours after he was initially paged, according to nurses' depositions, and prescribed an antianxiety drug over the phone. The combination of drugs -- the patient was already on an antihistamine and a narcotic pain reliever -- was known to suppress respiration in some patients, according to the depositions. The anesthesiologist did not come in to examine the patient. After he got out of bed to summon nurses, he collapsed and stopped breathing. The staff could not find resuscitation equipment, and no one in the area was capable of performing CPR. The patient died in a nursing home six months later, after incurring hundreds of thousands of medical bills paid for by, guess who? Your government.

Vista's inability or refusal to deal with emergency medical situations was well known to state and federal authorities even before the patient died. But Vista was never punished. On three occasions, state inspectors recommended to the federal Centers for Medicare and Medicaid Services that Vista's Medicare funding be terminated, one of the harshest penalties possible for a hospital. Vista retained its Medicare eligibility. In its first five years of operation, state inspectors conducted eight investigations into more than a dozen incidents. Each time, Vista promised to fix the problems and no punishment was given, but the problems persisted. In a period of only three years, Vista Medical Center Hospital or its outpatient clinic was named in at least fourteen medical malpractice lawsuits, including at least two cases involving patients who died. Vista has paid no federal penalties and has been assessed only one fine of $3,000 since it opened. The Texas State Board of Medical Examiners finally suspended one of Vistas most prolific spine surgeons after he had been sued for malpractice more than 78 times, finding that he was a "real and present danger to the health of his patients."

Can hospital inspectors do the job?

People believe that a hospital is a safe place. But, even in the face of serious deficiencies found by hospital inspectors, few hospitals are penalized. In Texas, the state hospital inspectors have the responsibility to investigate complaints for all hospitals, as well as surgery centers and other outpatient clinics. The most heavily populated area of Texas, Harris County (Houston) and the surrounding thirteen counties, has only seven inspectors to cover hundreds of facilities. This may explain deficiencies in 75% of nursing personnel files at one hospital; or why no penalty was imposed on the same hospital, even after an investigation concluded that a post-surgical patient who developed alcohol-withdrawal symptoms was transferred to another hospital with no paperwork, thus causing him to be abandoned on the ambulance dock of the receiving hospital; or why no penalty was imposed on the same hospital after its repeated failures to administer drugs and blood sugar tests prescribed for diabetic patients; or why no fines or penalties were imposed on the same hospital for failing to inspect emergency lifesaving equipment.

Remember Vista Hospital in Houston where the patient stopped breathing in postoperative recovery? Texas inspectors had learned that Vista had no physicians on call to treat people who came into its emergency room or Vista's own post-surgery patients who got into trouble during the night. Many of the doctors on call were unaware of the on-call list and didn't know their names were on it. Since no doctors were around to help that patient, inexperienced support personnel took fifteen to twenty minutes to get a breathing tube down the patient's airway.

<u>What is the best remedy for the conduct of errant doctors and hospitals?</u>

For in depth information about the argument over the question of who sets the standards for health care, you may consult the Public Citizen website at <u>www.citizen.org.</u> You will see a number of links to a good discussion of the debate.

The Texas Department of Health's hospital licensing and compliance division has never revoked a hospital's license or placed a hospital on probation. The public can't evaluate hospitals for potential problems because complaints not validated by state inspectors are not public record. And there are too few inspectors to cover all of Texas' hospitals, surgery centers, abortion clinics, rural health care clinics and other health care facilities.

In the 2003 session of the Texas Legislature, a bill was passed which limited the amount of damages that could be recovered for pain and suffering of a patient who was the victim of malpractice. Now bear in mind that the Texas Legislature did not have the constitutional power to enact such a bill, because the *Texas Constitution* has a provision that states that no one could be deprived of his right to redress his grievances in Court. That constitutional provision proved to be no deterrent to the Legislature. They passed the act, and then drafted a Constitutional amendment which was to be submitted to a vote of the citizens, so that the statute could be refractively approved. The constitutional amendment was passed by the voters by less than a 1% margin. The election date was in September, on a day when no other national, state or local elections were held for any office.

Now that Texans have put strict limits on damages for pain and suffering in medical malpractice claims, diligent oversight by state and federal authorities is the remaining bulwark between patients and abuse by reckless doctors, undertrained nurses and callous medical administrators. The general public -- perhaps naively -- perceives hospitals as benevolent institutions dedicated to patient safety. In light of Vista's example, it's a dangerous dereliction of duty when hospital regulators operate under similar assumptions. The state boards do not fill the void. The hospital boards and quality committees do not fill the void. None of these things has given bad for-profit hospitals incentive to make their care better. If they are not given the incentive of avoiding a financially devastating medical malpractice case, will their other incentives be sufficient to deter them from looking to profit above patient safety?

In the next chapter you will see how medical malpractice cases work. Contrary to what the doctors and insurance companies want you to believe, there are protections for the doctors, significant burdens for the injured victims, and safeguards to prevent frivolous lawsuits and to prevent verdicts that are out-of-control. You will see how specific cases work, and how it is no easy task for a plaintiff to get even adequate compensation.

CHAPTER FIVE

MEDICAL MALPRACTICE CASES-- A DIFFERENT ANIMAL

"The escalating medical malpractice crisis will not be resolved until the industry and regulators address the other, apparently more powerful, factors driving premiums higher." "Medical Malpractice Caps Fail to Prevent Premium Increases, According to Weiss Ratings Study," atwww.businesswire.com, June 2, 2003

        Medical malpractice cases are unlike other suits for personal injury in many respects. The evidentiary requirements are more strict on the plaintiffs, there are substantially fewer recoveries for plaintiffs statistically, and the cases are extremely difficult and expensive for plaintiffs to prosecute. What constitutes a "frivolous" suit depends upon the individual to whom you are talking at the time. There are, to be sure, such suits in the system, and their cost is unmistakable. We must find a way to prevent them. I will show you why those cases, however, are rare, and substantial recoveries rarely occur without clear negligence and devastating injuries. Punitive damages are awarded in only the most extreme cases. While it is true that frivolous cases are brought, almost all states have adopted ways to remove those cases from the system early on, to avoid needless costs and delays to other cases. One of the major problems with these cases is that often it is not what the juries decide that is wrong, but it is what the juries never even get to hear, because it was covered up, destroyed, hidden or altered.

There are abuses in every jurisdiction, and there are occasions where both sides have what is known as a "scorched earth" policy, which means that both sides will pull out all of the necessary legal stops, procedural and tactical, to win. Indeed, they will sometimes pull out many unethical and illegal ones, as well. The case of the "Smoking Guns That Would Not Stay Hidden" is a story of a real case, told by the authors Ralph Nader and Wesley Smith in their nonfiction work *No Contest*. You might say that you would not believe Ralph Nader because he is too much of a wacky consumer advocate, and he would be expected to take the side of the little guy over the insurance company or the medical product company, but if you look at the source of his information and how the information was acquired, you will see that the story is authentic. I have utilized here a large amount of the report that Nader and Smith give on the case, so that I can be true to the facts and not leave out details that demonstrate the sinister aspects of the plot told.

I could give multiple examples of personal experiences demonstrating the frustration, delay, expense and literal waste of judicial resources that I have been the brunt of in my career. It would better serve credibility for me to demonstrate from another verifiable source. In a medical malpractice and product liability suit filed by the parents of Jennifer Pollack in Washington state, plaintiffs alleged that one of the defendants, Dr. Klicpera prescribed Somophyllin oral liquid, marketed by defendant Fisons Corporation, for asthma. Jennifer suffered seizures that caused permanent and irreversible brain damage, caused by theophylline, the key ingredient in Somophyllin. In an opinion rendered over seven years after the devastating event causing the injury, the Washington Supreme Court detailed the fraud, abuse and evidence-hiding that ultimately resulted in hundreds of thousands of wasted dollars, delay, and outright contempt of the judicial process. *Washington State Physicians Insurance Exchange and Association v. Fisons Corporation*, 85 P. 2d 1054 (1993).

The main defense that the Fisons Corporation chose to assert, among many others, was that the doctor had mis-prescribed the medication. In other words, the drug company chose to turn on its customer, to whom it had the obligation to disclose the dangers of the drug. A fierce battle began over discovery(the process by which the parties learn from each other, and outside sources, the facts pertaining to the case), as it always does. Fisons was represented by Seattle's largest law firm, the 200-lawyer Bogle & Gates. In 1990, after four years of discovery and legal maneuvering, the plaintiff's lawyer received an anonymous envelope in the mail; the envelope contained a copy of a letter, dated June 30, 1981, which had been sent to a limited number of "influential physicians." That letter, however, had never been sent to defendant Dr. Klicpera. The letter warned of the side effect that later was, in fact, suffered by Jennifer. It noted an article that appeared in a medical journal not normally read by a number of physicians. That article warned of "life-threatening theophylline toxicity when pediatric asthmatics....contract viral infections." Most physicians never learned of this toxicity, since they were never told of it, and the warning did not appear on any labeling or package insert.

Why was it that the plaintiffs, in those first four years of the case, never learned of the existence of that letter? Good lawyers ask for documents that pertain to the medical issues in the case. One of the plaintiff's requests for information directed to Fison's lawyers was the following: "Produce genuine copies of any letters sent by your company to physicians concerning theophylline toxicity in children." The 1981 letter was never provided to the Plaintiff's lawyers in response to that request. When plaintiff's lawyers received the letter from the anonymous source, they asked the court to impose penalties against Fisons. This is the type of request that asks the judge to dole out some sort of punishment to the offending party and its lawyers for abuse of the litigation process. The trial judge did, in fact, order Fisons to turn over all documents requested by the plaintiff. Along with the letter was another document that had previously been withheld--a Fisons internal memo in 1985, six months before Jennifer's injury, noting a dramatic increase in reports of serious toxicity to theophylline. The memo said that prescribing the normal recommended dose of the drug was a significant mistake. The memo also reported that the physician who made the original dosage recommendation was a major holder of Fison stock. Along with other findings of the memo, its conclusion was that the epidemic of toxicity from the drug would justify stopping the drug's promotion.

Despite the recommendation to stop promotion of the drug, the company continued to promote it. After this evidence came out, Fisons settled the case for $6.9 million, an amount which was a small percentage of the profits Fisons had made from the drug, and still less than the future medical costs for Jennifer. What followed is out of the ordinary. The lawyers for Dr. Klicpera decided to pursue Fisons and its lawyers for their actions in the discovery abuse, as well as for Dr. Klicpera's damages incurred in having to defend himself when it was Fisons conduct that led to the suit. Ralph Nader, in *No Contest*, reports on his interview with the lawyers for Dr. Klicpera, who said that the reason they chose to go after Fisons and its lawyers was because this type of conduct makes litigation more expensive for everyone and that someone needed to bring this type of conduct to light. What Dr. Klicpera'a lawyers did not realize was how difficult that project would be. For the details of that projected skirmish, you can read the Washington Supreme Court's opinion or Ralph Nader's book.

The conclusion was that the case against Fisons and its lawyers ended up being settled, after a trial, an appeal, and then back to the trial court again. The impetus for settlement? The trial court directed that the lawyers disclose to the court evidence of how it ordinarily conducted discovery. Rather than do that, they chose to settle the case.

As an example of how things work in cases with which I am familiar, let's turn back to Dixon Klein's case. Wondering how it was that the two little blanks in the bottom right-hand corner got filled in after the record had been seen by both Dr. Test and Dixon, I, as Dixon's lawyer, asked to review the records of all of the other patients who had been seen by Dr. Lye during the time that he was serving as "locum tenens" for the clinic. You will recall that Dr. Lye had testified that one of the reasons that he knew that he had done the test on Dixon was that it was his habit, and since it was his habit, he must have done it. The theory is analogous to what you might do at your job every day. If you work on an assembly line at an automobile assembly plant, and you have to put bolt number 4-323 into a bumper coming down the assembly line, you do it many times a day, and it is your habit to do it a certain way, you can testify that you know you must have done it that way. With that testimony, the law allows the opposing party to do what I need to do to test the existence of the habit, so I asked to review all of the other patient records to see if it is true that he "always does it." The defense lawyers' response to that request was to deny my request, then, when I filed a motion asking the court to order my request, require me to have a hearing, taking my time, the court's time, and taking time from the system to adjudicate other legitimate issues. When the Court ordered them to show me the records, then they refused to schedule a time to do it. We had to file another motion with the court, and schedule another hearing with the court, before they finally relented and scheduled my opportunity to see the records.

The reason for their recalcitrance became clear when we finally saw the records. Nearly half of them had either no entries in the "tono" blank, or they were partially there, or completely illegible. It is no wonder they wanted no one to see them! The defense of "I know I must have done it because I always do it" took a large part of its trip down the drain the day I saw those other patient records. Once that defensive theory was dead, the doctor's lawyers took a new approach. They decided to contend that, even if no test was done, it must be true that Dixon had glaucoma at the time he first visited Dr. Lye, and that there would have been nothing that could have been done even if the test had been done and treatment would have been started back at the time that Dixon visited the clinic. More about that approach later.

Many of the delays and unnecessary costs are attributable to the actions of either the doctors or the lawyers who defend them. Most of the insurance policies that insure the physicians against medical malpractice claims have a "consent" provision, which provides that the insurance company cannot settle a case unless the physician consents to the settlement. There are no other such policies for any other profession, or for you or me if we are sued and believe that we have done nothing wrong. Since it is not the doctor's money that is paying for the defense of the case, the doctor can let a case go through all of the stages of the litigation in hopes that the plaintiff will run out of money to prosecute it, or the plaintiff's lawyer will make some mistake in jumping over all of the hurdles that are placed in the way of a successful prosecution. Then, if necessary, the doctor will finally settle a meritorious case on the courthouse steps, after his insurance company has shelled out tens of thousands of dollars in litigation costs that could have easily been avoided. Then, too, many other cases that should be settled early are not, because the insurance company lawyers milk the system to generate fees by keeping delaying the cases as long as possible.

Good doctors pay for the mistakes of the bad ones

The real problem with the medical malpractice system is twofold. First, good doctors are having to pay for the mistakes of bad doctors. Only five percent of the doctors are responsible for over one-half of the total medical malpractice payouts for settlements and judgments. Those bad doctors are either allowed to continue to practice in their own states, or they are allowed to freely begin practicing in other states or be accepted on the staffs of other hospitals. (See the Romero case below for an example of how that can happen without any responsibility to be placed upon the hospital). Second, the insurance companies have lost significant amounts of money in their investments in the last several years, and must, accordingly, raise their rates to recover from the doctors the money that they have lost in the stock market and in their mutual funds.

The insurance industry, which must

do something with its premium income, makes large investments in stock and mutual funds. The "hit" has been taken not just by all people and industry–it has also been taken by the insurance industry, one of the heaviest investors. They must recoup that money somewhere, so they turn to their only reliable source– the doctors and hospitals whom they insure. But they certainly cannot let the doctors think that their investment ineptitude was the problem, so they have to blame the easy enemy–trial lawyers. So even though caps on jury awards have never worked anywhere they have been tried, they cry for more caps on jury awards, claiming that juries are runaway and crazy, with no evidence to support that claim.

Doctor Vicodin

An all-too-real example of how the healthcare industry is given protections from liability much greater than those afforded to others is a recent case from Texas, entitled, KPH Consolidation, Inc. v. Romero, 102 S.W.3d 135 (Tex.App.-Hous. [14th Dist.] 2003). The suit was filed by a patient of Dr. Baker who suffered severe neurological and physical impairments after a relatively uncomplicated back surgery Baker performed. The Romeros sued Baker, a group of anesthesiologists, a certified nurse-anesthetist, and the Hospital. Before trial, the Romeros settled with the doctors; at trial the only defendants were the nurse-anesthetist and the Hospital. They proved that the Hospital credentialed (which means gives permission to practice in the hospital) Baker to practice medicine at the Hospital—even though it knew that he abused prescription drugs and was an incompetent surgeon. Plaintiffs proved that during the surgery Romero experienced significant blood loss. In fact, Romero lost almost all the blood in his body. Shortly after a blood transfusion, he went into cardiac arrest and had to be resuscitated. He suffered severe brain damage that left him totally disabled. In the trial court the Plaintiffs won a verdict against the hospital, but the Court of Appeals in Houston reversed the trial court, with a process that the Court characterizes as "reasoning," that really defies all reason.

A little bit of historical background is in order before you can see what is happening in this case. You will need to follow closely for the next few paragraphs, because, for even one trained specifically in the law pertaining to this case, the logic is difficult to trace.

First, in all hospitals the function known as "credentialing" is performed by a committee of the hospital deciding which doctors are competent to practice in the hospital and what duties they can perform. The credentialing committee looks at many different factors, including the educational background, performance in certain types of cases, record of malpractice cases and results, continuing training and education, and whether the physician has been restricted or prohibited from practicing in other states.

Because of the fact that the credentialing process is one in which the hospitals wish to encourage complete disclosure of all information pertaining to the doctor, many states (as well as Congress) have statutes which provide for confidentiality of the process. In other words, the information that is brought to light in the credentialing process is not subject to disclosure to any other individuals or entities, and specifically is not to be subpoenaed or disclosed in any legal proceeding. Second, the people who make the credentialing decisions, as well as the hospital, are provided civil immunity for their decisions. They cannot be sued by any doctor for being denied staff privileges, unless the denial was done with malice. In Texas, the statute is now known as Tex. Occ. Code Ann. § 160.007. The Health and Safety Code also provides that the records and proceedings of a medical committee are confidential and are not subject to court subpoena. Tex. Health & Safety Code Ann. § 161.032. These provisions are based on two premises: first, there is a need to have exacting, critical peer review of doctors' competence and performance results in order to improve standards of medical care; The Romeros showed that the database would have contained the malpractice actions against Baker that resulted in settlements, including one lawsuit in which Baker operated on the wrong leg of a patient and another in which he left a sponge in a patient. The last of these lawsuits was in 1993.

In mid-May of 1998, two months before Romero's surgery, a nearby hospital suspended Baker's operating privileges. Baker admitted that one of the reasons for the suspension was that he operated on the wrong leg of a patient. Baker tried to prevent disclosure of that suspension by obtaining a restraining order to prevent anyone at that hospital from discussing or mentioning that suspension. The Hospital's expert agreed that repeated instances of operating on the wrong limb was "not an acceptable outcome."

In light of this evidence, should the hospital be responsible for allowing Dr. Baker on its staff, and thus subjecting Mr. Romero to his irreversible and complete brain damage? You might argue that Dr. Romero would be found responsible, so why would Mr. Romero need to have liability imposed on the hospital. But, this argument fails to take into account the fact that there is no minimum requirement for liability insurance for a doctor in Texas. The insurance available from Dr. Baker could come nowhere near to even the medical bills to be incurred by Mr. Romero. So, when the hospital knew of Dr. Baker's drug abuse and incompetence, why should Mr. Romero bear the heartache of his condition without contribution from the entity that enabled the doctor to do his surgeries there?

It is with this tedious background that the Court of Appeals in Romero ruled that the plaintiff had not proved that the hospital acted with malice. The reason finally given is that the plaintiff had not proven what the hospital did or did not do to protect its patients from Dr. Baker's action, so the plaintiff had failed to prove that the hospital had acted with *conscious indifference* to the rights of Mr. Romero, and *conscious indifference* is one of the requisites of "malice." The catch-22, however, is that the confidentiality provided to the committee under Texas statutes absolutely prohibits discovery of any evidence about what the hospital did or did not do to protect its patients. So, Mr. Romero, and any other patient who might be injured by the conduct of Dr. Baker or any other such doctor in the hospitals of the state of Texas, will be without remedy against the hospitals who enable the doctor's conduct.

This example is one of the most recent of how the courts and legislatures have obfuscated the laws and bent over backwards to keep from imposing liability on health care providers. If there is a reason for the actions of the courts and legislatures, it must be, you say, so that there can be freedom from "frivolous suits." Can one say that Mr. Romero's suit was a frivolous one? Perhaps the reason for protection is that our healthcare individuals and entities are in a different class than others? Can one say that such separate classes should be recognized in a society that is based upon the rule of law and equality? Maybe the reason is that healthcare costs are too high and the way to cure it is to keep down the verdicts against hospitals and doctors. Even if this were sufficient justification, what about the cost of taking care of people who are permanent brain-damaged or quadraplegic–isn't there a cost both in taking care of these people and the loss of their productivity?

Will changes in the jury system lower the cost of healthcare?

Is the goal of lessening the cost of health care a goal that justifies taking away a crippled individual's right to recover adequate damages for his suffering and lifetime of misery? Anyone who follows the news on this issue is aware of the push that has been made in recent years for placing a "cap" on damages. This is the most brazen of the efforts that have been spoken, and in some instances, passed. Such a measure was passed in California way back in 1977, in what was known as the first "malpractice crisis." Such measures, and others less severe, are the reason why malpractice actions are different from other personal injury actions that do not involve health care. The California measure did not live up to its promised benefits. Costs of malpractice insurance in that state did not go down until more than a decade later, when the people of the state passed a Constitutional amendment containing insurance reform. Still, California is not in the best of shape in the area of medical malpractice premiums. (More on the California results later).

In the wake of the 1999 findings of the Institute of Medicine, which estimated that as many as 98,000 Americans died annually as a result of medical mistakes, two physicians, Dr. Robert M Wachter and Dr. Kaveh G. Shojania, wrote a book entitled Internal Bleeding. The authors state that the federal funding program designed to study the problem is inadequate, and that we are no safer than we were in 1999. The path to progress, they argue, is a "systems" approach, a coherent system that anticipates and prevents medical errors. Others have spoken of converting our medical records keeping system to a computerized and digitized one, so that there would be less error in reading, interpreting and following the direction given in, records.

These are all laudable measures that could go a long way toward helping the health care professionals in carrying out their responsibilities. But, does that do anything for the people who are still harmed by error, which we know there will still be? Shouldn't all of these things be on the table for consideration when we are trying to figure out how to deal with the crisis? Should we just look the other way when someone is crippled or brain-damaged, and play like they are not suffering, just because we think that we would like to punish others who might bring frivolous suits?

The authors describe the origins of the patient safety movement, which has drawn from a number of fields outside medicine — most notably, the aircraft industry. Errors during flights decreased only when pilots and other employees stopped keeping them secret. Disclosure taught experts a key point. Obvious errors, like plane crashes, generally did not result from a single human blunder. Rather, there was usually a series of mistakes. Any one of which, if detected, might have thwarted a tragedy. A systematic approach to discovering these events, therefore, was critical.

This approach is now important in patient safety, as most medical mistakes, they argue, "can be prevented by thoughtfully applying principles of systems thinking." Among the remedies they advocate is greater use of computers, which can detect dangerous drug interactions and incorrect dosages, enrollment of health professionals in "teamwork training" and more open disclosure of mistakes. This goal is, however, the hardest to achieve, since "Nobody," they admit, "likes a whistle blower." Since we are a long way from making the delivery of health care an error-free system, we must provide the patients a fair and balanced system to redress patient injuries.

"Fair and balanced" is a tricky phrase. Most of the states have enacted legislation that provides for certain safeguards that help provide some protection for the doctors against "frivolous" claims. One of the most common types of safeguards is the requirement of either an affidavit, letter, or other documentation of an opinion by a licensed physician certifying merit to the claims that the plaintiff has made. For example, when there is a suit against an orthopedic doctor alleging that he negligently injured a patient's spinal cord during back surgery, the law would require that the plaintiff obtain written certification from an orthopedic doctor or neurosurgeon that the defendant had failed to act as a reasonably prudent surgeon during the procedure, and that the failure was a cause of the plaintiff's injury. I would be one of the first to tell you that such requirements are needed, and I would not want to be a part of a system that did not have such a requirement, otherwise we would have lawyers deciding, on their own, what lawsuits to file. These certification requirements help us know that the suits have physician knowledge behind them.

So, is it "fair and balanced" if plaintiffs are not required to have such certification? I believe that it is not, because the system could otherwise be abused by plaintiffs. But I submit that it is not "fair and balanced" to limit a plaintiff who is rendered brain-damaged or quadraplegic to a sum that is less the cost of a 2002 Rolls-Royce. Courtside tickets to Los Angeles Lakers games are $1,750 per ticket. So, purchasing four season tickets would cost more than the Bush administration believes should be paid for having to spend the remainder of ones life being unable to breathe without a ventilator.

One might argue that we should not measure damages to injured victims in the same scale as we measure indulgences like fine automobiles and sporting events, and I would agree with that argument. However, these comparisons will help us understand how society measures the worth of certain things. Many doctors who injure patients and cause them pain and suffering, now argue for caps on pain and suffering, yet they own fancy automobiles and spend a lot of money on sporting events. So, why should we punish the innocent victim, who sits and watches from the sidelines of life, while the wrongdoer continues to enjoy life' pleasures in the middle of the playing field?

Do they really want fair and balanced reform?

If we want to find a way to construct some rules for handling medical malpractice cases that would make these cases fair for both sides, then we need to take a look back at some historical legal points where the battle over money damages has surfaced in the nations's mind. Ironically, a doctor, Dr. Ira Gore, was on the plaintiff side in the case of BMW of North America, Inc. v. Gore, 517 U.S. 559, 116 S.Ct., 1589 U.S.Ala.(1996). Dr. Gore brought his suit to find out why BMW was deliberately ripping off his customers.

Dr. Ira Gore, who treated cancer patients in Birmingham, Alabama, bought a new BMW 535i automobile in January 1990. He paid $40,750 for the car, which BMW marketed as the "ultimate driving machine," with "flawless body panels" that retain "their original luster" after many miles of wear. Dr. Gore wrongly assumed that since the car was new it had never been damaged. In fact, when Dr. Gore took his car to an auto detailing expert nine months after the purchase, he learned that virtually the entire car -- the top, hood, trunk and quarter panels -- had been repainted due to acid rain damage sustained in transit from BMW's factory in Germany.

BMW kept computer records of repairs to all of its cars, but no one from the automaker ever told Dr. Gore that the car he bought had been repainted at a company facility in Georgia. BMW even failed to disclose to its own dealers that cars had been repainted. So what''s the big deal? So, his car was repainted?

Several issues arise in this case. First, where is the "fraud" alleged by the doctor? 1. The repainted car -- although it looked "new" -- would always be unavoidably inferior. This is because the superheated painting process at the factory could not be duplicated once nonmetal parts were installed in the assembled car. Remember, Dr. Gore paid for a car that retains its "original luster" after many miles of wear. 2. Even if the repaint job was done as well as possible, the car still would be worth 10 percent less, a former BMW dealer testified. This is because the paint on the repainted car would begin to fade, reducing the value of the car. (In Dr. Gore's case, he was defrauded out of approximately $4,000, i.e., the $40,750 purchase price minus 10 percent.)

Dr. Gore approached BMW and asked them to simply exchange his car for another that had the original superheat paint on it. BMW refused. Feeling cheated, Dr. Gore sought legal help and filed suit against BMW for fraud. During trial preparations, Dr. Gore's attorney discovered that BMW's Executive Board had adopted a policy in 1983 to deliberately and fraudulently conceal from customers -- and even its own dealers -- that vehicles had been repainted, regardless of the extent of the damage or cost of repairs. A minimum of 983 other cars, each with at least $300 in damage, had been sold to unsuspecting American customers. BMW also sold more than 5,850 other repaired vehicles as "new" without disclosing repairs. These figures, though, vastly underestimate BMW's program of nationwide fraud. At a posttrial hearing, BMW filed a document indicating that repainting is required on two to three percent of all new BMW vehicles sold in the United States.

By selling damaged cars for more than they were worth, BMW reaped millions of dollars through this nationwide consumer fraud. The Alabama jury did not let BMW get away with it. The jury awarded Dr. Gore $4,000 for the diminished value of the car and $4 million in punitive damages to punish and deter BMW from engaging in fraud. Five days after the verdict, BMW dropped the policy and quit fleecing Americans. Because of this suit, BMW now discloses all damage to its cars. In upholding the award, the trial court found that BMW had fraudulently concealed the facts from a vast number of consumers and had profited from their fraud to the tune of millions of dollars. The Alabama Supreme Court agreed with the trial court that BMW's misconduct had been reprehensible and merited punishment. However, it reduced the punitive award to $2 million.

This case was about what it will take to punish and deter a multinational company that deliberately and intentionally defrauds its customers and reaps an unjustified windfall. Punitive damages are particularly appropriate where a defendant, such as BMW in this case, has fleeced unsuspecting consumers. That case was eventually appealed to the Supreme Court of the United States, which upheld the punitive damage award, while recognizing the plaintiff's very viable and persuasive position that such awards deter reprehensible conduct. Doesn't this conduct of BMW bear any resemblance to the conduct of the Houston hospital that charged hundreds of people for hospital services rendered to the patients operated on by its prized surgeon, the drug addict Dr. Baker? But, do you see the court order that hospital to do anything for anyone? NO, in fact, the Texas court overturned the award to the brain-damaged Mr. Romero, stripping him of the money to which the jury found he was entitled.

If we intend to make a fair and balanced effort to compensate victims, deter fraudulent or contemptible conduct, malpractice cases should not have different remedies than other cases that result from non-medical conduct. The conduct is the same. The damage to victims and society is the same. We just somehow want to protect doctors because we need to believe in our hearts that they want the best for their patients. We have to believe that, otherwise the confidence in our healthcare delivery system would stagnate. So, we look away from the bad doctors and bad hospitals, play like they don't exist, and try a one-size-fits-all remedy that puts a limit of $250,000 on the damages to be recovered, no matter how devastating the mistake or how uncaring the conduct. **This is wrong**. We should not stand for it, on the strength of the unjustified, unsupported, unproven and unreliable assertion that the insurance companies are being fair with us. It is just not true.

Getting Your Day in Court Isn''t Free

On average, it costs a complainant or plaintiff a minimal filing fee (usually less than $200) to file any type court action. Filing a lawsuit against an individual or a company does not guarantee you will be heard. If a case is filed that the Judge determines has no merit, he throws it out. Sometimes when this happens, the Judge will issue sanctions and/or fines against the attorneys who do this, if the suit was filed for the purposes of harassment or the suit was groundless. But, if a case has merit and it appears as though a plaintiff can substantiate his claims, a judge will allow it to progress. So, the statement that "anyone can sue anyone" is not necessarily the truth; our judges are the front line of defense against frivolous actions. Our Court system is a constant check and balance; through every step of the process both sides of a lawsuit get information from the other side. Good judges rule on legal issues, not facts. Judges are the ones who have to study the laws and apply them to each individual case. He or she determines whether or not a particular fact is entered into evidence (photos, statements, letters, etc.). Lawyers present the facts to the jury and the jury is the final determining factor. And this is the factor in a lawsuit that big corporations cannot control. That is why they are so afraid of it and why they will do anything they can to try to change it. They have been working on it for years, and much of their agenda has been accomplished. In fact, there have been some deserved and positively needed changes. But removing from the average jury of the public citizens' peers the right to determine reasonable compensation for devastating injuries is not the answer. This does not do away with trivial suits, where the damages are less than $250,000. It does punish those who are hurt the worst. What if it were you?

An item to note; often judges are criticized for verdicts in cases over which they preside in court; however, the fact is that the jury is responsible for the amount of a verdict. Ninety-five percent of all civil lawsuits settle or are dismissed in this country. Of the cases that make it to trial, usually half settle before closing arguments, thus the jury never assesses damage amounts. Of the percentages that do not settle, roughly half are defense verdicts. Therefore, the 1 to 1 ½ % that are awards for the plaintiff are the ones most widely publicized by the media, and that get all of the attention. *Alternative Dispute Resolution Handbook.*

"I consider trial by jury as the only anchor ever yet imagined by man, by which a government can be held to the principles of its constitution." -- Thomas Jefferson, President, Speech to Congress, 1801

The civil justice system is the only branch of government in which an average American can take on the wealthy and the powerful, where truth and justice still have a fair chance over money and influence. It is not easy for these average Americans, because they have to find a lawyer with the ability and the resources to go after the insurance companies. But our great tradition of unfettered access to an impartial trial by jury now faces an unprecedented threat from powerful corporations and their lobbyists. These special interests already dominate the executive and legislative branches through their campaign donations. Their agenda of deregulation, tax breaks and public bailouts, greased by campaign contributions to public officials, costs American consumers and taxpayers billions of dollars each year.

One of the types of lawsuits that the corporations do not want is class action cases. These type cases are probably the worst thing in the legal system, and they are often used for purposes nothing other than to line the pockets of the lawyers who bring them. Getting rid of class actions altogether, or severely restricting them in such a way that will hurt their usefulness of their best purposes, is wrong. If there were not class actions, your day may never come into court. In some of these Lawsuits you will have 20-30,000 plaintiffs. If the court system tried to hear all of the cases, one-by-one, from just one wrong, it would take 10-12 years to hear all of them in their entirety. For instance, in the Phen-fen litigation in which hundreds of people that were killed and/or permanently injured by following their doctors'' prescriptions, many of the cases were filed as class action lawsuits. These cases had to be certified as a class, because our court system cannot handle the case load and the voices of the victims would not be heard. And, most important, the manufactures of the drug would never be held accountable within a reasonable amount of time.

When you hear all of the bad things about class actions, one thing that you are not told is that EVERY PERSON has the right to, and is encouraged to "opt-out" of a case, which means they can choose not to be a member of the class and they may hire their own attorney to represent them individually. It is Federal Law that everyone is afforded this opportunity. Often cases in which doctors are involved can be brought as part of a class action, because those cases frequently involve claims against drug companies, medical product manufacturers, and surgical devices.

In these cases, if the class action is not available, the patient will be severely hampered in his ability to go toe-to-toe with the big guys.

Patients need that ability. That is what the jury system was designed to do. Every American has the keys to the courthouse and is protected by the principle of trial by jury -- in which ordinary citizens and their friends, neighbors, and co-workers hear all the facts and render appropriate judgments. This is the very foundation of our democracy and the envy of the world. While we should take pride in this uniquely American system, we can never take it for granted. The jury system should not be feared. It is always interesting when doctors like to have the jury system for themselves if they have a claim, but do not want to be the ones being questioned.

An op-ed in the *Fort Worth Star Telegram* on December 23, 2002 was written by a local doctor, Dr. Hugh Lefler, who claimed that the "Ministry of Medicine" that he and his comrades are practicing, is in danger if the jury system is allowed to stand. "Ministry of Medicine".12/23/2002. He claimed that doctors are too intimidated by lawsuits to provide optimal care. Whenever you read such editorials, you are entitled to check out the author. Ask questions about what that author would do if his loved one was negligently injured, and whether the author has ever availed himself of the benefits of the jury system by being a plaintiff. I wonder if he has ever used that system to try to protect himself and his family? You can always check those things out, since doctors are, at least for this purpose, just like the rest of us. If they are ever litigants, their suits will be listed in public records. One thing you can do is start asking these guys who like to vent–have they ever wanted the benefit of the system for themselves? If so, why do they think it should not apply to them?

Malpractice cases are not what we're told.

Claims against the medical industry as a whole have actually been flat since 1996. In Florida, a state insurers say is in crisis, medical malpractice claims rose just 3.7% from 1997 to 2000, according to the National Center for State Courts, a Williamsburg (Va.) research group. A broader as yet unreleased study of 17 states will show that filings remain stable, with an increase of about 5% from 1997 to 2001. No doubt there are frivolous lawsuits out there. But there are also plenty of medical mistakes. Doctors, many of whom are covered by physician-owned mutual insurers, traditionally have been loath to sanction colleagues by denying them insurance. "We're getting more aggressive" at weeding out bad doctors, says Dr. Richard E. Anderson, chairman of Doctors Co., a Napa (Calif.) insurer that covers 28,000 physicians in all 50 states. But Anderson and other insurers refuse to document that claim by releasing their nonrenewal rates. That makes it hard to tell if the profession is changing its culture. On this and many other key points, proponents of caps simply aren't coming up with the facts to make their case. Instead, they're relying on scare stories-- always a bad starting point for making serious policy decisions.

Doctor Intimidation of Patients

Ralph Blumenthal, in a March 5, 2004 article in The *Texas Lawyer*, wrote a story about a man who found himself the loser for his "litigious behavior." Greg Dawson, as domestic security director for sixteen north Texas counties, has many dealings with doctors and hospitals, preparing for a terrorism emergency he hopes will never come. So, Mr. Dawson said, he was stunned to find that his name had been added to a little-known Internet database for doctors. His offense: filing a medical malpractice lawsuit against a Fort Worth hospital and doctor over the death of his 39-year-old wife, whose brain tumor was missed, and winning an undisclosed settlement.

An obscure Texas company run by doctors started a Web site, DoctorsKnow Us.com, that compiles and posts the names of plaintiffs, their lawyers and expert witnesses in malpractice lawsuits in Texas and beyond, regardless of the merit of the claim. "You may use the service to assess the risk of offering your services to clients or potential clients," the Web site says. For fees listed as low as $4.95 a month for the first 250 searches and thereafter two cents a search, subscribers are invited to search the database "one person at a time or monitor any sized group of individuals for litigious conduct." They can also add names to the database "from official and unofficial public records." Whether that could include a doctor's own files is not clear.

"They can sue but they can't hide," says the Web site. A founder of the group, Dr. John S. Jones, a radiologist in Terrell, near Dallas, declined to respond to questions, saying through a lawyer, Vincent A. Bacho, that he had given one newspaper interview and had agreed not to give another before it was published. The sponsors draw no distinctions among cases in what they say is the first effort to use public sources to compile a list of litigants in "predatory lawsuits" that are causing a medical crisis. Do you remember Mr. Romero, brain-damaged from the drug-addicted surgeon in Houston.—he was put on the list after winning $40.9 million over his botched operation, which was later taken from him on appeal. Mr. Dawson, the security officer, said he recently had trouble finding a doctor for his son and considered it possibly retaliatory. "I thought how amusing, I'm blacklisted," he said.

Mr. Dawson said he learned he was on the list from Texas Watch, a consumer research and advocacy organization based in Austin. Dan Lambe, then the executive director of Texas Watch, said: "Medical malpractice patients need more care, not hurdles. It's offensive on different levels." One other doctor besides Dr. Jones, Hoyt Allen, is named on the Web site run by DoctorsKnow.Us, which registered with the State of Texas on Jan. 30, 2003. Dr. Allen did not respond to messages left by the *Texas Lawyer* reporter with his medical office in Kaufman, also near Dallas. The group lists an address in Mesquite, Tex., that has no telephone. No one responded to messages sent to the group's e-mail address.

The American Medical Association said that it had just learned of the group and that it saw no ethical issues at stake! So, the AMA, which says that it wants to do all that it can to weed out bad doctors, has chosen to attack the problem from the other end–just refuse to treat anyone who has ever filed a lawsuit, regardless of the reason or the merits of the case. "There's no question that physicians are totally frustrated by the relentless assault on the medical profession by trial lawyers," said Dr. William G. Plested, chairman of the A.M.A.'s board of trustees and a cardiovascular surgeon in Santa Monica, Calif. Dr. Plested said the government already maintained a database of doctors who had been sued, for use by medical professionals.

But Mr. Dawson, 42, director of Emergency Preparedness Department for the North Central Texas Council of Governments, said that since last month he had been seeking some minor medical attention for his 18-year-old son and been turned away by half a dozen doctors. They said they had full schedules or rejected his insurance, he said. Mr. Romero, who can barely walk or see and needs help feeding himself and using the toilet, is now blackballed for his irresponsible litigious behavior. The drug-addict surgeon, who is now practicing outside Houston, did not respond to a message from the reporter writing the story about the new doctors' website. I wonder why he did not want to tell us about Mr. Romero's frivolous suit?

Another couple listed, Rick and Sheila Beeson of Wichita Falls, Tex., also voiced dismay. Their son, now seven, suffered severe brain damage from untreated low blood sugar at birth. They settled with the hospital and doctors for $9.4 million. "All we did was try to help our son," Mr. Beeson said. "My job as father is to look out for him, his financial security since they took all that away from him. It's not fair to do what we have to do and be put on a blacklist."

Yes, malpractice suits are different animals. They are the height of drama, they make the "powerful" angry. They generate the most emotional of responses from the people involved. They are defended with vigor, and the courts turn upside down to help the doctors and the insurance companies. What is the reaction of the doctors, their insurance companies, the AMA? Try to make the law worse for the victims, and then band together on a website, threatening people who have the gall to go to the courthouse to exercise their right to trial by jury. Does this sound like an industry that wants to police itself?

In the next chapter you will see how the "medical malpractice crisis" does not exist, except in the ways that the insurance companies and drug companies earn and keep their profits, while maintaining protection from government regulation. Unless we find a way to correct these problems, the doctor's insurance premiums will go nowhere but up, along with your medical expenses. You will be the one to lose in the process.

CHAPTER SIX

INSURANCE COMPANIES HAVE CREATED THEIR OWN PROBLEMS

"I don't like to hear insurance-company executives say it's the tort system.... it'sself-inflicted," – Donald J. Zuk, chief executive of Scpie Holdings Inc.,a leading malpractice insurer in California

The *Constitution*'s authors believed the right to trial by jury to be as important as the freedom of speech, freedom of religion and the guarantee of due process. The Seventh Amendment provides: In Suits at common law, where the value in controversy shall exceed twenty dollars, the right of

> "trial by jury shall be preserved, and no fact tried by a jury, shall be reexamined in any Court of the United States, than according to the rules of the common law."

There is nothing in this Bill of Rights provision, coequal with the right to speech and religion, that says that the jury trial can be limited just because someone can get enough votes to make it go away. Democracy works best when the jury system is allowed to do its job. People have taken out their hate on lawyers by punishing the very people who need the lawyers help and need it in front of the jury. The corporations (with a little bit of inadvertent help from some not-so-altruistic plaintiff's trial lawyers) have been successful in bringing about the perception that we need to do away with juries. They have done that so that they can overwhelm the public's ability to take care of itself, leaving those corporations unchecked in their ever-increasing appetite for wealth at the expense of the public good.

The consumers, including consumers of everyday household goods, consumers of prescriptions that we need for our health, and consumers of healthcare services, have bought the corporate scheme, hook, line and sinker. We have partly done it to ourselves and we have partly allowed it to be done to us. However, if more of it is done, we will be left at the mercy of the corporations. We need to get the word out that the democracy, including the jury system, is put together for a reason. We need to let people know the motivation of the jury-spoilers, and the reasons for the falsities that we hear. There is nothing wrong with the jury system that cannot be fixed with some adjustments in thinking and some hard looks at the types of issues juries are allowed to decide. Most things are right with the jury system. There is no reason why the courts are not able to serve the function that they have always been called upon to serve. What it takes is a public willing to put in their service, and lawyers who are dedicated to making it work.

A government that runs with the influence of large monied interests will always work for the benefit of the large monied interests. The government is to be run not just for their benefit, but the benefit of all of us. Do you remember from your civics courses that the preamble of the *Constitution* stated the purpose for which the framers met: "to establish Justice, insure domestic Tranquility, provide for the common defence, promote the general Welfare, and secure the Blessings of Liberty to ourselves and our Posterity." Do you think for one minute that the statesmen would have said that they were going to take away the right to trial by jury for people who were rendered quadraplegic by a doctor's negligence, just because it cost the doctor too much money to pay his insurance? That turns the Seventh Amendment on its head. Yes–the corporations are "people" under the law, too. And in fact if corporations are happy, many people are employed and many people will be helped. Many of you can still remember the "company towns" of the oil business and the coal mining business. Those towns were built for a reason–the company's profit motive.

Just like the influence of the corporate owner of the company town, the influence of the large corporate interests may increase to the point that people allow them to surreptitiously and systematically fritter away our personal rights, which are the cornerstones of this democracy. If our Constitution's authors were right, and the right to a trial by jury is important, nothing should allowed to detract from that right, and nothing should be important enough to take it away or lessen its influence, unless it is doing so much harm that the *Constitution* is in need of amendment. If that becomes the case, then the amendment should be done in the manner prescribed by law.

Big companies telling stupid jurors what to do?

Placing a cap of $250,000 on the amount that a jury may award for noneconomic damages, besides being unfair to the victims, is also unfair to the millions of people who have served on juries in this country. One thing that a jury is charged with doing is applying the law, as well as society's norms, to the conduct of the parties in the case.

That is what damages are all about. The jury is the conscience of the community when it comes to determining values of lives, services, and disabilities. So, when the politicians pretend to be able to tell the jury how to function, those politicians are imposing their norms on society. I thought that politicians did that in the legislative process when they were making legislative decisions. Why are they now trying to make judicial decisions as well? We are constantly barraged with cries that liberal federal judges with no moral conscience try to legislate from the bench. Now, however, legislators are trying to legislate in the courtroom.

There is noting that is more antagonistic to our system of checks and balances than to rip from one of the three branches of government a function guaranteed to it under the United States *Constitution*–a right which the courts MUST preserve. This is the only provision of the Bill of Rights which necessarily must, if it is to be protected at all, be protected by the judiciary, because there is nowhere else that a jury exists. Should we allow the legislative branch of government to furtively purloin the right to trial by jury, based upon the bald, unproven assertion that the jury is doing a bad job of performing its function?

Even if we were to believe that juries were not performing their function, let's take a look at how the $250,000 cap stacks up against societal judgment about other commodities. Please compare one commodity, your health and well-

204

being (including all that would be taken from you if you were rendered brain-damaged or other such serious disabling injury), to the list of commodities below--some other commodities that our society has said are worth about $250,000. Let's see if you would agree to exchange your body, your well-being, or accept a life of pain, for any of the following:

1) Twice the amount of money that it cost Ken Lay in 1999 to dispatch an empty Enron Jet to France to fetch his daughter Robin home from Nice. The cost of that flight was $125,000, or one half of the proposed caps. Would Ken Lay's daughter have given up the lift to avoid a life of pain?

2) The Bush administration's latest tax cut would have reduced Dick Cheney's taxes by $220,000 in the last year he worked at Halliburton Oil. Would the Vice-President give up his tax cut to avoid brain damage?

3) Four innings of pitching by Braves pitcher Gregg Maddox (who earned more than $13,000,000 in one year). Averaged out over the year, he earned the cap for every four innings of pitching. Would the Braves' owner give up four innings of Greg Maddux's services to avoid becoming a paraplegic?

4) Former Tyco executive Dennis Kozlowski spent eight times the cap on a birthday party for his wife. This $2.1 is more than eight times what a brain-damaged patient could recover for his life of pain and anguish.

5) Less than the cost of a 2004 Rolls-Royce. Wouldn't every Rolls Royce owner give away their car rather than accept permanent disability?

6) A six-hour trip on Air Force One ($40,000 per hour to operate) would be worth the same as a lifetime spent without the use of arms or legs.

7) 70 brain-damaged children, at $250,000 per child, for their entire lives, are worth the same amount as the pharmaceutical industry gave ($17.5 million) to Republicans in one year in the 2002 election cycle.

8) A lifetime of suffering every day for a full year ($250,000 per day times 365) is less than Bill Gates annual Microsoft dividend. Bill Gates annual dividend in 2003 was $97.9 million. Put another way, Bill Gates, with his dividend (not including his eight figure salary) could pay the maximum award for a lifetime of suffering for 365 children.

9) Eight years of prep and Ivy League education. Andover and Yale, the President's prep school and college, charge $28,500 and $35,000, respectively. The eight years of tuition for the education Mr. Bush is in excess of the $250,000 cap that Mr. Bush thinks should apply to people whose life has been ruined by medical negligence.

The most recent news item that put this in perspective for me was a brief Associated Press report, May 14, 2005, from the tax returns of our two highest executives, the President and Vice-President. Among the $26,346 in gifts President Bush accepted last year were a $14,000 shotgun and a $2,700 mountain bike, according to his financial disclosure form, which also listed millions of dollars the president has invested in U.S. Treasury notes and certificates of deposit. The annual disclosures required by law offered a glimpse into the president's and Vice President Cheney's wealth and what they gave each other for Christmas last year. Bush's 1,583-acre ranch was worth between $1 million and $5 million, the president reported having at least $4.95 million in Treasury notes, $750,000 in certificates of deposit, and $217,000 in checking and money-market accounts. Bush owns the mineral rights valued at as much as $15,000 on property in Reeves County, Tex. He also owns a tree farm, which is not expected to have commercial sales until 2007, which has a value of just under $600,000.Bush received the shotgun from Roy E.

Weatherby Jr., head of a family-owned firearms firm based in Atascadero, California. These gifts were in addition to the ones received by the First Lady, who accepted $400 in salad plates from Tricia Lott, wife of Sen. Trent Lott (R-Miss.), and a $1,300 gold bracelet from the first couple's friends, Mr. and Mrs. Tom Bernstein of Riverdale, N.Y.

I do not state that there is anything wrong with the President receiving gifts. He obviously has many people whom he considers his "friends" and friends give each other gifts. Nor do I believe that baseball, basketball, plane trips or prep schools should be done away with. What I believe is more telling about this report is this–isn't it difficult for someone who receives more than $25,000 worth of gifts in a year to pretend to be able to state the value of someone else's happiness? If the President had the choice of paraplegia or all of the gifts he receives while in office, which do you think he would choose? The mere asking of the question dictates the answer. Bush has stated that $250,000 should be the cap for even the worst injury. How can he say that in the face of the fact that he will receive more than that in gifts during his presidency? What is wrong with our society that we would just accept the president's gifts as a fact of life, and all of the other expenditures as being ok with us, and then have the very politicians who give those gifts mandate that a brain-damaged child receive less for his entire life than one man gets in eight years worth of gifts. HYPOCRISY AT ITS WORST!

If a cap on non-economic damages is necessary or helpful, what if we tried a cap equal to one year's compensation of the most highly paid employee of the insurance company or hospital involved in the suit. Would any of those executives be willing to lose all of that salary, and be given $250,000 (of course it would then be reduced by attorney's fees and litigation expenses). If President Bush's daughter had been rendered paraplegic by the car wreck over which he hired a lawyer and sued, would he think that her life would be worth only his proposed cap? What if, in the labor and delivery of his first grandchild, the doctor caused permanent brain damage to the baby. Could he handle, after such an incident, looking his own daughter in the eye, next to that tiny baby in the neonatal care unit, and say, "I'm sorry, honey, I thought this damage cap would be good for our doctors and our country." Or, better still, does anyone believe that sending the daughter to Andover and Yale, taking her to a full year of Laker's games, or buying her a Rolls Royce would make her feel any better about her plight? An additional irony of that question is that a poor person, or even a middle-income person, if awarded that sum of money, cannot afford to turn it down as a matter of principle. The pain for indigent people, who desperately need financial assistance in such circumstances, is that they have to swallow their pride, take the money, and go away. Any wealthy family can easily just refuse the money, since they do not need it. The terrible thing, though, is the pain never goes away, whether they accept the money or not.

The legislatures' placing a cap on damages is wrong for two major reasons. First, it is a violation of the Seventh Amendment. Second, the moral judgment and societal value judgment of such a cap is simply wrong. The only real justification for placing such a cap is the claim that lawsuits are causing such huge malpractice premiums that doctors are leaving practice. Now that we have seen that lawsuits are not causing high premiums and that doctors are not leaving practice, the only justification that is in the mind and soul of the perpetrators of this fraud is that trial lawyers are bad. Even if you believe that trial lawyers are bad people, why would you want to punish the injured? Does not make sense, does it?

Why does the wheel squeak?

The insurance companies believe that if they can make it look like someone else is the problem in the system, then no one will look at them to make them change. So far, their plan has been very successful. But, if you will remember, the main thing that the insurance companies want the consumers to complain about is the high cost of health care. That is what they say is the reason that consumers should demand change, and put a cap on the jury awards, to lower the cost of malpractice insurance. But, who is making money on the system?

For the second year in a row, in 2004 the health plans turned in an impressive performance on the balance sheet, despite seeing enrollment numbers decline. In Texas, membership fell nearly 17 percent to 2.7 million in 2003, the result of growing enrollment in less costly preferred provider organizations. But having fewer enrollees didn't stop the plans from making a hefty profit. Even though in Texas, until very recently, an insured was able to sue his HMO, the HMOs in the state posted earnings of $166.6 million last year, according to figures released by the Texas Department of Insurance. That's a substantial jump from earnings of $20 million in 2002, and a far cry from the red ink that dogged the industry the previous six years.

The results offer fresh evidence that HMOs are pricing their products ahead. For many years, HMOs were in a race for market share, enrolling members as fast as they could but often failing to charge premiums that kept pace with medical cost inflation. That has changed, according to industry advocates. So, in addition to the fact that we now know (as we will see from studies discussed in Chapter 10) that malpractice verdicts only account for less than 1% of health care costs, we know that the HMO's are getting their fair share of the health care dollar pie.

Who gets the big fish?

We keep hearing that the jury awards are going up, that there are more of them, and that they are being given in frivolous cases. In addition to the fact that the reports of frivolous suits are fabricated, and that the average awards are down, there is ample evidence that reports of more huge awards are inaccurate, as well. In Lawyer's Weekly, USA, it was reported that the nation's Top Ten verdicts to individual plaintiffs came crashing back to earth in 2003, with the lowest total since 1997. That statistic is a bit deceptive, however, because the 2002 total was skewed by two verdicts that were quite literally off the charts (one for $28 billion and another for $2.2 billion, both of which were cut on appeal by huge percentages). But even if we eliminate those two verdicts and compare verdicts 3-10 for the past two years, there was still a 32 percent drop. You would have to go all the way back to 1993 to find a number one verdict that was smaller than the 2003 top verdict. "This could be just an aberration or a blip, and go back up again next year, or it could be the beginning of a long-term trend which would be good for society in general," said Richard Samp, chief counsel for the American Tort Reform Association (ATRA). "From a common sense perspective, you can make an inference that tort reform has had an impact on attitudes. Even if we don't enact concrete reforms, it has an impact on how people perceive the impact of large verdicts," he said.

There is no way of knowing whether the 2003 ten largest verdicts typify big verdicts as a whole. However, jury consultant Richard Gabriel said that, based on conversations with hundreds of mock jurors and focus groups, the tort reform message is getting through."We've seen more jurors talking about windfalls and lotteries and

McDonald's coffee," said Gabriel, cofounder of Decision Analysis, which has offices in San Francisco, Los Angeles and Chicago. "Jurors are influenced by the debate about tort reform. The perception that there is a med-mal crisis is having an effect." He said the tort reform rhetoric - such as a recent publication by ATRA which targets the nation's 13 "judicial hell holes" - sinks into the public consciousness.

There is also growing concern among potential jurors that a large portion of these giant verdicts go to lawyers. This is particularly true of punitive damages, which are intended to punish the defendant but ultimately send hundreds of millions of dollars to plaintiffs and their lawyers. "They don't think plaintiffs should get large windfalls," said Gabriel. "They should get their lost wages, medical bills. But as far as punitives, they are very skeptical unless there has been very egregious behavior - and even then, they are concerned that too much of this money is going to lawyers. There has been a lot of talk of wanting to distribute the money differently."

Victor Schwartz, general counsel for the American Tort Reform Association, also believes there we are witnessing a fundamental change in the public's attitude toward punitive damages. He said that plaintiffs' attorneys have been less successful in portraying "certain sectors of corporate America as Saddam Hussein-type wrong-doers."

So, the true facts do not demonstrate that verdicts are on the rise. On the contrary, some verdicts have some motivational elements. The number 10 verdict was returned on behalf of an academic All-American diver who was rendered quadriplegic during a stunt diving accident, but went on to develop a new career painting magnificent portraits holding a brush in his mouth. The number five and six verdicts also have an element of hope. Both involve swimming pools and both were litigated by the same small-firm attorney, Michael Haggard of Coral Gables, Fla. Haggard, who has since used his money and time to launch a legislative campaign aimed at improving pool safety. Why did he do this? Because he discovered during his representation of the victims that, "In Florida, for children under age five, drowning is the number one cause of accidental death." Not only are huge verdicts not the rule, they are often the impetus for much better things.

The legal safeguards which are in place to counter frivolous lawsuits have increased in most states. Tort reform measures have been enacted with increasing frequency, so that the injustice of unjustified recoveries may be avoided. When unjust results occur, those results get published, but often the correction of that result goes unpublished (such as the true facts regarding the infamous McDonald's coffee case). Whenever there is a large and unjustified verdict, it is most often substantially reduced either by the trial court or on appeal. Although huge verdicts are always reported, the plaintiff's losses or minimal recoveries are never published. The corporate mistakes or actual malicious conduct that result in crippling injuries, have often been corrected by the jury system. If it were not for our justice system working the way it does, many people will be left to be wards of the state, at a price the economy can ill afford at a time when we are at war and our national resources are increasingly burdened by other necessities.

Bedpan Mutuals wreak havoc

If the top verdicts are not higher, settlements are not on the rise, and the vast majority of lawyers do not file frivolous suits, then what is the reason for the increase in medical malpractice insurance? In a story by Steven Brown of the Dallas Morning News, it was reported that "Homeowners who've watched their annual insurance premiums skyrocket can empathize with the owners of big skyscrapers, shopping malls and hotels." Premiums for commercial real estate insurance almost tripled in that year. But it had as much to do with the stock market as Sept. 11. "Before 9-11, we were already looking at insurance price increases across the board," said Randy Kostroske, director of risk management for Crescent Real Estate Equities, one of the country's largest owners of commercial real estate. "Even before the terrorist attacks, the insurance market was hardening; 9-11 just made matters worse," he said.

While it's easy to blame terrorism coverage

for the spike in commercial real estate insurance costs, the big landlords and insurance industry representatives say that's only part of the story. The insurance industry is seeing reduced income from its outside investments, so losses on Wall Street are probably more to blame for the run-up in cost than Sept. 11, Mr. Kostroske and others said. Major insurance companies are substantial investors in securities, and some of them also provide debt, including mortgages for commercial real estate. Through most of the 1990s, the insurance companies were making a lot of money on their investment income. Insurers could afford to pay more out in losses than premiums, and investment income covered the difference. With a downturn in the stock market, and corresponding lower interest rates and thus much lower returns on debt instruments, insurance companies don't have that luxury. When premiums have to be raised, the blame must be passed along to someone, and that someone is you, the potential victim of negligence.

While the stock market was going downhill, some of the nation's health insurers were feeling no pain. In a September 4, 2002 wire report, Reuters' noted that profits at the nation's health insurers jumped 25% in 2001, led by Blue Cross plans, though earnings from traditional HMO plans slumped.

All Blue Cross Blue Shield plans--led by Anthem Inc. and several nonprofits– reaped $2.9 billion in profit in 2001, a 70% increase from 2000, according to a survey by Weiss Rating, an independent insurance rating firm. Health insurers in the aggregate earned $4.1 billion in 2001. Remember, these guys are the ones that pay the doctors their fees, but they say that increased medical costs are due to trial lawyers!

New York Times staff writer, E. Scott Reckard, in an October 5, 2002 report, states that far more than they publicly admit, home and auto insurers are raising rates to cover their losses on risky corporate securities, according to a controversial study released today by a Santa Monica consumer watchdog group, The Foundation for Taxpayer and Consumer Rights. In 1998, with the bull market still roaring ahead, the insurance companies covered in its study held 48% of their investments in stocks and corporate bonds. By 2001, when the market had turned, corporate stocks and bonds had climbed to 57% of the insurers' portfolios, including major stakes in now notorious companies such as Enron Corp. and WorldCom Inc. The huge losses in both of those stocks, now known to have been caused by pure corporate greed and corruption, led to horrendous losses by heavy investments of the insurance industry. Douglas Heller, a senior consumer advocate for the group, said insurers built up their emergency reserves and fought for market share in the 1990s as they enjoyed the fruits of the bull market. But when their investments soured, "they came back and demanded that policyholders make up the difference."

During the first half of 2002, the nation's property and casualty insurers suffered $8.6 billion in paper losses on investments, according to the Insurance Services Office, which tracks the industry's returns. Those still-unrealized losses eclipsed the industry's reported profit of $4.6 billion during the first half of 2001, the ISO said.

We all know that the *Wall Street Journal* is not a trial-lawyer loving, consumer advocate publication. If anything, it is inclined to lean toward the conservative, big business and insurance view of things. Yet on Monday, June 24, 2002, the *Journal* reported, in an article entitled "Assigning Liability: Insurers' Missteps Helped Provoke Malpractice" that lawsuits did not cause the premiums of malpractice insurers to skyrocket. The article states, "As medical-malpractice premiums skyrocket in about a dozen states, across the country, obstetricians and doctors in other risky specialties, such as neurosurgery, are moving, quitting or retiring. Insurers and many doctors blame the problem on rising jury awards in liability lawsuits." Yet, the authors conclude, despite the claims of David Golden of the National Association of Independent Insurers, the real sickness is not that people sue at the drop of a hat, or that judgments are going "up and up and up," or that "the people getting rich out of this are the plaintiff's attorneys." A major part of the problem is the insurance companies' investment losses.

Following a cycle that recurs in many parts

of the business, a price war that began in the early 1990s led insurers to sell malpractice coverage to obstetrician-gynecologists at rates that proved inadequate to cover claims. Some of these carriers had rushed into malpractice coverage because an accounting practice widely used in the industry made the area seem more profitable in the early 1990s than it really was. A decade of shortsighted price slashing led to industry losses of nearly $3 billion last year. "I don't like to hear insurance-company executives say it's the tort [injury- law] system -- it's self-inflicted," says Donald J. Zuk, chief executive of SCPIE Holdings Inc., a leading malpractice insurer in California.

In addition to pointing out the insurance companies investment problems, the *Journal* authors point out the misleading claims of insurance companies regarding the "out of control" jury verdicts. Although the American Medical Association says Florida, Nevada, New York, Pennsylvania and eight other states face a crisis because the legal system produces multimillion-dollar jury awards on a regular basis, the truth is that the litigation statistics most insurers trumpet are incomplete. Those statistics have large gaps. Award information is collected unsystematically, and much information is missed. The major tort reform groups admit that they can't calculate the percentage change in the median for childbirth-negligence cases, which are the largest damage cases. More important, the database excludes trial victories by doctors and hospitals -- verdicts that are worth zero dollars. That's a lot to ignore. Doctors and hospitals win about 62% of the time, according to Jury Verdict Research, one of the largest collectors of date. They also admit that a separate database on settlements is less comprehensive. A spokesman for Jury Verdict Research, Gary Bagin, confirms these and other holes in its statistics. Some doctors are beginning to acknowledge that the conventional focus on jury awards deflects attention from the insurance industry's behavior.

The American College of Obstetricians and Gynecologists for the first time is conceding that carriers' business practices have contributed to the Current problem, says Alice Kirkman, a spokeswoman for the professional group. "We are admitting it's a much more complex problem than we have previously talked about," she says.

No one disputes one thing–malpractice insurance rates have increased. The question is how and why. Understanding the full reasons would take a lot of time. One thing that we know for sure is that in the early 1980's the frequency and size of claims rose significantly for several years, industry officials say. St. Paul Insurance Company, previously the largest malpractice insurer in the nation, and its competitors raised rates sharply during the 1980s to cover these claims. Expecting malpractice awards to continue rising rapidly, St. Paul Increased its reserves (the amount of money it holds in an account to pay future claims it anticipates it will have to pay). But the company miscalculated, says Kevin Rehnberg, a senior vice president. Claim frequency and size leveled off in the late 1980s, as more than thirty states enacted curbs on malpractice awards, Mr. Rehnberg says. The combination of this so-called tort reform and the industry's rate increases turned malpractice insurance into a very lucrative specialty. A standard industry accounting device used by St. Paul and, on a smaller scale, by its rivals, made the field look even more attractive.

Realizing that it had set aside too much money for malpractice claims, St. Paul released $1.1 billion in reserves between 1992 and 1997. The money flowed through its income statement and boosted its bottom line. St. Paul stated clearly in its annual reports that excess reserves had enlarged its net income. But that part of the message didn't get through to some insurers -- especially "bedpan mutuals"–the smaller companies that are actually owned by their doctor members. They were dazzled by St. Paul's bottom line, according to industry officials. In the 1990s, some bedpan mutuals began competing for business beyond their original territories. New Jersey's Medical Inter-Insurance Exchange, California's Southern California Physicians Insurance Exchange (now known as Scpie Holdings), and Pennsylvania Hospital Insurance Co., or Phico, fanned out across the country. Some publicly traded insurers also jumped into the business. With St. Paul seeming to offer a model for big, quick profits, everyone wanted to get into the game.

As they entered new areas, smaller carriers often tried to attract customers by undercutting St. Paul. The price slashing became contagious, and premiums fell in many states. Says Tom Gose, President of MAG Mutual Insurance Co., which operates mainly in Georgia. "They came in late to the dance and undercut everyone." The newer competitors soon discovered, however, that profitability of the '90s was the result of those years in the mid-80s when the actuaries were predicting the terrible trends, according to Donald J. Fager, president of Medical Liability Mutual Insurance Co., a bedpan mutual started in 1975 in New York. Except for two mergers in the past two years, his company mostly has held to its original singlestate focus. The competition intensified, even though some insurers knew rates were inadequate from 1995 to 2000 to cover malpractice claims, according to Bob Sanders, an actuary with Milliman USA, a Seattle consultancy serving insurance companies.

In at least one case, aggressive pricing allegedly crossed the line into fraud. Pennsylvania regulators last year filed a civil suit in state court in Harrisburg against certain executives and board members of Phico. The state alleges the defendants misled the company's board on the adequacy of Phico's premium rates and funds set aside to pay claims. On the way to becoming the nation's seventh-largest malpractice insurer, the company had suffered mounting losses on policies for medical offices and nursing homes as far away as Miami. Pennsylvania regulators took over Phico last August. The company filed for bankruptcy-court protection from its creditors in December. A trial date hasn't been set for the state fraud suit. Phico executives and directors have denied wrongdoing.

By 2000, many companies were losing money on malpractice coverage. The losses were exacerbated by carriers' declining investment returns. Some insurers had come to expect that big gains in the 1990s from their bond and stock portfolios would continue, industry officials say. When the bull market stalled in 2000, investment gains that had patched over inadequate premium rates disappeared. Some bedpan mutuals went home. New Jersey's Medical Inter-Insurance Exchange, now known as MIIX, had expanded into 24 states by the time it had a loss of $164 million in the fourth quarter of 2001. The company says it is now refusing to renew policies for 7,000 physicians outside of New Jersey. It plans to reformulate as a new company operating only in that state. St. Paul's malpractice business sank into the red. Last December, newly hired Chief Executive Jay Fishman, a former Citigroup Inc. executive, announced the company would drop the coverage line. St. Paul reported a $980 million loss on the business for 2001. So, the best way to recoup the money is to raise rates, lie to their clients (the doctors), and blame it on the trial lawyers.

A big irony here is that the doctors

have been convinced this is all the fault of the trial lawyers. I think that many doctors truly believe that lie. The ultimate burden, though, comes back on the patients–the very ones that the doctors claim they are trying to protect by keeping their costs down. This problem, if there is one, could be fixed if the focus were on the real cause. So long as we do not look at the insurance industry investment decisions, or the premium pricing policies, we will not be looking at the entire picture. If we do not look at the statistics on claims payment and jury verdicts, we will not be looking at the full picture.

Washington–we have a drug problem!

When Tom Hanks played the part of the Apollo 13 astronaut in the movie of that name, his famous line "Houston–we have a problem" was referring to a problem that could have killed three people. What the writers of that movie did not know, and what most people do not know, is that we have a serious problem in this country that someone needs to talk about, that has already killed thousands and will continue to kill more. That problem is the amount of money that is thrown away each year on marketing drugs in order to make them the bestsellers.

What makes drugs so expensive? Do you think that a new drug comes on the market and all of the doctors just start using it? We now see huge marketing television campaigns targeting the consumers and patients. Are you, like I, sick and tired of the warning stating "if your erection lasts more than eight hours, call your doctor!" You end up paying for that little piece of advice that sounds pretty much like commonsense. But, the TV ads are only the tip of the iceberg of costs for the promotion of drugs that the manufacturers pay every day. In "Drug Makers Battle Plan to Curb Rewards for Doctors," appearing in the *Washington Post,* (Dec. 25, 2003), writer Robert Pear reports that drug companies and doctors are fighting a Bush administration plan to restrict gifts and other rewards that pharmaceutical manufacturers give doctors and insurers to encourage the prescribing of particular drugs. This is one area where the president has had some very constructive plans. In October, the Department of Health and Human Services said many gifts and gratuities were suspect because they looked like illegal kickbacks. Since then, a few consumer groups, including AARP, have voiced support for the restrictions. But they are outnumbered by the drug makers, doctors and health maintenance organizations that have flooded the government with letters criticizing the proposal.

Drug makers acknowledged, for example, that they routinely made payments to insurance plans to increase the use of their products, to expand their market share, to be added to lists of recommended drugs or to reward doctors and pharmacists for switching patients from one brand of drug to another. Insurers, doctors and drug makers said such payments were so embedded in the structure of the health care industry that the

Bush administration plan would be "profoundly disruptive." Wouldn't it be a shame if we disrupted their profit plans, all in the name of reasonable costs?

In its guidance to the industry, the government warned drug makers not to offer financial incentives to doctors, pharmacists or other health care professionals to prescribe or recommend particular drugs. The government said the industry's aggressive marketing practices could improperly drive up costs for Medicare and Medicaid, the federal health programs for 75 million people who are elderly, disabled or poor. The payments and incentives to which the government objects are "standard in the drug industry." Merck & Company said it routinely gave such payments to health plans to reward "shifts in market share" favoring its products. Merck complained that the administration proposal would "criminalize a wide range of commercial conduct" that the industry regards as normal and entirely proper. The Pharmaceutical Research and Manufacturers of America, the chief lobby for brand-name drug companies, acknowledged that these payments created a strong incentive to prescribe certain drugs, or to shift patients from one drug to another. But, it said, that did not make the payments "illegal kickbacks." Solvay Pharmaceuticals of Marietta, Ga., told the government: "We understand that bribes and other hidden remuneration should be prohibited. However, a policy statement that declares well-established commercial practices potentially criminal creates a chilling effect on commerce and ultimately harms all consumers."

There are specialized companies that manage drug benefits. These companies, known as pharmacy benefit managers, can exert immense influence over what drugs are prescribed and dispensed. H.M.O.'s and pharmacy benefit managers said they typically received money from the manufacturer of a drug if sales of that drug reached a certain level — say 40 percent of all the prescriptions for cholesterol-lowering agents. The manufacturer may agree to a higher payment if the drug achieves a larger share of the market. If these companies pay money to get their drugs prescribed, don't you think that the cost comes out somewhere? If that cost is passed onto the HMO or PPO, and you, the consumer, pay the premiums, or your employer pays the premiums as part of your benefits, who do you think ultimately bears the burden? If it is passed on to you, you pay. If it is passed onto an employer, and anyone in this country is a consumer of that employer's products or services, then those consumers pay. More cost, more price, more inflation, more dollars out of your pocket.

The administration proposal received support from one H.M.O., the Great Lakes Health Plan, which serves more than 90,000 Medicaid recipients in Michigan. Eric J. Wexler, general counsel of the Great Lakes plan, said pharmacy benefit managers sometimes sent letters to doctors recommending that they shift Medicaid patients from generic drugs to brand-name medicines. In many cases, Mr. Wexler said, the brand-name drugs cost more, but are less effective. For each letter sent to a doctor, Mr. Wexler said, "the pharmacy benefit manager receives an administrative fee, and it may get additional remuneration for converting patients from one drug to another."Advance PCS, a pharmacy benefit manager based in Irving, Tex., confirmed that it received payments from drug companies for letters sent to doctors and patients urging them to use particular drugs. But it said the payments — typically a flat fee for each letter — were for educational services that could help control drug spending.

Why do we even need pharmacy benefit managers? Did you even know that there was someone out there who was in the line between the manufacturer and the insurance company who was trying to "move market share?" I learned in high school economics that, for every middle man, there was an extra cost. Who pays for that? YOU DO. You pay extra because your HMO or PPO has chosen to approve a certain drug or your doctor gets a golf trip to make a recommendation of that drug. Then, if that drug causes you brain damage, you are limited to $250,000 in damages. Why? Because the doctor's insurance rates are too high!

The $800 toilet seats

Remember the series of articles that was so much in the news back in the 1980's about government waste. Among the things discussed was the fact that some government contractors were allegedly receiving as much as $800 for a toilet seat on a toilet installed in a government building. One thing that we need to be aware of if we are going to try to help provide for some affordable quality health care is the place in the system where extra costs can be reduced. When a commodity required a lot of extra spending on marketing that is not directly related to the quality of the product, the cost of that commodity goes up. In her well-researched article appearing in AMNews, January 6, 2003, Victoria Stagg Elliott, wrote about some of the advertising campaigns that our major drug manufacturers feel compelled to generate in order to keep up with their competition. Advertisements for "Talk IBS," a campaign to inform women about a specific type of irritable bowel syndrome, appeared in many major media markets in major newspapers. The advertisements featured a celebrity -- Lynda Carter, television's Wonder Woman -- whose mother had the condition. The ads listed the condition's symptoms, with the tagline: "Talk to your doctor."

In the marketing biz, this type of effort is known as "an unbranded educational campaign." The campaign was funded by Novartis

Pharmaceuticals, in the hope that raised awareness of the disease will trigger an increased demand for their new drug, Zelnorm. The medication, approved by the Food and Drug Administration in 2002, was the only treatment for the particular IBS variant targeted. Marketing geared to physicians started in September 2002. But name-specific advertising directed to consumers did not start for months.

According to the drug companies, the first priority has to be to get physicians comfortable with the product. The second phase is to raise awareness and educate consumers about the condition and ask them to go in to see their doctor to get diagnosed. If they are diagnosed with it, the doctor will see if there are any treatments that can help them. Such efforts are a common practice within the pharmaceutical industry. The plan is usually put into action years before the drug is even approved. And it comes with a price tag in the millions, on top of the investment necessary to research and develop the drug scientifically. But doing it right can make an enormous difference in how the pharmaceutical is received. Estimates of the cost of drug development including both research and marketing range from $110 million to $900 million per drug. Industry-wide, according to IMS Health, a pharmaceutical market research and consulting firm, drug companies spent $19.1 billion in 2001 on promotional activities, including $2.7 billion on direct-to-consumer advertising. This amount is above and beyond the $30.3 billion invested in research. In other words, 39% of the cost of the drugs is marketing. That percentage far outpaces the increases in malpractice insurance, but we do not hear anyone screaming about it.

On top of that is the cost of nagging the doctors. Physicians are no strangers to marketing messages. Drug reps show up regularly at their offices, keeping them supplied in pens and Post-it notes. Advertisements appear in publications they read, such as the one in which Elliott's article appeared. But sometimes the messages are more subtle. Physicians are invited to educational sessions sponsored by drug companies that, even if they do not mention a specific drug -- much like the "Talk IBS" campaign, are designed to increase sales. According to the Society for Academic Continuing Medical Education, more than 40% of funding for continuing education at medical schools is funded by commercial sponsors -- an increase from just 17% in 1994. Drug companies may also fund the development of treatment guidelines. But while many physicians have concerns about these practices, there are few other options.

Increasingly, drug companies also fund much of the research into their products, either by making grants to universities or by owning their own labs. And it is this last bit that is generating controversy. There is concern that these studies may be designed to show drugs in their best light. According to a paper presented at the American Geriatrics Society in May 2002, drug studies presented at scientific meetings are uniformly positive if research is funded by a drug company. Of those funded independently, one-third were negative. "It doesn't mean it's invalid," said Chad Boult, MD, MPH, lead author and a professor at Johns Hopkins Bloomberg School of Public Health. "But it should be put in a different context. ... It should be taken with a little more skepticism."

And, although medical meetings and peer-reviewed journals insist that authors make clear their funding sources, this is not always simple. When Dr. Boult was researching his paper, he ran across posters funded by organizations of which he had never heard, only to have the money trail lead to a large drug company. Although 80% of a drug's marketing budget targets physicians, consumers are also targeted with unbranded awareness campaigns as well as direct-to-consumer advertising.

Drug marketing is a reality, and many maintain that it serves an important purpose. But there are also ongoing efforts to ensure it doesn't go too far. The FDA, for instance, regulates direct-to-consumer advertising. However, a General Accounting Office report released in December 2002 found this oversight insufficient. And doctors often become frustrated. In September 2002, the Dept. of Health and Human Services Office of the Inspector General issued a document outlining exactly what would make a drug company subject to a fraud or abuse investigation. Even the

Pharmaceutical Research and Manufacturers of America, weighed in with guidelines on gifts to physicians.

In a review reported in the Journal of the AMA, two Yale University researchers found that one-fourth of university researchers receive funding from drug companies. These companies want the good seal of approval from the researchers. When drug companies fight over good press and market share, the cost to you goes up. In one of the drug industry's most bitter rivalries, Amgen Inc. and Johnson & Johnson have struggled for 18 years over the market for a blockbuster drug they both sell. Now a medical mystery is opening up a tense new front in their battle. About 180 patients, mostly on a J&J version of the drug, have developed a severe blood illness. The companies are locked in a high-stakes dispute over whether just J&J has a problem or whether something is more broadly wrong with the entire class of drug. The drug is EPO, which treats anemia. Amgen invented it in the 1980s and developed it with funding from J&J, ceding a chunk of the market to J&J in the process. The two have battled ever since, sometimes in court, over how to divide a market now valued at more than $7 billion a year, according to a story printed in the *Wall Street Journal* on January 29, 2003, written by David P. Hamilton and Scott Hensley, *Journal* reporters.

Another common practice in the marketing of drugs is the use of intermediaries to market drugs and pharmaceutical devices to mass users, such as HMO's and PPO's. Merck and Company, one of the nation's largest manufacturers of drugs, announced in 2003 that it had agreed to pay $42.5 million to settle long-running class-action lawsuits against its pharmacy-benefit unit, Medco Health Solutions. Medco had pocketed billions of dollars in rebates from manufacturers and other fees that, according to the lawsuit filed by Medco drug card holders, should have gone to thousands of health plans and millions of consumers. Medco has 65 million holders of its drug cards. Medco is one of the largest of a handful of pharmacy-benefit management companies, including AdvancePCS and Express Scripts, that negotiate with drug manufacturers to obtain products for employers and health plans. In lawsuits across the country, Medco, AdvancePCS and Express Scripts were accused of violating fiduciary duties to customers under the federal Employee Retirement Income Security Act by failing to disclose the extent of their financial ties with the manufacturers.

The Right and Power to Make decisions, without responsibility for those decisions.

The drug companies, malpractice insurance companies, doctors, and hospitals not the only ones fighting for their share of your health care dollars. Do not forget the HMO's and PPO's. But there is one big difference between those guys and the other decision makers– if your HMO makes a bad decision about your care and you end up getting hurt over it, they cannot be held responsible. Congress, those guys who now want to cap your damages, have given HMO's immunity. The U.S. Supreme Court last year struck laws that allow patients to sue their managed-care organizations, as provided by a Texas law that makes employer-paid health insurance plans liable for negligence when they wrongfully refuse to pay for medical care. The Texas law and similar statutes in nine other states had been hailed by supporters as a necessary means to hold managed care accountable for denials of coverage that sometimes result in pain, suffering and even death.

The health insurance industry claimed that states are forbidden to subject health plans to liability because of a 1974 federal law that encouraged the formation of employee benefit plans by making them subject only to federal regulation, rather than a patchwork of state rules. In 1987, the court said that the 1974 law, known as the Employee Retirement Income Security Act, precluded state suits against employee benefit plans. But the court has chipped away at that holding in more recent cases. In oral arguments before the Court, Texas Assistant Attorney General David C. Mattax told the justices that the state's law was necessary because times have changed since the court's 1987 ruling, and that now "HMOs are making medical decisions." But Chief Justice William H. Rehnquist, agreeing with the HMO lawyers, replied that HMOs and other managed-care firms do not decide on treatment. "Their statement is they just won't pay for it," he said. Mattax countered that a payment decision, based in part on a judgment about what the necessary and appropriate treatment would be, "is still a medical judgment."

Justice Stephen G. Breyer, while expressing sympathy for patients who are denied benefits, said that state lawsuits "seem to be the thing this [federal] statute forbids, and I don't see a way around it." The court's ruling arose out of two consolidated cases. The first case involved a man who participated in an employee health plan insured by Aetna Health Inc. His doctor prescribed Vioxx for arthritis pain, but Aetna Health said it would pay for only a cheaper alternative, Naprosyn. Several weeks later, Davila developed a severe bleeding ulcer, which he attributed to side effects of Naprosyn.

The second case involved a lady member of Cigna HealthCare of Texas through her husband's employer. Her doctor recommended several days in the hospital following a hysterectomy, but Cigna said it would pay for only one day. Calad developed serious complications and had to return to the hospital.

The fox guarding the hen house

Should we allow the insurance companies to be in charge of lessening your healthcare costs? Should they be the ones to tell you how you should spend your healthcare costs? If there is a certain amount of money that is available in the pot, would you rather some of it be spent for insurance to assure that if you get hurt, you will be compensated; or would you prefer that it be used to pay for TV ads for Vialis? If insurance companies have made bad investments, should that take away from money you or your loved one may need to have a nurse get you out of the shower if you cannot do it on your own? If you are unable to comb your own hair, and need a helper to do it, should you be deprived that helper so that your doctor's drug representative can take your doctor on a golfing trip?

Industries that have problems do not often regulate themselves very well. In the December 9, 2002 edition of the *Washington Post*, an article discussed some lessons that we can learn from the Enron scandal–one should be skeptical of highly qualified professionals -- in those cases, accountants who promised to regulate themselves. This skepticism should now be applied to doctors. As The Post's Sandra G. Boodman reported the medical profession is making scandalously slow progress in reducing the rate of medical errors in hospitals. According to the article, the largest single source of error stems from faulty drug prescriptions. One recent study found that one in five doses of medicine dispensed to patients involved an error. Either the wrong drug was given, or the wrong dose, or it was given at the wrong time.

These various errors reflect the arrogance of the medical priesthood. The article states that even though doctors themselves have produced studies showing how fatigue erodes worker competence, they persist in thinking that it's normal for junior members of their profession to put in more than 100 hours of work a week. Even though every other profession has embraced computers' ability to enhance human performance, doctors persist in scribbling prescriptions in illegible handwriting rather than punching them into a computer that might alert them if the dose is wrong. Studies of hospital infections find that junior workers are most likely to wash their hands properly. It is doctors who are most likely to forget this chore.

The article is not one-sided, noting that there are honorable exceptions. Some private hospitals, such as the Luther Midelfort Hospital in Eau Claire, Wisconsin, have made big strides in safety. But in general the problem does not get much attention. The national system for reporting medical errors is voluntary, so few errors get reported. A few states have mandatory systems, but most still do not. So long as patients have no way of finding out which hospitals are unreliable, bad hospitals will face minimal incentives to invest in the solutions that could drive error rates down. Computer systems that track medications going to each patient can eliminate dangerous interactions between drugs prescribed by two different doctors; they can screen for possible allergic reactions; they can query odd dosage levels. But such systems are expensive. Somebody must force hospitals to admit to errors, or hospitals won't invest in reducing them. The author of the article says that the obvious somebody is government, which is easily the biggest payer for health care. The Medicare authorities need to insist on proven safety procedures, such as computerized prescription systems, which currently exist in only about three percent of hospitals. They should extend their efforts to publish quality reviews of medical providers. Meanwhile state or federal regulators should require the reporting of errors and should make some of this information public. Otherwise thousands will continue to die needlessly and with no one held to account.

The administration proposal that would stop some of the drug company giveaway programs has some enforcement provisions. The administration proposal says that when drug executives discover evidence of illegal conduct, they should report it to federal authorities within sixty days. Also, it said, drug makers should consider offering rewards to whistle-blowers and should prominently display the phone number for reporting Medicare fraud to the government. The coalition of drug makers objected to these recommendations, saying they would undercut the companies' efforts to police themselves.

The so-called "solution" to high health care costs proposed by the President doesn't address the main root of the problem - skyrocketing insurance costs. The real culprit is the insurance industry, which controls virtually every aspect of America's health care system and is forcing doctors to pay for its recent investment losses. The insurance lobby, one of President Bush and the Congressional leadership's biggest campaign contributors, operates with a free hand because it is exempt from antitrust laws. Here's the evidence:

FACT: The lobbyists say lowering premiums will help average people, but the cost of medical malpractice liability premiums amount to less than one percent of total health care costs. The Consumer Federation of America reports that medical malpractice premiums comprise only 0.59 percent of national health care costs - so even if every single medical malpractice case in the country were eliminated, less than one percent of health care costs would be saved.

FACT: The lobbyists say jury verdicts drive up premiums for doctors, but consumer groups, a bipartisan legislative committee, and even the insurance industry say insurers' bad business practices, not jury awards, drive up premiums: "I don't like to hear insurance-company executives say it's the tort system - it's self inflicted." - Donald J. Zuk, Chief Executive of Scpie Holdings Inc., a leading malpractice insurer in California. Wall Street Journal, June 24, 2002.

FACT: The reformers say frivolous claims drive up the cost of doctors' insurance, but insurers themselves admit that they don't settle frivolous claims. "In interviews with liability insurers that I undertook, the most consistent theme from them was: 'We do not settle frivolous cases!' .

. . [Insurers'] policy on frivolous cases is based on the belief that if they ever begin to settle cases just to make them go away, their credibility will be destroyed and this will encourage more litigation." Neil Vidmar, Ph.D., Russell M. Robinson II Professor of law at Duke Law School.

FACT: The reformers say caps will lower doctors premiums, but experience in states with caps has shown - and insurers and tort reformers admit - that caps and tort reform won't lower doctors' premiums. In California, which limits non-economic damages to $250,000, the average actual premium is $27,570, eight percent higher than the average of all states that have no caps on non-economic damages. Medical Liability Monitor, 2001. Malpractice premiums in California increased by 190% during the first 12-years following enactment of the $250,000 MICRA cap. It took California's Proposition 103 - insurance reform - to lower and stabilize malpractice premium rates.

Remember Linda McDougal, 47, a U.S. Navy veteran, an accountant, wife and mother of three from the Woodville, Wisconsin, who had a double mastectomy, and then was told the cancer diagnosis had been wrong. Linda, who was mutilated for no reason, knows that the President's recommended legislative surgery to take away the legal rights of patients injured by malpractice is dangerously wrong and puts insurance company profits over the lives of injured people. McDougal said, "President Bush wants to put through rather rapidly a cap on medical malpractice [compensation]. His intent is to harm me. It's not to make doctors accountable for their actions. Don't penalize the patients. Don't penalize the victims."

Policing their own--We have now learned how well that works!! It has not worked in the past, and it will not work now, especially since the corporations are running things in the halls of power, whether at the state legislature or in Congress. In the next chapter, you will see some of the facts of how that system works. It is a system that continues to grow and feed on its own power. You do not have a voice except in your vote. If you want to preserve your right to trial by jury, you must learn how a few of the facts of the corporate power world functions.

CHAPTER SEVEN

WILL THE DOCTORS POLICE THEMSELVES?

"Enron should teach us that one should be skeptical of highly qualified professionals who promise to regulate themselves." "A Medical Enron," *Washington Post* **(December 9, 2002)**

Every state has a board that licenses and disciplines its doctors. In addition to looking at the qualifications of physicians that they license, they accept and act upon the complaints that are made by patients of the doctors in that state. Each of these boards has the authority to terminate the license of a physician if that physician is a danger to his patients. One of the categories of doctors that might be considered a danger to the patients is the category of doctors who repeatedly commit malpractice. The most recently available statistics from the U. S. Governments National Practitioners Data Bank, which is the clearing house for information on malpractice payments by physicians, show that 5.4% of the doctors in this country are responsible for 56.2% of the total malpractice payments. What better evidence could there be that a few bad doctors are causing the vast majority of payment? Does that type of physician often get his license terminated? Not if you look at the records in Texas, which just two years ago placed a $250,000 cap on non-economic damages that a patient could recover from any of those physicians who commit malpractice.

Even more surprising than the fact that just 5.4 percent of doctors have been responsible for 56.2 percent of all malpractice payments to patients, just two percent of doctors (each of whom has made three or more malpractice payments) were responsible for 31.1 percent of all payments; and only 0.9 percent of doctors (each of whom has made four or more malpractice payments), were responsible for 18.8 percent of all payments. A whopping 83 percent of doctors have never made a medical malpractice payout since the National Practitioners Data Bank was created in 1990. *Source*: National Practitioner Data Bank, Sept. 1, 1990 – Dec. 31, 2003.

More than eight out of ten doctors have not even had to pay any claims, and over one-half of all payments result from only one-twentieth of the doctors. These statistics alone demonstrate that it is more likely that some bad doctors are allowed to keep on practicing medicine, rather than that patients and their lawyers are suing doctors at random just to make a windfall.

Twelve strikes and you're out

Doug J. Swanson, and investigative reporter with the *Dallas Morning News*, another one of your not-so-liberal newspapers, did a series of articles in 2003 on this subject. He concluded that The Texas State Board of Medical Examiners, the agency that pledges to protect the public, "has shown routine mercy to doctors whose negligence killed the people they were treating. It has granted second and third chances to surgeons who were thrown out of hospitals because they botched operations. It has forgiven physicians who overlooked cancerous tumors, who maimed infants or whose mistakes left women sterilized. It has refused, in the last five years, to revoke the license of a single doctor for committing medical errors." Not only did the board fail to take action to discipline physicians, it failed to investigate the deaths of more than 1,000 patients that were reported to it in one year's time. Thousands more may have been ignored over the last decade. "We didn't do as well as we should," said Dr. Donald Patrick, who became the board's executive director in September. He said he had begun making sweeping improvements that target laggard workers, chaotic record-keeping and regulatory breakdown.

Even the legislature, charged with the oversight of the board, stated that "The board of medical examiners is badly broken," said state Rep. Ray Allen, R-Grand Prairie. "They should understand that the Legislature will be looking very hard at whether they need to continue to exist."

For years, the board has been unable – or unwilling – to crack down on physicians who commit serious, repeated medical errors. Some agency staff members and officials blame bureaucratic inefficiency compounded by a reluctance to confront doctors who injure patients. Though it has the power to cast troubled Texas physicians from the profession, the 18-member voting board – 12 of whom are doctors – does so infrequently. During the six-year period of 1997 through 2002, out of the total of 42 licenses being "surrendered," only one was for the category known as "repeating liability claims." Out of that 42, here are the others: 10 for substance abuse; 7 for scientifically unproven or non-therapeutic treatment; 2 unprofessional conduct; 3 criminal conduct other than drugs or sex; 7 for health, incapacity or other infirmity; 1 inconsistent with public health or welfare; 1 retirement; 1 abetting unlicenced practice; 2 failure to comply with rules on records or registration; 4 prescription of narcotics irregularities; 3 sexual misconduct. The list was compiled from the Board of Medical Examiners' disciplinary orders, databases and press releases. It includes only physicians who were practicing in the state of Texas at the time of their disciplinary proceedings. Over the last five years, the board has taken more than 700 disciplinary actions against physicians. In that same period, it permanently revoked the licenses of only 18 doctors practicing in the state: three committed mail fraud; several failed drug tests; one didn't pay his income taxes; not one of those revocations, *News'* analysis found, was directly related to medical errors of any sort, including patient death.

In addition to the forced surrenders during this time frame, the board has accepted the voluntary surrender of licenses from 44 physicians in Texas, many of them elderly practitioners ready for retirement anyway. None of those surrenders was attributed in the board's public records to mistakes that harmed patients.

The *News* reviewed thousands of pages of board disciplinary orders and more than 100 malpractice case files in 18 county courthouses across Texas, and concluded, "The pattern was one of state-sanctioned tolerance for serious medical mistakes." Even the board's own executive director during that time, Dr. Bruce Levy, admitted that, "The board was less interested in revoking somebody on a quality-of-care case than they were on a behavioral issue such as drug abuse." The reason? Investigations into cases of patient harm 2000 are "laborious and complicated," according to the current director, who also admitted that those cases were not "popular" to work, even though he further admitted that an investigation of that type is the way the board is supposed to protect the public.

By law, every medical malpractice suit filed in Texas must be reported to the state board, but it has been too short of money, manpower and institutional will to examine them closely. In 1998, agency figures show, more than 4,500 malpractice claims or suits were filed against Texas doctors. The state board (consisting of 18 members, 12 of whom are doctors) investigated only 121 of the 4,500. And it began actual disciplinary proceedings against only three of those physicians. In May of this year, the governor's office gave the board a $200,000 emergency grant to reopen abandoned cases. The following month, the board sent a progress report to the governor, which was released to the *News,* after a request under the state Public Information Act. The board reported that it had reviewed 6,038 malpractice claims that had been entered into its database from January 2001 to May 2002. Not one of those cases had been investigated, the agency revealed. And, it said, 1,068 of them involved patient death. The board has disclosed in other records that it did not investigate 46,276 malpractice claims or suits reported to it from 1991 to 2000. Roughly 18 percent of all malpractice cases not investigated by the board since January 2001 involved patient death. If the same percentage applies across the years, the state board has neglected to investigate more than 9,000 malpractice cases involving patient death since 1991. Most of that 2003 legislature, whose members overwhelmingly endorsed and passed the cap on non-economic damages, knew, when they passed that cap, what members of its House Appropriations committee knew-"we want a board that actually functions, and does its job and merits the public's confidence," a member of the House Appropriations Committee. "The board has not succeeded at any of these expectations. Does anyone think that will change?" That same member also predicted, "I don't think you'll see the Legislature throwing good money after bad."

It was almost always my experience that my clients who sought action against a doctor wanted to know what the Board would do about that physician. Some patients, or their surviving family members, assume that winning a large malpractice settlement guarantees that the medical board will discipline a doctor. Debby Stanley made that mistake with Dr. Charles C. Bittle Jr. "I thought they took that son of a bitch's license away forever," she said. Dr. Bittle, of Sanger, had problems with at least two cases. One of which was the 1991 death of a 3-yearold boy whom he treated in the emergency room of a Lancaster hospital. Dr. Bittle diagnosed the child with gastroenteritis and sent him home with medicine for nausea. Actually, the boy had intestinal blockage. He died five days later, after emergency surgery, of blood poisoning. The child's parents said that Dr. Bittle misread the X-rays. Their suit against him was settled. The medical board took no action. The other case was Mrs. Stanley's son, Jody. He was 19, a college student on a Thanksgiving visit home, when he saw Dr. Bittle in 1989 in his Sanger office for a painful lump on his left hip. The doctor told him he had a strain from crossing his legs. Four months later, home for spring break, Mr. Stanley complained that the lump was larger and more painful. Dr. Bittle did not palpate the swollen area, according to court papers, but prescribed an anti-inflammatory medication. A year after his initial visit, the lump was still growing and hurt more. His mother insisted that Mr. Stanley see another doctor. The second physician discovered a malignant growth on Mr. Stanley's hip. Worse, the cancer had spread to his lungs. He had chemotherapy, then surgery for a tumor. Jody's chance of survival had been reduced, by the delay, from very good to very bad. The case was settled for much less than the family believed they could have gotten in court, so Jody could enjoy it while he was alive. He died at the age of 23. Even though the matter was reported to the state board, no investigator ever contacted her any of the family, and the board took no action on the case.

The medical board did discipline Dr. Bittle in 1994, but not for the two death cases. He was cited for not performing sufficient follow-up visits on nine geriatric patients. The board ordered him to take courses in risk management and record keeping. In 2000, the board acted again, this time over numerous questions about Dr. Bittle's prescribing of narcotics. A review of his medical records, investigators said, showed that he had over-prescribed addictive drugs to 49 patients. The board placed him on probation. Dr. Bittle, 42, later moved from Sanger to Lubbock, where he continues to practice medicine.

Even the best doctors make mistakes, and almost no one – including the most aggressive of plaintiffs' lawyers – suggests that a physician should lose his license for a catastrophic but solitary error. Most reasonable people would agree with that belief. That is where the benefit of a civil justice system exists. The board should be concerned with weeding out physicians who demonstrate a pattern of problems. But the task of defining and identifying patterns has sometimes proved impossible.

Reasonable minds could differ over what is just a human mistake and what is a pattern of conduct demonstrating incompetence or lack of caring. Dr. Jasbir Ahluwalia of Stephenville, Texas was sued by a husband and wife who alleged that he caused severe and permanent brain damage to their child during delivery. At six years, the boy was determined to have the mental functioning of a 4-week-old. Dr. Ahluwalia settled the suit in 1989 for more than $1.3 million. In the course of the suit, lawyers for the couple raised questions about the quality of Dr. Ahluwalia's medical training, much of which he received in Uganda.

The board took no action. In March 1991, a Dallas woman sued him, accusing the doctor of perforating her uterus during a procedure. As a result, surgeons had to remove her uterus. That same year, another Dallas woman sued him. She, too, said he perforated her uterus. Dr. Ahluwalia settled both suits in 1993. The medical board took no action on either one. In 1995, he was sued by a woman on whom Dr. Ahluwalia had performed a hysterectomy. She alleged that he mistakenly

252

blocked a ureter with stitches. The complications were so severe that, four months later, another surgeon had to remove her kidney. Board members voted to require him to take 50 hours (about one of his normal work weeks) of continuing medical education and keep adequate patient records. And he was ordered to subscribe to the journal Obstetrics and Gynecology. The board even had the good conscience of requiring that he read it. Dr. Ahluwalia, 63, still practices gynecology in Stephenville.

"We'll give you just ten years to quit killing people"

In what the *Dallas Morning News* report called a decade of tolerance, Dr. Jerry Wayne Biddix was given chance after chance to become a better physician. The problem with that approach is it also gives him chance after chance to hurt or kill someone. Biddix had his first encounter with the board in 1988. He had lost his privileges at two East Texas hospitals and was facing questions about his treatment of 12 patients. One had been improperly committed to a psychiatric hospital. Four of them sued him for malpractice. Another had died during an arthroscopic knee operation."The allegations were basically, I guess, that somehow the surgery caused the ... anesthesia death," Dr. Biddix recalled in a deposition for an unrelated case.

The board ordered Dr. Biddix to stop performing surgeries but allowed him to maintain a general practice. "At that point I'd already given up surgery, so it was no big deal," Dr. Biddix said in the deposition. By 1991, he had moved to Winters, about 200 miles southwest of Dallas, and was working at hospital emergency rooms in the region. In 1996, he was in trouble again. A man who had been in a motorcycle accident came to the emergency room at Dyess Air Force Base in Abilene. Dr. Biddix, the board said, failed to take his blood pressure, determine whether he had worn a helmet or ask whether he had lost consciousness. He also discharged the man without performing a neurological exam or ordering X-rays. Two days later, the board said, the patient was hospitalized by different doctors for "extensive wound care." He spent six days in the hospital. As a result, the Air Force revoked Dr. Biddix's hospital privileges. The state board only ordered him to take and pass a standardized medical knowledge exam.

The *Dallas Morning News* article also referred to a case in which I represented the widower of one of Dr. Biddix's patients. I will only talk about the newspaper version, rather than what I know, in order not to violate confidentiality provisions my client agreed to. The case also arose in 1996, concerning my client's wife, who had been taken to a hospital emergency room in Winters, Texas. The woman suffered from severe head pain, nausea and elevated blood pressure. Biddix, the physician on call, would not get out of bed and come to the hospital to treat the woman. She died of an aneurysm hours later. The suit was settled out of court. In a deposition, a hospital nurse testified that on at least three other occasions, Dr. Biddix refused to come to the emergency room to treat sick or injured patients. The medical board did nothing. But in 2000, the board accused Dr. Biddix of mishandling another patient. That patient had diabetes and coronary artery disease, and Dr. Biddix neglected to perform timely lab tests or diagnostic exams, the board said, treating the patient chiefly by prescribing painkilling narcotics. The symptoms did not improve in the course of such unconventional therapy. In late 2000, a board attorney filed additional papers saying the agency was investigating "other claims of improper conduct" against Dr. Biddix. And there it ended. Twenty-one months later, at the time of the *News* report, the board had still taken no further action, and Biddix's name was included on a recent list of abandoned cases that the board plans to revive. Dr. Biddix, 59, remains in practice in Winters. Although he claimed that his past conduct was "no big deal," since he has now been ordered to refrain from surgery, it seems that some of his later patients might believe that it is a bigger deal than he believes.

In the case of Dr. Jack Franklin Hardwick of Fort Worth, witnesses were ready to talk, but no one from the board wanted to listen. Dr. Hardwick had been accused in four lawsuits of refusing to refer seriously ill patients to specialists, because the referrals would cut into the bonus he received from his HMO. His former nurse, Rosemary Dudley, said in a sworn affidavit in 1999 that he "indicated to me that he refused to send patients out for necessary referrals to specialists because of the effects ... on him financially."

Ms. Dudley herself had a history of breast and thyroid cancer, and was a patient of Dr. Hardwick's. She sued him in 1998, alleging that he discontinued her visits to an oncologist despite blood tests that indicated a recurrence of cancer. When he finally relented and referred her to a specialist, Ms. Dudley said, malignancies were found in her lungs and bones. She died last year at 68. Her daughter, Gail Dudley, said her mother complained to the state board, "but we never got the impression they were interested."

Fort Worth attorney George Parker Young said he told the state board he had "at least seven or eight" former patients of Dr. Hardwick's who were willing to talk. One was Jerry Batson. He said Dr. Hardwick diagnosed pneumonia in his 70-year-old wife, Pauline, in 1997. Days later, the doctor pronounced the pneumonia "all gone" and refused to put her in a hospital for additional tests, Mr. Batson said. She died several months later of lung cancer. "He was just trying to make money at other people's expense," Mr. Batson said of the doctor. Mr. Batson said he was willing to tell the board his story, but no investigator ever contacted him.

Others had similar accounts. "I gave the board their names," said Mr. Young, the Fort Worth lawyer. "I offered to hunt these folks down for them. What's really egregious is that the board

256

didn't follow up." In 2002, the board took up Dr. Hardwick's case. It cited him for his treatment of an 11-year-old who had to be hospitalized after the doctor missed his case of diabetic ketoacidosis, a life-threatening condition. The board also found that he "failed to meet the appropriate standard of care" with one of the patients who had sued him – a woman whose bowel cancer went undetected because Dr. Hardwick did not order the proper tests. No mention was made of any of the other patients, or of any financial incentive related to referrals. The board ordered Dr. Hardwick to have his practice monitored by another physician and to pay a $5,000 fine. He remains in practice in Fort Worth.

Late in 2002, the board issued a temporary suspension of Dr. Billy R. Ringer of Houston. The 36-page list of allegations against Dr. Ringer included: • He is addicted to narcotics.• He has injured numerous patients during penis enlargement surgery. In one patient's postoperative records, the complaint said, "there are a series of photographs showing a twisted, s-shaped, curved, scarred penis." • Many of his breast augmentation patients have suffered serious infections and complications. • He has had brain surgery, and several employees resigned because they feared he would suffer a seizure while operating on a patient. • He repeatedly injected narcotics into his girlfriend's groin. An abscess developed, and "this may lead to the amputation of her leg." The *News* reporter attempted to interview Dr. Ringer to allow him a chance to tell his side of the story. He did not respond to a telephone call, and his lawyer, declined to comment. But, you ask, aren't the plaintiff's trial lawyers the ones who are to blame?

Much of the damage Dr. Ringer is accused of inflicting on patients might have been avoided. The state could have put his license on ice long ago but refused to do so. Eight years ago, a board attorney drew up a formal complaint accusing Dr. Ringer of botching several surgeries and molesting female patients. One patient alleged that he bit her breast. In addition, at least 12 malpractice suits had been filed against him between 1991 and 1993, causing his insurance company to cancel his coverage. And he had resigned from a Houston hospital "while under investigation for quality-of-care issues." But after a 1994 hearing, a three-member medical board panel voted unanimously not to take any action against Dr. Ringer. "There is insufficient evidence," explained one panel member at the time, that Dr. Ringer "is a real and present danger to the health of his patients."

Remember that the legislature was going to increase the budget of the board, and they were going to give better oversight? The director of the board, in his interview with the News reporter, said that all of those problems were in the old days. The new board, members say, is a new era, as seen in their pledge in May of 2003 to renew their commitment to protect the public. On the same day they adopted that pledge – in fact, only a few hours later – board members encountered the matter of Dr. Dennis B. Dove. Dr. Dove used to practice in

Broward County, Fla. Since 1998, he has been a professor and chairman of the surgery department at the Texas Tech University Health Sciences Center at Amarillo. After holding a teaching faculty permit, he applied for a Texas medical license.

Here is Dr. Dove's malpractice history in Florida, according to that state's Department of Insurance records:

• A 49-year-old woman accused him of damaging her ureter during surgery for an ovarian cyst. Dr. Dove settled the suit in 1996 for $125,000.
• A 31-year-old male patient alleged that the doctor partially cut the artery to his liver during gallbladder surgery. Dr. Dove settled the suit in 1996 for $185,000.• A 48-year-old man died, a lawsuit contended, after Dr. Dove failed to take him to the operating room for drainage of a pancreatic abscess. The suit was settled in 1997 for $200,000. • A 41-year-old woman died, a lawsuit alleged, because Dr. Dove did not diagnose a perforated peptic ulcer. It was settled in 1997 for $238,000.• A 61-year-old woman died, according to a suit, of complications from colon surgery. Dr. Dove settled in 1999 for $205,000. • And a 37-year-old woman alleged that Dr. Dove damaged her laryngeal nerve during thyroid surgery, leaving her with no voice. Her suit was settled in 2000 for $300,000. Dr. Dove, in a written response to questions from the News, said that settlement of the cases had been directed by his insurance carrier. "It was cheaper for them to settle than to ... risk the unpredictable verdict of the jury," he said.

New state-- new record

In "Bad Doctors Do Keep on Practicing,"
Jim Edwards, *mailto:jedwards@amlaw.com*New
Jersey Law Journal, December 17, 2003, wrote
about the way that some doctors can move to a new
state, or even country, and start over. You get more
strikes that way. Dr. Richard Kaul went before the
New Jersey Board of Medical Examiners to plead to
keep his doctor's license. Kaul had been convicted
in England of negligent manslaughter after a dental
patient died under anesthesia. His British license
was revoked when he admitted that his "inattention"
allowed the patient's blood oxygen to drop low
enough to cause brain hypoxia and, finally, cardiac
arrest.

But the New Jersey board allowed Kaul to
keep his state license if he agreed to a six-month
suspension. Kaul, of Convent Station, N.J., believed
the decision was too strict, so he appealed. "If
anything, the six-month period of active suspension
was lenient," the New Jersey Appellate Division
ruled on Dec. 5, 2003. The discipline was especially
lenient considering that Kaul had lied about the
death on his applications to St. Clare's Health
System, where Kaul is on staff, and Hackensack
University Medical Center, the court noted.

The board rarely bans doctors from
practicing, even when they kill people, a review of
the board's discipline records, dating back to 1972,
shows. In fact, doctors who repeatedly commit
malpractice or engage in behavior that could harm

patients on multiple occasions are about twice as likely to be allowed to continue practicing than to be banned, the records show.

The survey discovered 290 cases in which doctors are described as repeatedly committing malpractice. In only 90 of those cases -- about one in three -- were the doctors permanently prevented from continuing to practice. In all other cases they were fined, reprimanded or given temporary suspensions, but were allowed to continue working. The *New Jersey Law Journal* undertook the study to test a key argument in the debate over the medical malpractice insurance crisis: Whether the medical profession allows bad doctors to continue practicing after they commit malpractice, thus increasing malpractice insurance premiums. Doctors, who nearly succeeded in convincing the state Legislature to cap damages for pain and suffering at $250,000, have contended that the malpractice insurance crisis is caused largely frivolous suits and jackpot jury awards, not bad doctors.

Overall, the survey found that since 1972, the New Jersey Board of Medical Examiners has disciplined 800 doctors for activity harmful to patients. About 32 percent of the 3,461 discipline reports issued by the board describe cases in which the board has found that a doctor has harmed a patient. The numbers are surprisingly low -- only about 26 cases a year. By contrast, 1,650 to 2,000 medical malpractice suits are filed every year, according to the Administrative Office of the

Courts. Settlements in such cases are often secret, but the federal National Practitioner Data Bank of Rockville, Md., tracks malpractice insurance payments. In New Jersey, insurers made 940 malpractice payments in 2001, the most recent year for which figures are available, according to the data bank. Put simply, the disparity between 940 payments and 26 disciplinary actions means that only about 2.7 percent of malpractice payments result in doctors being disciplined.

The fault is in our courts, they say

Juries are bad at deciding malpractice cases, the medical society argues, because once they see a patient's injuries, their hearts blind them to the medical facts, and they decide for the plaintiffs.

By statute, if an insurance company makes a malpractice payment, it is automatically referred to the Board of Medical Examiners, which then reviews the case to decide whether discipline is warranted. Once the board -- a 21-member panel dominated by doctors -- has heard the evidence, it frequently concludes that despite the jury verdict the doctor did not deviate from the appropriate standard of care. Hence, it is not the board but the court system that needs fixing, the medical society says. "The survey results are some of the best proof that the system is broken," says Robert Convoy, a partner at Kern, Augustine, Convoy & Schoppmann in Bridgewater. Conroy is general counsel to the medical society and specializes in defending doctors before the Board of Medical Examiners. Indeed, according to cases in which that "blue-ribbon" jury has found malpractice or harmful behavior, **none of the following fact patterns guarantees a total ban on medical practice**:

1. Killing a cancer patient with a dose of chemotherapy 10 times the correct strength, at the same time as prescribing antibiotics to which the child was allergic;

2. Deliberately dropping a fetus in the trash instead of following proper disposal laws;

3. Being convicted as a cocaine dealer;

4. Allowing a patient to bleed to death internally in the emergency room as she lay unexamined overnight -- and then filling out the postmortem paperwork to say she was seen before her death;

5. Anesthetizing a patient in an MRI machine and then abandoning him so that he dies when complications go unattended;

6. Repeatedly sexually abusing multiple patients.

In these examples, the doctors were allowed to continue practicing. The doctor who killed the cancer patient, for instance, was fined $5,000, which was less than the amount of the charges for his services to the dead patient. If these types of behavior, according to "blue-ribbon" panels of experts at the Board of Medical Examiners, are not malpractice, then it is no wonder that the doctors think that juries should not be deciding such things!

For the disciplined doctor, however, there is one refuge that will allow them to continue seeing patients -- a private, cash-only practice. That scenario happened in the case of Dr. William Kellogg. In 1986, the Board of Medical Examiners cited Kellogg for "alleged unnecessary surgery and indiscriminate C.D.S. [controlled dangerous substance] prescribing." The surgery was for cataracts. He was restricted from performing surgeries without the supervision and approval of another doctor and the state Attorney General's Office. In the early 1990s, Kellogg was again accused of performing unwarranted eye surgeries -- by 37 patients. The board resolved those cases in 1995 when Kellogg's license was revoked and he was fined $140,000. That did not end Kellogg's career. He went into business as a "technician" at Dr. Joseph Dello Russo's New Jersey Eye Center in Bergenfield, and was then sued for consumer fraud by patients who believed he was a fully licensed doctor. Oral arguments in the case -- on the issue of whether physicians can be sued for consumer fraud -- were heard at the state Supreme Court on Dec. 1 in Macedo v. Russo. Last April, the Board of Medical Examiners reinstated Kellogg's license without restriction. Take Dr. David Bradway, for instance. In 1980 his license was surrendered with prejudice -- meaning he could not practice at all -- based on a variety of allegations regarding his handling of drugs. Between 1986 and 1988, however, the board gradually restored his license, granting him more and more practice privileges. By November 1997, he was granted an unrestricted license. Two years later, however, after seven patients had died in Bradway's "Ultra-Rapid Detox" drug treatment program in Merchantville, the board put him back on restricted practice, and banned him from drug rehab remedies.

Interestingly, lawyers on both sides of the bar are unhappy with the board. They have similar criticisms: Its processes are too bureaucratic, it takes too long to make decisions and it does not have enough resources to examine cases in the depth required. Many doctors complain of administrative delays caused by state lawyers employed by the board. "I don't think the board is invested with sufficient resources to appropriately prosecute investigations and admin actions," says a partner at Red ,Banks, Drazin & Warshaw. "They get themselves into an administrative quagmire. They have a cumbersome process," It's not a perfect system. It can take several years before license removal occurs.

Other states have the same problems with disciplining their physicians. More than 250 doctors are licensed by the Virginia medical board despite records of serious mistakes or misconduct, actions of a review of board since 1990 shows. They work in every corner of the state, in virtually every specialty. Their ranks include sex offenders, swindlers, tax evaders, felons, former drug dealers and even a convicted murderer. Some have been rejected by a string of hospitals or insurance companies. An analysis of the National Practitioner Data Bank, which tracks physicians, found at least 70 Virginia doctors who have been disciplined five or more times by state and federal authorities, hospitals or professional societies. Only 28 of them lost their licenses.

A ray of sunshine in the sunshine state

The antidote that Florida's doctors hope will cure what they claim to be the soaring malpractice insurance rates - a $250,000 cap on pain and suffering damages -- won't work, the state's largest malpractice insurer said. "No responsible insurer can cut its rates after a bill passes, and we will have to see what the Florida Supreme Court does," Bob White, president of First Professionals Insurance Co., told 600 Palm Beach County doctors. "Even if a cap is approved by the legislature and survives, the likely legal challenge - which could take three to five years to play out - it would yield on average only a 16 percent premium cut," White said.

That cap would barely make a dent in the problem for area doctors, many of whom have seen their malpractice rates double and triple in the past two years. White's comments came a day after Florida Medical Association President Robert Cline said his group would fight any malpractice reform bill that did not include a $250,000 cap on damages.

In his January 29, 2003 article in *The Palm Beach Post*, Phil Galewitz, stated that the Palm Beach County doctors at the meeting appeared stunned to learn that limiting damages might not work, and several physicians called for their leaders to come up with a new strategy. According to an editorial appearing at the same time, the Florida legislature was considering the cap on damages in medical malpractice suits,

> "the Legislature is likely to take the wrong approach in dealing with the latest flare-up in medical malpractice insurance premiums. That would be to crack down on lawsuits, as urged by the doctor and insurance lobbies, and call it a day. It would be like prescribing a medicine for pain without looking for the fracture or malignancy that is causing it....Florida's malpractice problem goes beyond the fact that some doctors are paying too much for their insurance....There has been no showing of a sudden spike in the frequency of lawsuits.....To the contrary, the weight of evidence available to legislators points to low interest rates, poor management of reserves and other nonmedical market factors as the main reasons the insurance companies are tightening the screws so severely....It would be a dangerous delusion for legislators to assume that [the problem] is only because Florida has hungrier lawyers. It is as possible that Florida physicians, nurses and hospitals are not as careful as they could

be....[A]ny 'remedy' that consists only of cracking down on lawsuits - such as the $250,000 cap on non-economic damages...would be an incentive to even less caution on the part of care givers. Worst of all, the arbitrary damage cap would make the lives of children and elderly people virtually worthless in the eyes of the law....[T]he cap would likely reduce payouts by insurance companies and make them even more stingy about settling cases without trial. This does not necessarily mean lower premiums for doctors. When a more severe cap was undertaken 20 years ago (it was eventually struck down by the Florida Supreme Court), two major insurance companies said it would have no effect on premiums.... [M]ost instances of malpractice never get to the lawsuit stage.... Many are not even suspected, because hospitals are not required to disclose adverse incidents except in secrecy to the state....[The] best defense against malpractice litigation is a combination of strict oversight and public accountability on the part of the various medical licensing agencies. But in Florida, it is impossible to judge the quality of that oversight. Complaints against hospitals and doctors are kept secret forever....The governor's malpractice task force appears to be taking an indefensibly narrow approach to the problem. Nearly all of the recommendations to which it has tentatively agreed have to do with hampering lawsuits.

Legislators should treat the ultimate report as worthless if it does not incorporate at least some of the preventive reforms urged by patient advocates. Among them: Require hospitals to share their adverse incident reports with victims as well as with the state. Publish comparative statistics on hospital safety records. Put teeth, including deadlines, in the law requiring doctors to report information (which the state does publish) on malpractice claims and disciplinary orders. Open all complaint files once the decisions are made to pursue cases or to drop them....[T]he people of Florida surely would be more trusting, and forgiving, if the medical community didn't react to every surge in insurance premiums by trying to suppress the message and kill the messenger."

At the same time as the Florida debate, the same thing was going on in the halls of Congress in Washington, D. C. Richard A. Oppel Jr., wrote in *The New York Times*, January 24, 2003, that Senate Democrats were planning to push for a curb on the insurance industry's longstanding exemption from antitrust laws, in an effort to hold down rising medical malpractice premiums. Senator Patrick J. Leahy of Vermont, the ranking Democrat on the Judiciary Committee, plans to introduce a bill to make it illegal for malpractice insurers to collude in setting rates or otherwise engage in "price fixing, bid rigging or market allocations." Mr. Leahy and some other Democrats say they believe that the antitrust exemption allows insurers to act in concert in a manner that would be illegal in other industries and that removing the exemption would be an important step in controlling malpractice premiums. Democratic leaders say the legislation will be a counter to a proposal by President Bush that seeks to rein in malpractice premiums solely by limiting jury awards.

Past efforts to curb the antitrust exemption have failed, and the Democrats' legislation would face a difficult battle. But Democrats say the push by insurers and doctors to limit awards by state judges and juries in malpractice suits has opened the door for lawmakers to reexamine the wide exemptions in the federal law.

In "A Medical Enron," *Washington Post* (December 9, 2002), the writer stated that Enron should teach us that one should be skeptical of highly qualified professionals who promise to regulate themselves. The article claimed that this skepticism should now be applied to doctors. The evidence that supported this position--the medical profession is making scandalously slow progress in reducing the rate of medical errors in hospitals:

"   – errors that, according to an Institute of Medicine study three years ago, Kill between 44,000 and 98,000 patients annually while injuring perhaps 1 million more. The sources of error are various. Surgeons mix up patients' X-rays or look at them the wrong way up; as a result, they operate on the wrong patient or the wrong body part. Doctors and health workers fail to follow basic hygiene procedures such as washing hands or changing gloves; the consequent infections account for thousands of deaths a year. The largest single source of error stems from faulty drug prescriptions. One recent study found that one in five doses of medicine dispensed to patients involved an error. Either the wrong drug was given, or the wrong dose, or it was given at the wrong time.

These various errors reflect the arrogance of the medical priesthood. Even though doctors themselves have produced studies showing how fatigue erodes worker competence, they persist in thinking that it's normal for junior members of their profession to put in more than 100 hours of work a week. Even though every other profession has embraced computers' ability to enhance human performance, doctors persist in scribbling prescriptions in illegible handwriting rather than punching them into a computer that might alert them if the dose is wrong. Studies of hospital infections find that junior workers are most likely to wash their hands properly. It is doctors who are most likely to forget this chore.

There are honorable exceptions. The government-run veterans' health system is a pocket of excellence; some private hospitals, such as the Luther Midelfort Hospital in Eau Claire, Wis., have made big strides in safety. But in general the problem does not get much attention. The national system for reporting medical errors is voluntary, so few errors get reported. A few states have mandatory systems, but most still do not.

So long as patients have no way of finding out which hospitals are unreliable, bad hospitals will face minimal incentives to invest in the solutions that could drive error rates down. Computer systems that track medications going to each patient can eliminate dangerous interactions between drugs prescribed by two different doctors; they can screen for possible allergic reactions; they can query odd dosage levels. But such systems are expensive. Somebody must force hospitals to admit to errors, or hospitals won't invest in reducing them.

The obvious somebody is government, which is easily the biggest payer for health care. The Medicare authorities need to insist on proven safety procedures, such as computerized prescription systems, which currently exist in only about 3 percent of hospitals. They should extend their efforts to publish quality reviews of medical providers. Meanwhile state or federal regulators should require the reporting of errors and should make some of this information public. Otherwise thousands will continue to die needlessly and with no one held to account."

The sentiments expressed by the Florida and D.C. editors are examples of some of the voices that have now appeared in opposition to the insurance industry's claims that doctors should be exempt from the laws that others live by. The insurance industry wants doctor exemptions for one reason–so that they can continue to charge their exorbitant premiums, unfettered by government regulation, to cover their speculative and risky investments, and leave the injured holding the bag. This windfall to the insurance companies will result in the government picking up the tab for uncompensated medical expenses resulting from malpractice, which can only be paid by you, the taxpayer, through your Medicare and Medicaid dollars.

How else might this affect your pocketbook? Let's just take a simple example. If you have medical insurance with Aetna, Pacificare, Blue Cross, Humana, United, or any of the large HMO's or PPO's, your premiums are based upon health care costs (plus a tidy profit for the company and a multi-million dollar salary and fringes for the CEO and CFO). If another policy holder of your medical insurance company is injured as the result of the malpractice of his doctor or hospital, would it be fair for your insurance company to pay for those expenses? Isn't it more fair for the malpractice insurance carrier of that doctor or hospital to pay, so that your insurance carrier is not stuck with the bill, raising your rates to cover the cost?

This debate is not about doctors versus lawyers. It is about how the insurance companies have distorted the facts to pit everyone against the justice system which is supposed to be there for everyone. If they are allowed to continue to do that, frittering away the *Constitution* bit by bit, one day you or your loved one will suffer the consequences. One of the tools they use is their

political influence. Read on into the next chapter to
see the tools they use to accomplish their objectives.

CHAPTER EIGHT

CORPORATE INFLUENCE —THE DESTRUCTION OF THE PEOPLE'S POWER

expenditures on malpractice premiums reported to the National Association of Insurance Commissioners ...... constitute about .62 percent [less than one percent] of national health care expenditures. National Association of Insurance Commissioners, "Medical Malpractice Insurance Net Premium and Incurred Loss Summary," 2003 edition.

Should businesses have the courts to themselves, while the average, everyday American

can not buy his way into the courthouse? The corporate influence over the political system in our country is at an all-time high. Billions of dollars are spent each year by the corporations in an attempt to influence not only the outcome of elections, but the enactment of legislation limiting the rights of the average person. A large part of the dollars spent create publicity campaigns designed to influence people that their interests lie commonly with the corporate interests, when nothing could be further from the truth.

If the people of this country allow the monied conglomerate interests to inflict tunnel vision on us, we will surely pay with the forfeiture of our freedoms protected under the Seventh Amendment. From 1999 to 2002, the CEO's of firms now being investigated for accounting fraud pocketed $1.4 billion in salaries and fringe benefits. Does that create public confidence in the corporate world? When public confidence in the corporate world is eroded, so is confidence in the stock market. All markets run on confidence. So what does our government do to help us get back the confidence? Before you answer that question there are some fact that you should consider.

We know that Ken Lay has contributed over $550,000 to George W. Bush over Bush's political career, and during the 2000 presidential campaign Enron (Ken Lay's company) contributed over $1.3 million to Bush and the GOP. That secured Enron a big place at the government's table–veto power over Bush's nominees to the Energy Commission and an invitation to Dick Cheney's White House Energy Task Force. When we later learned that Enron defrauded all of its investors while rewarding Lay with billions in stock payments, the government takes no action to even slap Enron's wrist. One might wonder why? Especially if one does not know Enron and Lay's ties with the Republican Party and our President.

Is it any wonder then that we see President Bush, Vice-President Cheney, Senator Bill Frist (a physician) and other powerful political figures, taking the side of the corporate world in the debate over the power of the jury to determine damages a corporation should pay for an injury to a victim? There was significant note taken at the president's inaugural of 2005, at which donors contributed more than ever in our history to get a "seat at the table." An article appeared on January 20, 2005 in *USA TODAY,* entitled "Donors get good seats, great access this week" The article is quoted here in its entirety, so that you can judge what it means after the dust has settled and the corporations and their government go back to work the following week:

WASHINGTON — This week's presidential inauguration marks more than the start of a new term. It's also the kickoff for a new lobbying season, a chance for the capital's permanent influence class to cement its status with money and entertainment. Police motorcycles lead an inaugural parade rehearsal down Constitution Avenue in Washington, D.C., on Sunday.

To that end, corporate America has showered the inaugural organizing committee with money. It has given $25.5 million so far [the ultimate contributions were reported to be in excess of $45 million] to help pay the costs of a week of parties, balls, receptions and other official functions. The money has comemostly in six-figure chunks from companies and their executives — nearly all of them with business before the government that affects their industries. Heavily regulated sectors such as finance, energy, tobacco, pharmaceuticals and telecommunications are as prominent on the list as they are in the capital's lobbying circles. Donor companies such as ExxonMobil, ChevronTexaco, Cinergy, Occidental Petroleum and the Nuclear Energy Institute are looking for passage of a long-stalled energy bill. Financial services firms are keenly interested in the prospects for tax cuts and the creation of Social Security private investment accounts. Drug companies are wary of how Congress may respond to a recent spate of bad news about medicines such as Vioxx and Celebrex. ....

With thousands of Americans, including many politically active supporters of President Bush, flocking to Washington, this week's festivities also provide an opportunity for a mammoth schmooze-fest sponsored by interests hoping to stockpile goodwill in advance of the year's policy battles. "From a lobbyist's perspective, having an opportunity to further build your relationships is always good," says lobbyist Wright Andrews, whose fifth-floor office overlooking the Pennsylvania Avenue Inaugural Parade route gives him a prime spot to entertain clients and policymakers.

"If you look up and down Pennsylvania Avenue on Inauguration Day, almost all of us will be having parties," Andrews says. The benefit of a prime location is made even more attractive because of the tighter-than-ever security along the parade route.

The revelry begins well before Thursday's swearing-in at the Capitol. At a nightclub a few blocks to the south, the Nashville band Big & Rich will entertain hundreds of guests Monday night, including members of Congress. The tab will be paid by sponsors that include the electric utility Southern Co., tobacco and food giant Altria Group, and UST, which markets smokeless tobacco and wine. Each was also a $250,000 donor to Bush's official inaugural committee.

Other sponsors include MCI, Pfizer, Corrections Corporation of America, R.J. Reynolds, Hospital Corporation of America, the Generic Pharmaceutical Association and the Managed Funds Association.

THE NAMES BEHIND THE BIG BASH

If you are chairing an inauguration, it doesn't mean that you've ordered the cocktail napkins or made the seating arrangements; it means you've raised a lot of cash for your party. Chairs and co-chairs of the Presidential Inaugural Committee:

Jeanne Phillips, chairwoman
Résumé: Dallas businesswoman; former U.S. ambassador to the Organization for Economic Cooperation and Development; executive director of the 2001 presidential inauguration Party contribution: Helped raise $300 million for Republican elections in 2000; organized Dallas political fundraisers for George H.W. Bush and George W. Bush;

Brad Freeman, co-chairman
Résumé: Founding partner of Freeman Spogli & Co., a private investment firm with offices in Los Angeles and New York; co-chairman of the 2001 presidential inauguration. Party contribution: Co-chairman of a Republican National Convention gala in 2000 that raised $10.1 million; "Super Ranger" for President Bush's 2004 campaign, meaning he raised at least $300,000

Mercer and Gabrielle Reynolds, co-chairs

Résumé: Co-chairs of the 2001 presidential inauguration; Mercer Reynolds runs a Cincinnati-based investment firm with William DeWitt; former ambassador to Switzerland and Liechtenstein ; national finance chairman of Bush-Cheney 2004. Party contribution: Raised at least $100,000 for Bush's campaign in 2000.

William and Kathy DeWitt, co-chairs

Résumé: Co-chairs of the 2001 presidential inauguration; William DeWitt runs a Cincinnati-based investment firm with Mercer Reynolds. Party contribution: Raised at least $100,000 for Bush's campaign in 2000; "Super Ranger" for Bush's 2004 campaign, meaning he raised at least $300,000

Reported by Melanie Eversley, USA TODAY. Sources: The Associated Press, Republican National Committee, Presidential Inaugural Committee

On the night before the inauguration, the U.S. Chamber of Commerce teamed up with the

American Continental Group, a Washington lobbying firm, to throw a party for a crowd that includes lawmakers, administration officials and Republicans who played key roles in financing Bush's re-election campaign. *Atop the Chamber's legislative wish list: limits on damage awards in lawsuits, which also is a Bush priority.*

Business software company SAP hosted a reception the same day at the Corcoran Gallery of Art for Sen. Bill Frist of Tennessee, leader of the Senate's newly bolstered GOP majority. On Tuesday, United Parcel Service threw a party for House Speaker Dennis Hastert, R-Ill.

Among those watching the Inaugural parade from prize vantage points were guests of the Financial Services Roundtable, a trade group for the banking and investment sectors; the lobbying firms Thelen Reid & Priest and Valis Associates; pharmaceutical maker AstraZeneca; and rum maker Bacardi.

Some saw the occasion as an opportunity to raise more money. A group supporting Bush's goal of remaking Social Security to include personal investment accounts, For Our Grandchildren's Team Grandparent, held a $500-a-ticket parade-watching party. The invitation that went out to Republicans notes that Karl Rove, Bush's chief political adviser, was asked to attend.

Donors to the official festivities had full social calendars. Major contributions— which the fundraising committee capped at $250,000 — came with packages of tickets to dinners with Bush and other officials, tickets to the parade and the swearing-in, and admission to one of nine official balls.

Inaugural fundraisers Dawn and Roland Arnall found a creative way to pump more than the $250,000 limit into the event. Their mortgage firm, Ameriquest Capital, contributed the maximum, as did three subsidiaries, for a total of $1 million. The company declined to comment on its political giving.

Even more rewarding than the social whirl was the gratitude of the administration and the party that will be in power at least for the near future. "Clearly, the influence these people are seeking has to do with government decisions," said Steve Weissman of the Campaign Finance Institute, which studies the role of money in politics. Andrews said, "They hope that they are favorably noted by party officials and elected officials for having supported the inauguration."

Among the list of the fifty-three largest contributors, each of whom gave $250,000 toward the inauguration, were several providers of health care products or services or their insurance companies.

What does money get them? What access does it buy? Why would we assume that these contributions are in some way sinister? We have only the facts that show what that access can do. That is what this chapter can shed some light upon. We cannot ever know exactly what is in the mind of our government servants when legislation is enacted, because they certainly are not going to tell their constituents that they had anything on their minds and hearts other than the purest of motives and the intended beneficial effects of their actions. So, characterizing them as having other interests would be unfair unless we could see some pattern of activity or other habit of action that suggested differently.

What we have, so far, not touched upon is that segment of the law and lawyers that have not been so much in the public eye and the subject of so much public scorn. Those are the lawyers who run the corporate world. What most of the public does not see is the way in which those lawyers control the direction that we take. In her book *The Case Against the Lawyers*, Catherine Crier lumps together as a group all lawyers, without distinction as to the roles that different types of lawyers play in shaping public policy.

Pinstripes or Khakis

Let's take a look at the differing functions of two different lawyers. First, the lawyer who brings a suit to recover damages for the client who has been injured by the exploding gas tank on the GMC pickup; second, the lawyer who wrote the memo telling the CEO of General Motors that the company need not remedy the defective gas tank, since the cost of remedy would be far more than would be potentially awarded in damages by juries who considered the defect. Can it be said that the lawyer for the victim should be compared in the same sentence with the lawyer for General Motors? Many other examples would be appropriate to serve the purpose of differentiating the roles of these two different types of lawyers. Placing the comparison in the realm of the medical system is easy. Compare the role of the plaintiff's trial lawyer in the Romero case, who took the hospital to trial for its malicious credentialing of the drug-addicted surgeon, to the role of the hospital lawyer who writes the policies of the hospital which confer confidentiality upon the hospital's decision to retain that surgeon on its staff of physicians. Which lawyer would you want to represent you?

That is not to say that all trial lawyers are noble while all corporate attorneys are corrupt. Certainly such a proposition would be ridiculous. However, when an author, such as Ms. Crier, undertakes to author a book, and casts a net over the legal profession as if they were all the same, she does that very thing. She fails to even note for the reader that there are differences in the roles of the two different types of lawyers. If we had hundreds of thousands of lawyers who brought legitimate, worthy cases over serious injuries, then those lawyers would deserve their credit, even if there were hundreds of thousands of corporate lawyers who were sycophants for their conglomerate clients and sought only to strengthen their pocketbooks. Considering the two different types of lawyers all in the same boat is like talking of teachers and their societal role in comparison to toymakers, just because their jobs have something to do with children. Why would anyone be so shallow as to say that both types of lawyers should bear the blame or shoulder the shame of all, when they serve totally different functions, totally different interest and totally different people?

Corporate lawyers are at the center of the movement by the corporate-owned power plants to try to persuade the Bush administration to ease rules that would force power plants to reduce mercury emissions. A December 2000 EPA ruling would have required the plants to install new equipment in order to achieve the strict emissions rulings. But that ruling was reversed by the decision of the Energy Task Force led by Vice-President Cheney as soon as the new administration took office in 2001. Corporate lawyers are the catalysts for much of the criticism of trial lawyers who bring suits to recover damages for people who have been seriously injured by defective products or errant medical care. However, the legal reforms that these lawyers advocate do nothing to curb the ridiculous lawsuits filed by businesses against each other, which we saw in Chapter Two.

Why should businesses have the courts to themselves, in deprivation of the rights of the average, everyday American who can not buy his way into the courthouse? In the *New York Times* of August 8 23, 2002, it was reported that Fox News sued Al Franken for using the term "Fair and Balanced" on his book cover. Calling the case "wholly without merit, both factually and legally," the judge, Denny Chin of United States District Court, threw out the case. Judge Chin said the decision was an easy one, and chided Fox for bringing its complaint to court. The judge said, "Of course, it is ironic that a media company that should be fighting for the First Amendment is trying to undermine it." But the Fox News networks all over the country every day in daytime talk radio promote the tort reform measures that would keep the injured victim from his day at the courthouse. A Fox franchise in the Dallas-Fort Worth Metroplex, AM Radio 570, has a daily commentary from its right-wing host, who was constantly promoting Texas Proposition 12, which ultimately paved the way for the $250,000 cap on non-economic damages in Texas in suits against doctors and hospitals.

The *New York Times* also reported, on November 13, 2002, that Victoria's Secret went all the way to the Supreme Court in an effort to sue Victor's Little Secret, a gift and novelty shop selling sex toys and "Everything for Romantic Encounters" from a strip mall storefront in Elizabethtown,

Kentucky. Victor Moseley, who opened the shop in 1998, named it Victor's Secret after himself, but changed the name to Victor's Little Secret a few months later in a futile effort to satisfy a sharply worded complaint from Victoria's Secret. *Moseley v. V Secret Catalogue, Inc.,* No. 01-1015. This is a true story of a true lawsuit, but we did not hear our President or any other of our elected representatives complaining about the wastefulness of such a suit, or the unfairness of the corporate power of Victoria's Secret against a one-store small businessman, who did nothing more than use his own name to promote his business. By the way, his business went under.

We did not hear a public outcry over the role of the juries or the ridiculous waste of judicial resources when toymaker Mattel spent five years litigating until the Supreme Court turned down their request to reopen a trademark suit against MCA Records. In that suit, Mattel claimed that the preteen girls who buy Barbie dolls were duped into thinking the song "Barbie Girl" was an advertisement for the doll or part of Mattel's official line of Barbie products. The song, by a Danish group called Aqua, includes the lyrics, "I'm a blonde bimbo in a fantasy world/Dress me up, make it tight, I'm your dolly." *Mattel Inc. v. MCA Records Inc.,* 01-633, Associated Press, 2/22/03.

Wal-Mart Stores Inc., the world's largest retailer, is going to court to prevent wares bought at rival Kmart Corp. from going for a spin at the register. Bentonville-based Wal-Mart has a patent on its carousel that holds its blue plastic shopping bags. The cashier drops items into bags as merchandise is rung up, and spins the rack to make the effort easier for both the cashier and the customer lifting out the bags. Wal-Mart is suing in a Delaware court to keep Troy, Mich.-based Kmart from using a similar device. The Associated Press, 7/17/03. And when you hear insurance companies promoting the theory that lawsuits should not be filed to recover damages for injuries received in vehicular collisions, ask yourself the question about why this suit was filed--An 81 year old woman stepped in front of a truck on a Missouri highway and was killed. The trucker's insurance company charged the elderly woman with negligence, and is suing her estate for damages. That story comes from the January 15, 1999 issue of the *Wall Street Journal*, not exactly your average consumer-oriented business bashing publication.

When the insurance companies complain that they are going out of business because of the "skyrocketing" jury awards, or the manufacturers complain that they are the victim of frivolous suits over their defective products, or hospitals or medical malpractice insurance carriers complain that anyone can bring a lawsuit and make any kind of complaint that they wish, we are not told of the types of cases that are brought by these huge companies. The legislatures are not asked to curb lawsuits filed by businesses. No one complains of the millions of dollars wasted on judicial resources for cases filed by businesses against businesses. Should the judicial system be there to decide disputes over business interests, or disputes over whether someone has used another's slogan or jingle, but not be there to remedy wrongs done to people, or for just compensation for a lifetime of pain or disfigurement?

In Chapter Nine we will talk about the story of Louis Brandeis. He made the following observation about corporate lawyers in an address to a gathering of lawyers at his alma mater, Harvard Law School, nearly one hundred years ago:

"Instead of holding a position of independence, between the wealth and the people, to curb the excesses of either, able lawyers have, to a great extent, allowed themselves to become adjuncts of great corporations and have neglected their obligation to use their powers for the protection of the people. We hear far too much of the corporate lawyer and far too little of the people's lawyer."

If that was the opinion of Justice Brandeis then, imagine his reaction to the ethic so prevalent today in our modern corporate law culture! Giant corporations tend to hire giant law firms, which themselves "have become like business corporations in their structure, management and goals," according to Peter Megargee Brown, former partner in charge of litigation with the law firm of Cadwalader, Wickershan & Taft, in his book *The Selling of the Legal Profession*. Brown commented that the changes brought about in large corporate firms also carry "deep troubles to the Bar as a whole. Becoming an efficient machine and urging every partner to be a 'profit center' has its own special consequences on how the partners behave, how they go about counseling clients and how they serve community interests.....to do so is directly counter to the essence of what the profession is about."

In their book *No Contest,* Ralph Nader and Wesley J. Smith write about the giant corporations' tightening grip on American society by virtue of the large corporate law firms, who have perfected the art of nullifying, misusing, or breaking the law, while pretending to uphold it. They state that:

"the corporation is emerging as a private legislature–imposing private legal systems under one-sided agreements of "fine print" between sellers and consumers, employers and employees, companies and government departments, and in the burgeoning taxpayer subsidy areas, between corporations and communities. The incremental nature of this process obscures the advancing surrender of Americans' rights as they have been delineated by our nation's unequaled system of civil law torts and contracts."

Some of the specific matters about which Nader and Smith write are the influences that corporate lawyers have on the safety policies, or lack thereof, of their corporate clients. One such example is that of corporate lawyer Lloyd N. Cutler, founding partner of the Washington, D. C. firm

Wilmer, Cutler and Pickering. Cutler (now
deceased and acclaimed by the *Washington Post*
obituary as one of the most influential lawyers of
the latter half of the twentieth century), representing
major auto industry clients, masterminded years of
delay for his clients to keep air bags out of any
federal safety standards, while more than 100,000
Americans lost their lives and many more were
seriously injured. Cutler also represented Ford
Motor Company in the early seventies, lobbying
against air bags when General Motors was touting
the devices. He worked against air bags even as they
were installed in some twelve thousand automobiles
in the seventies and demonstrated their reliability
during actual crashes.

Cutler represented the Automobile
Manufacturers Association back in the late 1960's,
and persuaded the Justice Department's antitrust
division to drop a pioneering criminal prosecution
of the automobile industry for "product fixing,"
which meant conspiring to restrain competition by
agreeing to freeze technological innovations related
to vehicular smog controls. After the Justice
Department had convened a grand jury and
concluded that it had evidence to prove the
existence of a conspiracy among the auto
manufacturers, Cutler was able to resolve the matter
by means of a civil consent decree with the
government, under which his clients admitted no
wrongdoing but promised not to violate the law in
the future. Cutler's firm still lobbies to weaken the
Drug Safety Act of 1962, to block auto safety
standards, to advance the interests of banks,

telephone companies, broadcasters, steel companies, airlines, and chemical manufacturers, as their efforts are aided by political action committees and other corporate campaign contributors every step of the way. Members of Congress give him their attention not just because of the wealth of his clients but also because these same clients grease the legislative wheels with their campaign dollars.

Was Lloyd Cutler alone in his effect and ability as a corporate lawyer? Not by a long shot. There are hundreds of law firms whose sole job is the representation of corporate clients in their everyday wrangling. These lawyers run the gambit of all three branches of our government. They work on legislation, executive regulation, and judicial decision-making. The substance of their work touches anything and everything that interests their corporate clients, whether it be taxation, environment, civil justice, education, government contracts, industry oversight, or any subject that needs to be addressed in such a fashion that their clients can gain some favor over the interests of the guys who can not afford their representation. That is why it is so ridiculously disingenuous for these corporate lawyers to complain about the contingent fee system which allows the little guy to afford representation in his quest for justice. You see, that contingent fee system is what puts the little guy on an equal footing in terms of being able to pay for a lawyer.

The listing of corporate law firms and their billings per annum is available to the public. It is very interesting to note that the cry for limiting contingent fees is founded upon the assertion that the fees charged by contingent fee lawyers are excessive, and that they result in some sort of huge tort tax upon the public. But no one complains that the lawyer fees charged by the lawyers for corporations or insurance companies or hospitals are in some way unfair to the consumer of the goods or services that are provided by those institutions. If the government was to determine that it had the right to tell lawyers what they could charge their corporate clients, we would most certainly hear that determination was a violation of the private right of contract between the business and its lawyers. However, when a private citizen chooses to pay a fee to his lawyer based upon the value of the services rendered and the benefits obtained for that private citizen, the government argues that it must follow its public duty by limiting the amount that the private citizen can agree to pay the lawyer he chooses to represent him.

Is there any difference between a consumer agreeing to pay a fee and a corporation paying a fee? The only difference is that the corporation charges as a business expense the amount that they pay the lawyer, thus lessening their ultimate tax burden and accordingly increasing your tax burden. In addition, the corporation passes on the charges of its lawyers to you, the consumer, in the form of prices for services rendered or goods sold. So, you pay twice for those lawyers' services. But you are told that you are powerless to affect anything that the corporation does because the government can not interfere with their private contracts.

I do not know of any trial lawyer who really wishes to enter the world of corporate lawyering. I hated corporate law courses in law school. I never wanted to be a corporate lawyer, and I do not think that I would be good at it. Nor am I saying that the corporate lawyers are not worthy of every penny that they get paid to do what they do. I just believe, and I think most consumers who knew the true facts would believe, that large corporations are being extremely hypocritical when they malign the contingent fees that trial lawyers rely on to be paid for rendering services to consumers, while paying their own lawyers each hundreds of thousands of dollars per year to try to defeat those same consumers.

If I were a corporate lawyer representing Ford Motor Co., receiving $400 per hour to help my client shield from discovery the internal memo that showed Ford knew that the Pinto gas tanks would explode in a rear impact, I think I would find it difficult to argue that the lawyer who found that memo should not receive a percentage of the recovery, as agreed upon by his client, the widow of the charred passenger. Is it that Ford thinks the plaintiff's lawyer should charge by the hour, thus the client could never have afforded to hire him? How convenient for Ford that would be!! Or would it be better that we simply let the government decide, after the case is over with, how much the plaintiff lawyer earned, thus creating yet another agency to monitor someone's conduct?

What would be a better way to insure that injured victims have the ability to bring meritorious suits to the courthouse? Should we give some government entity the power to pick out, in advance, which people should get to go to a lawyer and get representation for a contingent fee? Would the corporations like to decide how much a private citizen can agree to pay to hire a lawyer to sue that corporation? A good rule here is what is good for the goose is good for the gander. Corporations choose to pay their lawyers what they deem appropriate. Consumers, who can not afford to pay a lawyer unless they get a recovery, have the same right. That right is the freedom to contract with whomever they wish for whatever price they wish for their suit. How can we justifiably take away that right, when the corporation against whom they are in a legal fight is using that very right to defeat their legal claim?

"That's not my dog"

There is a funny line in the first <u>The Pink Panther</u> movie. Inspector Clousseau is at the front desk of a hotel in France, where he is talking to the check-in clerk. There is a little scottish terrier standing next to the clerk. Clousseau points to the dog and asks the clerk, "Does your dog bite?" After the clerk tells Clousseau that his dog does not bite, Clousseau feels safe enough to pet the dog, for which he is rewarded with a vicious attack on his hand. When Clousseau says "I thought you said your dog did not bite," the clerk replied, "that's not my dog."

I am reminded of <u>The Pink Panther</u> episode when I see some of the antics that lawyers play in the pre-trial phases of the case. Since we all now know that only a very small percentage of cases ever go to an actual trial, we can surmise that there is a high level of importance to what goes on in the pre-trial phases, where most cases are won or lost. Here is where the corporate guys have their finely tuned machine in high gear. When I first got out of law school, stating my intentions to be a trial lawyer, one of the senior partners in my first firm (a firm representing exclusively corporations, insurance companies and banks) told me, "You do understand, don't you, that trial lawyers never go to trial?" It was more of a declaration than a question. He knew what all corporate lawyers know–you win or lose on what your opponent learns about your case in pre-trial.

Discovery is the part of the litigation where the lawyers for both sides are supposed to have the opportunity to find out what the claims of each side are. That is how the parties evaluate what their chances are of winning at trial, and allows them to make decisions about resolution of the case. The dog bite administered to Inspector Clousseau came about becuase he did not ask the right questions. So, in discovery, the lawyers had better ask the perfect questions and ask them perfectly, or the answers will lead to an ambush at trial, just like the bite administered to Inspector Clousseau.

In *Hickman v. Taylor*, 329 U.S. 495, 507 (1947), the United States Supeme Court stated that free and open discovery is essential to fair and honest litigation process. That case, in 1947, was shortly after the courts had first authorized the discovery process. Prior to that, the trials that went on in this country were done primarily on a trial by ambush basis, meaning that the evidence was what it was, and the litigants went to trial with only the knowledge that they could get on their own. The abuses of discovery that have arisen in the past fifty years have taken on a life of their own. Making spurious objections to legitimate discovery requests, stonewalling when one does not want to give up harmful information, and obstructing the flow of information has become a major way of gaining an advantage. Which side of a medical malpractice case do you believe it most behooves to engage in such activities? Two clues-First---it is always the defense lawyers who are billing by the hour; second, it is usually the health care providers who have the most access to the documents and testimony that is necessary to prove the case. Who, then, has the most incentive to obfuscate, delay, object and stonewall?

That is not to say that every case involving doctors and hospitals is one in which the defendants engage in such conduct. However, if it were to be known that delaying tactics, discovery disputes, frivolous objections and obfuscation were everyday, common activities, then does it make sense to believe that it would ordinarily be the plaintiff who was engaging in such activity. Remember, it is the plaintiff lawyer who works on a contingent fee. The more that he can get done in the shortest amount of time, the more money he makes.

On the other side of the coin, the more time it takes to go through the litigation process, the more money the defense lawyers make. It is also true that the more the defense lawyer makes the plaintiff and the plaintiff lawyers work, the better chance the defendant will have of getting the plaintiff to give up and go home, or to settle for an amount less than what they believe to be a fair amount.

The American Bar Association has passed model rules pertaining to discovery that it suggests the states adopt, which many states have, in fact, adopted. One of the rules they suggest is Rule 3.2, which states "A lawyer shall make reasonable efforts to expedite litigation consistent with the interests of the client." The one phrase that is open to a large amount of interpretation is "consistent with the interests of the client." What if it is in the best interest of the client for the plaintiff not to know information that is within the defendant's possession? The comments to the rule give the answer to that question, stating that "financial or other benefit from otherwise improper delay in litigation is not a legitimate interest of the client." In his book, *No Contest*, Ralph Nader reports an interview with a leading professor of law and ethics at New York University, Stephen Gillers, discussing the issue of defendants' discovery abuse, who states that "the client's incentive is to avoid loss. The lawyers incentive is to avoid displeasing the client. It is consensual wrongdoing between the lawyer and the client, with the victim being the 'other', the person or entity on the other side of the lawsuit." Nader, at 104.

Let's assume that there is some evidence that a hospital does not want to be disclosed to the other side because it is both embarrassing and would be of assistance to the plaintiff in their case before the jury. Next assume that the client and the lawyer sit down in a meeting and decide to try to find a way to keep that information from being disclosed, even though it is clear to both that the information has been requested and that the law requires its disclosure. If they determine that they will not turn over the evidence, then who is to know that it ever existed. According to Gillers, if the client approves of the refusal to disclose, then it does not get reported. University of Washington School of Law ethics professor Robert Aronson opines that discovery abuse is one of the major causes of court congestion. He says that "an overwhelming amount of time is spent by judges and clerks in dealing with these discovery disputes." Nader, at 105.

In Chapter Five we discussed the case of "The Smoking Gun that Wouldn't Stay Hidden," where Jennifer Pollack was brain-damaged as a result of complications from a drug deceptively marketed by the Fisons Corporation. There are four things about this case that are alarming to me and should be extremely alarming to anyone who might ever be injured by hospital or doctor error:

First, the firm that represented Fisons in this litigation also represents a large number of physicians. Commonly the firms who have pharmaceutical companies for clients also have malpractice insurance companies for clients. The fact that they were so willing to hide evidence in this case, and then settle when they were about to have to show their practices, suggests that their conduct was part of a pattern. In fact, that was their defense to the claims by Dr. Klicpera--that "everybody does it." So, we must believe that the Fisons case was not an isolated event. If they did it there, they likely do it everywhere.

Second, there were no fewer than fourteen lawyers who came to the aid of the Fisons lawyers, supporting them and giving sworn testimony that the practice of being an advocate for your client when it comes to disclosure of information is appropriate and expected. So, we know from this show of support from their brethren, the Fisons lawyers' conduct is the type of conduct approved by many other corporate lawyers who believed that it was appropriate to refuse to turn over the document in question.

Third, you will recall that the plaintiff had asked Fison to "Produce genuine copies of any letters sent by your company to physicians concerning theophylline toxicity in children." The reason that Fison and its lawyers claimed for failure to turn over the 1981 smoking gun letter and subsequent memo was that these documents were not relevant to the case, since they did not concern the product in the litigation, Somophyllin, but only concerned its primary ingredient. Plaintiff's lawyer should have taken a lesson from Inspector Clousseau, and asked "Is that your scottish terrier?" Even "Is that your dog?" would not have been sufficient. No plaintiff could be as precise as the Fisons lawyers wanted, unless he was already holding the offensive document in his hands.

Fourth, a lesson can be learned from the conduct of the lawyers for Dr. Klicpera. These lawyers were representing Physicians Insurance Exchange, and they pursued a claim on behalf of Dr. Klicpera for his damages resulting from the conduct of Fisons and Fison's lawyers. One of the damage claims was for "emotional distress." In the trial of that part of the case, the jury awarded to Dr. Klicpera the sum of $3.3 million. This was for the emotional distress of being involved in a suit rightfully brought by his patient. Apparently those lawyers did not see anything wrong in asking for such damages, or in using that award as leverage later to recover money on behalf of Dr. Klicpera. To be sure, Dr. Klicpera was wronged by the conduct of Fisons and its lawyers. He was, however, never physically harmed. He can walk, talk, see, eat, stand and function as a normal human, unlike his patient. Yet his insurance company, Physicans Insurance Company, although seeking damages on his behalf then, is now among those who clamor for a cap of $250,000 on emotional damages sustained by people like his patient, Jennifer, who have the misfortune, through no fault of their own, of being brain damaged. HYPOCRICY AT ITS UGLIEST!!!

Hospitals playing mission impossible

Remember the TV show "Mission Impossible," or the movie by the same name, where the audio tape disappeared in a cloud of smoke after the secret agent listened to it. Some hospitals have learned a lot from this. In addition to the widespread game-playing that goes on in a large number of cases, there are also those cases where certain documents or records never get seen, because they are "deep sixed;" "filed in the round file;" "sent to a better place;" or otherwise disposed of, so that they will never have to be produced. What would be a smoking gun turns becomes a mirage. You see, if a document does not exist, no one needs to make a decision about whether to turn it over to the other side.

What is unknown is the number of documents we never know about that get destroyed, lost, altered, or defaced. We do have some cases where they are learned about. Again I think a real reported case will lend itself to a more credible discussion. In *New Jersey Law Journal*, (May 4, 1992) an article appears regarding a case in which a New Jersey hospital was sued as a result of failure to timely perform a caesarean section delivery, resulting in severe brain damage to the baby. During the course of discovery, plaintiff lawyer requested the baby's fetal monitor strips, which are the strips that are printed from the monitors reporting heart rate and breathing of the baby. In response, the hospital replied that there were no such strips.

That made no sense to the plaintiff's lawyer, so she went to the hospital to look at the medical records. She looked at all fetal monitor strips, strip by strip, for five hours, finding nothing. She then found one of the baby's strips (there would normally be dozens for each child) buried in another baby's file. Even more strange, the package containing the strip, once sealed, had been opened, suggesting at least the possibility that there were other parts of the record gone

Additional requests were then made by the baby's lawyer for other records that would normally have been maintained by the hospital in a patient of this nature. None existed!! After multiple hearings at which the hospital lawyers reported to the judge that such records did not exist, the hospital finally settled the case for $1.35 million. See, *No Contest* p. 157.

It would not be fair of me to state, suggest, imply or otherwise maintain that all lawyers for insurance companies, hospitals, doctors and corporations act in such a manner. It would not even be right for me to suggest that even the parties, without the knowledge of their lawyers engaged in such behavior. As I said in my preface, I have met far more lawyers whom I like and respect than lawyers for whom I feel differently. I have, however, been involved in my share of cases where I have seen, and have had to deal with, disruptive refusal to comply with court orders, or at a minimum, abject and unwarranted refusal to respond appropriately to legitimate requests for information. What these cases, and far too many others to detail here, tell us is that a large part of the justice system is plagued by this type of legal, and illegal, maneuvering. We have no way of knowing even its full prevalence, much less its full effect.

One question I would ask is this-- Could it be possible that these defendants blame the cost of medical malpractice litigation on plaintiffs so that the true cost of their conduct will not come to light?

I could give you numerous examples of cases where I know in my heart I have been lied to about the existence of certain documents, the statements of certain witnesses, or the truth of certain allegations. I can give you less numerous examples of cases where I can prove it. One example is one that I will always remember, where I knew that a doctor had altered, after the case started, medical records of an elderly gentleman who went blind after cataract surgery. The doctor altered the records to demonstrate that he had done a series of tests, over several months, that he did not do. When he came to his deposition, what he did not know was that I had copies of the true, unaltered records that my client had obtained before the suit started. While taking him through his deposition, I allowed him to tell me about how he knew he had done the tests, how important the tests were, how careful he was in doing them, and how important it was that the testes be documented when done, since they involved very precise numbers and important timing. He also testified that the patient could have gone blind if the tests were not done. He gave all of this testimony while reviewing his altered records, which he was trying to pass off as accurate. When I placed copies of his true office chart in front of him, and began juxtaposing each office visit with the lack of the test documented on the true copies, a silence fell over the room. I asked the deposition videographer to hone the camera in on the doctor's forehead, where beads of sweat formed and then fell to saturate the pages of altered records.

The next day I got a call from his lawyer, asking me to let him know what it would take to get the case resolved. I tell this story not to say what a great lawyer I am. Any lawyer could have done what I did. I would just like for you to wonder--what if my client had not gotten copies of his records before the case started?

Witness protection programs

To whom do witnesses belong? If a person has knowledge about something that is of some interest to the public or to the judicial system, should it be the obligation of people involved in a lawsuit, if they know of the whereabouts or knowledge of these people, to disclose the knowledge? Our court rules of procedure say that if a party to a lawsuit knows of someone with knowledge of relevant facts they must disclose that person and the persons whereabouts, if asked to do so. Therefore, it is uniform procedure in every lawsuit for both sides to ask each other to disclose the names and whereabouts, if they know, of "people with knowledge of relevant facts." Too often this disclosure is given less freely than you would hope, as you would see from General Motors attempts to silence it former engineer from testifying about is knowledge of dangerous side gas tanks on its pickup trucks. See, Trisha Renaud,, "Silenced GM Engineer Still In Great Demand." *Texas Lawyer*, September 27, 1993.

It was always strange to me when I was representing people who had been injured in hospitals how the hospital protected the knowledge of their former employees. By the time an injured patient gets out of the hospital, heals, goes to see a lawyer, and the case gets into litigation, it is often that case that nurses, orderlies, record personnel, and others have left the employ of the hospital. When I would ask the locations of former employees, I would never be told until after the employee had been contacted by the hospitals lawyers and "woodshedded." Even if I had located them before the hospital got to them, they would very rarely agree to talk to me before they got to talk to the hospital lawyer, even if the employee was not a defendant in the suit, nor was their conduct being questioned. What was even more strange was how statements that former hospital employees would make to me would often change by the time they gave their deposition or their trial testimony.

Dixon Klein–a victim of the witness protection program

An interesting twist in the Dixon Klein case. You will recall that there was a receptionist who met Dixon when he appeared at the clinic asking for his records. You will also recall that there was a manager, the wife of the clinic owner, who refused to allow Dixon to take copies of his record. Both of these individuals needed to give their depositions so that I could question them about how the record looked at the time and what the record-keeping policies were. When I requested to find out the name of the receptionist and to take her deposition, and requested the deposition of the manager, I learned that the name of the manager was Ms. Little, which happened to be the name of the owner of the clinic. I took those depositions on the same day, back to back. When I took the deposition of the manager, I learned that she was the wife of the owner–I asked her, since she had the same last name, whether she was the wife of the owner. When I took the deposition of the receptionist later that day, I asked her if she knew Ms. Little or Dr. Little (the owner) socially, she said that she had been to their home "at a Christmas party once." She testified that she did not know them socially other than that. When I asked if they were friends, she said that they were not. When I asked the receptionist if they socialized together other than that, she testified, under oath, that she did not.

I accepted that testimony as the truth.

After all, it was given under oath, subject to the penalty of perjury. It was not until several days later that I talked to another former employee that I learned that the receptionist was, in fact, the daughter of the manager and Dr. Little, the owner. She had a different name, since she was married, so I would not have known unless I asked specifically if she was a family member. Recall her answer about whether she knew them socially, she only acknowledged she had been to their home once for a "Christmas Party." So much for the oath "to tell the whole truth and nothing but the truth" That phrase is not just something you heard on Perry Mason. It is still the oath given in a court of law, and one that the court reporter gives, and is by law required to give, at a deposition. No wonder the receptionist and the manager wanted so badly to protect the records from Dixon's curious eyes!! The defendant's lawyers, knowledgeable about the relationship of the receptionist and the owner, sat next to me at the deposition, heard the same testimony. Don't you know that the receptionist asked for their guidance on how to answer the questions that they knew were coming? The receptionist had been instructed not to tell me that she was a family member unless I asked that specific question. Yet it is the plaintiffs who are always accused of frivolous activity!!

The issue of the accuracy of the medical record, who had access to it, and what it said at what time was extremely important to the outcome of the case. The issue of the credibility of the witnesses was more important because of the fact that the contents of the crucial document were so seriously in issue. Everyone knew that, including both of the defense lawyers. "Do you ever see them socially? Only once at a Christmas Party." Was that the truth?

Whose pot of gold is it?

One thing that is often discussed in the tort reform circles is the amount of money that trial lawyers make when they win a case and get a percentage of the recovery. What is always left out of that discussions the number of hours that lawyers spend when talking with clients about cases that they never take, or investigating, analyzing, or spending money on cases that are never even filed, or for which claims are ever made. When I was a medical malpractice lawyer, I usually received between 150 and 250 calls from potential new clients every year. Out of those cases, I averaged around five cases that were ever filed, or for which claims were ever made. The reason--many people would call a lawyer, but would not have a case that was either provable, or for which the damages were significant enough to warrant litigation. I, like most others who do that type of work, served as a screener for meritorious cases, since all of us knew that it would not help us or our client to bring cases that were not provable, of which had damages that would be eaten up by expenses.

Often times it would take dozens of hours of lawyer time, paralegal time, or nurse time to determine whether a case was meritorious. No money came in for that time--in fact, lots of dollars in employees salaries and expert consultant fees went out the door. No fee was ever guaranteed, since the lawyers got paid only if the case prevailed. Defense lawyers get paid for every minute that they think about, look at, talk about, or go to lunch over a file. A beautiful comparison between the two types of work, and the hypocrisy is seen in two different cases. One of the complaints made by Catherine Crier in her book *The Case Against the Lawyers* is about the money that some trial lawyers received in compensation for suing tobacco companies on behalf of the state of Texas in its suit to recover Medicaid money the state paid for smoker's ill health. What Ms. Crier does not mention is that the state could not have funded the litigation itself, nor could it have garnered the manpower itself, nor does she state that the state welched on the deal after the lawyers had recovered $246 billion dollars from the tobacco manufacturers, a feat that the state was not prepared to even come close to doing on its own without outside counsel.

Juxtapose that situation to the one which Ms. Crier does not discuss--the case where the Federal Deposit Insurance Corporation and the Resolution Trust Corporation (the entity created to gather the assets of insolvent banks and savings and loans) sought to recover from private companies for junk bond losses. *RTC Office of Inspector General*, "Legal Fees Paid to Cravath, Swaine & Moore,"September 28, 1992. In that matter, the government agreed with a private law firm for a guaranteed fee, regardless of results, for $300 per every hour of every senior partner, $250 for other partners, $180 for associates, and $50 for paralegals. Taken without any other information, this is a large amount of money to be guaranteed, regardless of results. Examined only in this context, most of those associates earned less than $100,000 per year and were expected to bill 2000 hours per year. The firm's annual take from each associates work at that rate would be $360,000. Thus, even if their salaries were $100,00 per year, which they were not, the firm made a hefty 360 percent return on their non-speculative investment. On top of that, the firm extracted this agreement from your government--if the award from the case was $200 billion or more, the fees would double. Just on associates salaries--that is a 720 % return on investment. But they clamor about the fees charged by medical malpractice lawyers!!

Just one more observation about this situation--the government agreed that if the law firm obtained a recovery of $200 million or more, the lawyers fees would double. Why was the $200 million dollar level chosen? That was only 10 per cent of the *claimed* damages. In other words, the government must have believed that there was an insignificant chance that the $200 million figure would ever be achieved, or they would not have so freely agreed to it. But the government wanted to give their lawyers an incentive to kick some rear end. Why was the trigger point only 10 percent of the damages claimed in the suit? Could that mean that the government asked in the lawsuit for at least ten times what they expected to receive? Why did the government and their lawyers ask for ten times the amount that they believed themselves entitled? Yet they claim that medical malpractice lawyers should not get paid for good results for the client, and that trial lawyers ask for damages that are too high. HYPOCRISY AGAIN!!

The role of the corporate world in medicine

Let us look, for a moment, at the concept of the corporate delivery of medicine. It was not more than twenty years ago that a decision on the part of your doctor to prescribe for you a prescription, a diagnostic tool, a test, or a procedure, was a decision that was made by two people–you and your doctor. When was the last time, if you are covered by any form of medical insurance, that you and your doctor made those decisions without some input from an insurance company?

Every decision regarding choice of treatment must be approved by your medical insurance company. Think how many millions of dollars are spent every day in this country on people who do nothing but look over the shoulder of your doctors, all in the name of saving money so that they will not have to pay for what they consider unnecessary tests or procedures! When you go to the hospital, the insurance company wants to know, before you go there, the reason you are going, what is going to be done for you there, and how long you will be there.

In the January 23, 2005 issue of the *New York Times*, a report was made on the disappearance of what was thought to be a very beneficial new test that could discover disease processes early in their development. You may recall that in 2000 a new form of radiological exam became possible, known as the whole body scan, which was capable of detecting cancers, heart disease, organ dysfunction, or other debilitating and deadly physiological problems, long before any other type of exam ever known or devised. Reports of the new testing capability appeared on the Today Show, Good Morning America, *USA Today*, and in *Men's Health*. Dr. Thomas Giannulli, a Seattle internist, opened a company that would offer the CT scans to the public, with no doctor visit required. The demand for the scans was so great that when he opened his center in 2001, he had waiting lists and cold not keep up with the patient load.

Three years later, the center was down to one or two patients a day and Dr. Giannulli was no longer getting a paycheck from the business. Two other such businesses, CT Screening International, which screened 25,000 people at 13 centers across the nation, as well as AmeriScan, another national chain, also closed. The closings of these potentially invaluable businesses, all dedicated to the early detection and prevention of diseases with significant morbidity and mortality rates, was not due to lawsuits by greedy trial lawyers, not due to frivolous lawsuits by someone looking for the "lawsuit lottery." The closings were due to the medical market–when insurers refused to pay, requiring patients to dig into their pockets, scanning centers found themselves cutting prices to compete, and then doomed to fail from disuse.

This scan was not the product of some fly-by-night snake oil salesman promising miracle cures that he could not deliver. Many academic medical centers, where our fresh young doctor minds are molded and primed for new cures and ideas, got into the business of whole body scans. Beth Israel Deaconess Medical Center at Harvard, opened the "Be Well Body Scan", owned by the Beth Israel Radiology Foundation, a nonprofit organization that supports the hospital's radiology department. Dr. Max Rosen, the medical director of the group, says that he has saved lives, finding lung cancer at a stage when it could be removed, and a heart problem that led to a bypass opertation, rather than a heart attack. But the professional medical societies, who control large groups of physicians and consult directly with the insurance carriers on the efficacy of new treatments, made the argument that the tests would find too many problems in healthy people that would need working up, at too large a cost.

Never mind the fact that when a deadly disease process was found, it would always be well worth the money! If it costs too much for the insurance companies to screen hundreds of well patients, or to check out something that appeared to be a problem when it really was not a problem, then we should certainly not want the insurance companies to pay for the possibility of saving a few lives!

Dr. Giannulli has now moved on to other things. He founded a company that sells software for medical record keeping to doctors offices. That is the new direction of the money in healthcare, because it makes the doctors' offices more efficient. We should be glad that medical record-keeping is going in new directions, but we can not ignore the fact that the business side of medicine runs the minds of the decision-makers when it comes to the cutting-edge technology. A new device must be measured not just on the test of whether it can save lives or reduce significant illness or injury. It must be measured on the test of whether it will cost too much money to do those things.

What we do not yet know is the standard used by decision-makers for how many lives are worth how much money. Let's assume that a whole body scan will save the lives of two people out of 1,000, and that fifty people out of that 1,000 end up having a problem area found on the test, and that problem costs some insurance dollars spent on ruling out serious illness. What amount of insurance dollars spent on the extra testing is worth saving those two lives?

Do you remember the little girl (Baby Girl Jessica) in the eighties who got stuck deep in a well in Midland, Texas? That little girl has been on my mind on many occasions for over twenty years for two reasons. First, the innate courage and stamina for life that she displayed in her fight; second, and more pertinent to the discussion in this book, the amount of resources, human emotion, time, energy and money that everyone agreed, without hesitation, should be devoted to saving that little life. No one questioned whether it was worth the money. No one sat down and said "let's figure out our chances of success and the cost of getting there;" no one measured the dollar value of the girl's life, or tried to figure out whether she was going to be a homemaker or a school teacher or an astronaut or a nuclear scientist. Everyone knew what had to be done back in Midland, Texas, the hometown of our current president.

Does that mean that we should require insurance companies to pay for every dime of healthcare that a doctor prescribes, no matter the cost and no matter the potential benefit to the patient? Of course not. We would not have a method of paying for medical costs if we did not have health insurance carriers willing to insure people. But should we be placing as much power and unfettered decision-making capability into the hands of the people who have only a profit motive as a basis upon which to measure decisions? We will never go back to the days, that even I remember, when the family doctor would come to my bedside with his bag and stethoscope. However, shouldn't the doctor-patient relationship, and thus the doctor's decision making on a patient-by-patient basis, carry more weight than the economic basis upon which insurance companies make their day-today decisions about coverage and payment?

Healthcare is not the only thing over which there is vast corporate control. The lawyers of the corporate world make sure that they put their imprimatur on most everything. Big money is made practicing power corporate law. *The National Law Journal* reported in 1995 that economic census data shows that the legal services industry had $108 billion in revenue in 1992. That does not include the figures of in-house corporate counsel, which means lawyers who work full-time for a corporation that it serves. General counsel for the investment firm of Merrill Lynch & company earned $2.8 million in 1994. Many other corporate counsel make in excess of one million dollars each and every year, not to mention the various other benefits of stock options (the right to purchase stock at very favorable prices) retirement benefit packages, vacations, free meals at fine restaurants, or other entertainment. In contrast to these lawyers, the federal judges who serve our nation for life, earn around $150,000 per year, and the non-profit public interest lawyers earn far less than that.

The corporate influence on medicine is the very thing that is driving many doctors from the profession. Even some of the doctors say that the rewards that they sought as some of the main motivating reasons for going into the profession, are now overcome by the burdens the corporate world is placing on health care. In the January 31 issue of *U. S. News and World Report*, in an article entitled "Doctors Vanish from View," the authors state that those rewards–satisfying relationships with patients, autonomy, high status and high pay–are now outweighed by the reality of the 21ˢᵗ century U. S. medical practice–reams of time-consuming paperwork that is out of proportion to the time spent on caring for patients, declining reimbursements from insurers, and loss of autonomy from managed care. These downsides are increasingly becoming larger issues in the retention and recruitment of good quality physicians.

Insurers, the doctors say, keep reimbursements so low that it is not possible for a primary care doctor to practice with fewer than several thousand patients on the rolls. That leaves the doctor, even if he works extremely long hours, with only 17 minutes per patient visit, which is not enough time to ask all of the questions that need to be asked to cover all of the health issues that they are supposed to bring up. When a primary care doctor is required to see 25 patients a day, it is often a brand new patient, since every time an employer switches health plans, or a patient switches jobs, the doctors are different. When a patient sees a different doctor each time in the office, respect is eroded. When most of our fathers and mothers were living, they saw the same doctor for decades, and that doctor knew them and everything about their bodies.

The *U. S. News and World Report* article states that, although it is still very difficult to get into medical school, many professionals worry that the best and the brightest will avoid the profession altogether. Medical school applications in 2004 were more than 10,000 below their peak of 47,000 in 1997. In a 2001 survey of California doctors, two-thirds of them were not advising their children to go to medical school. Some of the worst shortages of physicians, and particularly specialists, are in California. What is interesting about that is that the tort reformers cry out that the high cost of medical malpractice insurance is driving good specialists out of the practice, and that caps on damages should be passed to keep them in. However, California passed a $250,000 cap on damages, and caps on attorneys fees, in malpractice cases, in 1976. Yet, California is among the worst in terms of specialist availability for handling the patients. "The wait is three weeks to see a pediatric neurologist," says Harvey Cohen, head of pediatrics at Stanford University School of Medicine. Merritt-Hawkins, an Irving, Texas, physician search firm, says that the average wait to see an obstetric-gynecologist (the profession allegedly hit the hardest by the claimed medical liability "crisis") is 31 days in San Diego.

Putting caps on damages has had no beneficial effect in terms of keeping the doctors in California practicing in the high risk specialties. Although supporters of the cap claimed that it would lower malpractice insurance rates in Texas, malpractice rates in Texas are rising despite the passage of a constitutional measure that placed caps on verdict awards. Out of all of the carriers in Texas, however, only one major carrier has promised to lower premiums. *Houston Chronicle*.

11/19/2003.

Look every gift horse in the mouth

The delivery of health care is not always treated like other commodities or services when it is done in the corporate world. The billing, accounting and tax practices of hospitals known as "non-profits" belie their description. One example is the North Mississippi Medical Center, which has grown into the largest non-metropolitan hospital in the country, a booming enterprise with a complex of glass and marble buildings and 40 satellite clinics stretching into Alabama and Tennessee. The company, incorporated in Delaware, has nearly $300 million in the bank and "exceptional profitability," according to one Wall Street rating agency. The hospital is exempt from federal, state and local taxes by taking charity cases. It pays no taxes of any sort. *Washington Post,* Janurary 29, 2005; "Tax-Exempt Hospitals' Practices Challenged."

As one of 4,800 nonprofit U.S. hospitals, North Mississippi Medical Center receives this exemption from federal, state and local taxes in return for providing care to "charity patients." When Tim Gardner was born at the hospital 53 years ago, it was just a little building in a town best known as Elvis Presley's birthplace. Now Gardner, according to the *Post* article, and hundreds like him are at the center of a nationwide battle over whether nonprofit hospitals -- often flush with cash, opulent buildings and high-paid

322

executives -- are fulfilling their mission as charitable institutions.

"I was paying the best I could," said Gardner, who receives $18,000 a year as a cook, and had managed to pay $1,000 in small amounts from each payroll check. "I'm not trying to run. At the end of that week I was going to pay them some more." But when Gardner, who is uninsured and suffers from heart trouble, asked for more time to pay off a $4,500 bill, the response came in the form of a summons. The hospital sued him for the balance plus $1,100 in legal fees.

North Mississippi is not the only beneficiary of the tax exemption. Forty-six suits have been filed in 22 states, alleging the hospitals violate their tax-exempt status by charging uninsured patients the highest rates and employing abusive tactics to collect. "Their goal is to discourage these uninsured patients from returning," said Richard F. Scruggs, the lead attorney. "If they paid taxes, I couldn't complain. But these hospitals are given freedom from taxation for doing something."

One of the hospital defendants is a California hospital with $1 million in an offshore bank account, another in Louisiana that owns a luxury hotel and health clubs, and a Georgia hospital that flew its executives on private jets to meetings in the Cayman Islands and Florida's Amelia Island. Because private insurers and the government negotiate deep discounts for their clients, the uninsured are usually the only ones charged the list price -- up to six times as much as for insured patients. The feeble response of the American Hospital Association to these allegations is this: "Mr. Scruggs is seeking to use the courts to reform the health care system," said AHA executive vice president Rick Pollack. "We don't think lawsuits are the answer to the problem of the uninsured." The problem with that response is clear–the legislative and executive branches have not figured out a solution, so why shouldn't we let the courts go to work? With an entrenched, vested, financial interest on one side, versus no organized national effort on behalf of patients, the effort is not likely to succeed in Congress. Says Scruggs, "Courts have traditionally stepped in to the breach as a safety net when the political branch couldn't act."

It appears that the suit may be headed toward a very positive outcome. In a tentative settlement, North Mississippi agreed to provide free care for patients earning less than 200 percent of the poverty level (about $18,000) and low-priced care for those with incomes up to 400 percent of poverty. The hospital proposed to issue refunds to patients in those categories who were treated in the three previous years and would revise its collection practices, according to court documents.

The tentative agreement would also be a good one for the hospital, which collects less than four percent of what it charges indigent patients, and collects about $650 million annually. There was a delay in finalizing the settlement, since U.S. District Judge Michael P. Mills wanted some tightening of conflict-of-interest provisions governing relationships between the hospital and its board members. According to the *Post* article, while the case is hanging, nothing has changed for people such as Kathy Millican, 50. After an emergency hysterectomy, she was billed more than $11,600, which she was unable to pay. She was sending periodic checks for 50 or $100.

Bill collectors began calling at odd hours, suggesting she put it all on a credit card or deliver a bank note. After her second request for charity care, the hospital forgave $700 but added $1,000 in finance charges. Frustrated and without anywhere to turn, she delivered a large plastic bag bulging with medical bills to Scruggs's office and joined the lawsuit.

The hospital fights back in the media, saying that North Mississippi provided $26 million in charity care last year. But the term "charity care" can be misleading. In most instances, the figure is based on the sticker price for a procedure rather than the much lower amount it accepts from private insurers and Medicare or Medicaid. It's like the New York department stores that buy hundreds of dresses wholesale at $18, mark them up to $90 for retail, and have a 50% discount to sell them to you at $45, still nearly three times their cost. Who is the real winner in this deal? You judge for yourself. North Mississippi Medical Center's tax exemption was worth about $29 million, according to Mississippi's tax commissioner. IRS filings for fiscal 2003 show that the CEO of the hospital was paid more than $600,000, in a state where the average salary was $33,000. Maybe that is why the hospital tries to deflect attention back to the trial lawyer, saying the suit is just Scruggs's latest money-and-publicity grab. When you have no substance, attack the other side's lawyer. Seems that the approach often works well!!

Should low-income people get free or reduced-rate health care? *That is not my point, either pro or con.* The point of discussing this "charity" hospital (of which there are an average of nearly 100 for every state in this country) is that the consumer is again taking it on the chin here. People with health care coverage pay only their deductibles and co-pay amounts, and Medicaid and Medicare recipients get virtually all of their bills paid. Hospitals, as well as large physician practice groups have made reduced-fee deals for these patients.

Hospitals and doctors get paid; Medicare, Medicaid and insurance companies get good deals. Jane Doe, either poor, elderly, or disabled, gets free care, and the government pays $5,000 for her emergency hysterectomy. Sarah Roe, covered by health insurance, pays a small deductible, and her insurance company pays $6,000 for the same surgery. But, down the hall– same hospital, same surgery, same length of stay (unless they threw her out early for lack of payment), Kathy Millican, 50, after her emergency hysterectomy, was flooded with bills totaling more than $11,600. With her husband making $12 an hour hauling rocks, the best Millican and her mother-in-law could do was send in periodic checks for $50 or $100, bill collectors calling at odd hours, suggesting she put it all on a credit card or deliver a bank note. After her second request for charity care, the hospital forgave $700 but added $1,000 in finance charges. Her only choice, join the lawsuit brought by Scruggs on behalf of others in her same boat.

Gerard Wages, the hospital's chief operating officer, complained that after word of the potential settlement got out, North Mississippi has seen its volume of charity care jump, with patients traveling from outside the region for care and some locals "bypassing other hospitals." Mr. Wages, who, according to IRS filings for fiscal 2003, was paid more than $600,000 as CEO, in a state where the average salary was $33,000, does not believe the hospital can afford this additional volume of charity care.

There is no doubt that health care is expensive. There is no doubt that we need to pull our forces together in a very determined effort to bring reduce the rate at which the cost of health care is climbing. We can not do that, however, unless all participants in the debate are willing to be honest about where the skeletons are, and are willing to do their part to bring thins under control. Instead of spending time and money ridiculing the lawyer who is trying to bring some fairness to the lower-middle class of uninsured patients, why don't these 4,800 hospitals consider allocating some of their resources for a program to modify some elements of the system. For example, if every CEO made $600,000 annually (I have no idea whether the median is more or less than that figure), that is 2.88 **Billion** (yes, with a **B**) in salaries for CEO's of these institutions. A mere 17% reduction pay to approximately $500,000 (not a shabby sum), would generate nearly $500 million dollars annually.

There is nothing to be gained from pure partisanship. I realize that many of these CEO's are hard-working, intelligent, dedicated servants who have the best of intentions, just like many trial lawyers. In Chapter Eleven I have some suggestions for change that I think would help both sides do something to benefit the people we all should be trying to benefit–the patients who can not afford to go to these hospitals and obtain the care that everyone else can obtain.

328

The mother of corporate wrongdoing

We build memorials to implant a marker on the minds of future generations. We do not want our society to forget Washington, Jefferson, Lincoln. That is why our capital is so patently marked with larger-than-life symbols of their contributions to our ways of thinking, our institutions and our government. We love to go to see and experience the good memorials. Only a few of those who go to the ground at Jamestown do not shed tears walking where we have a modest, but compelling, memory of the 1607 settlers; their determination to start a new society led to the House of Burgesses just a few miles from there, which led to a Congress, just a few more miles from there. But we only need to take a few steps from Congress to be at the site of the type of memorial we wish we would never see--National Highway Traffic Safety Administration. One of my worst memories, and a memory that serves as major boil on the face of corporate America, was played out there. Ford eventually recalled 1.4 million 1971-76 Pinto's for safety modifications under pressure from the National Highway Traffic Safety Administration, after prolonged investigation and hearings uncovered one of the worst frauds ever worked on the American people. We, however, have forgotten that event much more quickly and easily that we should.

In 1971, Ford Motor Company released the Ford Pinto which became the best-sold subcompact car on the market at the time. By the middle of the 1970's, though, reports showed that Pinto's tended to catch fire in rear-end collisions. Over 100 lawsuits against Ford forced the auto maker to pay out millions of dollars in damages. At least fifty-nine people burned to death in rear-end collisions. Ford had been losing market share to small imported cars. So after the Ford Mustang was produced, Lee Iococca, Executive Vice President of Ford Cars and Truck, realized that Americans wanted small cars. The Pinto was engineered as a totally new car and there were many challenges to overcome, not just safety. Ioccocca wanted to market an "econocar" which sold for less than $2,000 and weighed less than 2,000 pounds. The goal was put in jeopardy when the manufacturer discovered in its own testing that the gas tank was found to catch fire in rear end collisions at speeds as low as 21 miles per hour. Repairs for the problem would have been an estimated ten to fifteen dollars per car. Ford thought this cost would be more than it would have to pay out in accident-related lawsuits. So, Ford decided to make the car and worry about the fires later.

The Center for Auto Safety began receiving significant numbers of complaints about the Pinto. Within a few years, the Center for Auto Safety expressed concerns to the government. The government then began a "defects investigation" through the National Highway Safety

Administration. Many flaws were found in the Pinto. Some compounded problems caused a fire in the rear-end. These include the gas tank being about six inches from the flimsy bumpers, the back end not containing rear sub-frame members, and doors tending to jam shut in an accident. The fuel filler tube was prone to separate and create spillage. Engineers at Ford developed a variety of ideas that would have corrected the gas tank problem, all of which would cost too much money.

When confronted about the problems, Ford argued that all the federal safety requirements were met. That was easy because there were no standards for withstanding rear-end collisions of a specified number of miles per hour until a few years later in 1977. In June of 1978, Ford voluntarily recalled 1.4 million 1971-76 Pintos and 30,000 similar make 1975-76 Mercury Bobcats. Ford had decided to make changes to "end public concern". In August of the same year as the recalls, three teenage girls died in a Pinto that was struck in the rear-end. The fire started in the rear-end, causing the death of the girls. Ford was charged with reckless homicide and this case would set legal precedent. The prosecutor charged that Ford allowed the Pinto to remain on highways, knowing full well its defects. Ford was found innocent on the charges. Ford continually had a bad name for the Pinto and finally dropped it out of the product line. Ford put dollars ahead of lives.

The first fundamental canon in the

Accreditation Board for Engineering and Technology code of ethics of Engineers, states that engineers shall hold paramount the safety, health, and welfare of the public in the performance of their professional duties. Was this canon upheld? No way. The Ford company knew that the back end of the Pinto was weak, and that the gas tank was in a vulnerable location. If the executives would have upheld this canon, lives would have been saved, because an alternative solution for the gas tank would have taken place. The thoughts and actions of these few people influenced many lives, including the families of those who died.

At least 59 people were burned to death by Ford. A big difference, besides the obvious race difference between the cowards who lynched other human beings in the South, and the cowards who made the Ford Pinto is that Ford's victims never had the opportunity to even look their murderers in the eye. When Ford decided to market the car, fires be damned, they perpetrated 59 deaths, and hundreds of other burnings of nameless, faceless, powerless victims. Who started the investigation ball rolling? The lawyers for the victims in 100 private personal injury lawsuits.

A generation exists now that never witnessed such a fraud that killed so many people. Of course we have a far larger number of people who lost their life's fortune in Enron or WorldCom, but at least those cases cost no lives, as far as I am aware. Ford is different now, we hope and believe. But, the current generation should remember bad things from the former, just as we remember the good called to mind by our memorials. We should learn from both the good and the bad in our history and our national conscience. My point, simply put, is that people tend to remember things in their own generation, since that is what they live and experience. In this one generation, the tort reformers have found a way to get the public to forget the Pinto, and all of the other products of corporate America that were removed from the market, many of which were removed only because of the tenacity and determination of trial lawyers. Even if you think that money was the only motivation of these lawyers, the result of their work was still to society's benefit. In all of these cases, the one solace for victims who died or were maimed at least could be that they were a memorial for those in the future.

It is unfortunate that the archives of the Pinto deaths at the National Highway Traffic Safety Administration are a different type of memorial than nearby Washington, Jefferson, and Lincoln. We do not have a fondness for erecting memorials to our failures. The closest that we have come to that is the Viet Nam Memorial, just yards away from those of our nation's best. You will never see a granite Ford Pinto erected in our national mall in Washington, D. C. That does not mean that we should not learn some lessons from that episode, which, though not as devastating to our psyche as Viet Nam, still should serve as a reminder of what corporate greed has the capacity to do when unchecked by some power in the hands of the potential victims. We should not take that power away by destroying our best means of protection. Remember that Ford thought the cost of paying for victims' injuries would be less than it would have to pay out in accident-related lawsuits. Ford learned otherwise, and that's what led to the recall. Don't let any potential corporate wrongdoer believe that they can gamble with your loved ones lives.

In addition to our court system's ability to right wrongdoing, in the next Chapter we will see some other historical developments in our courts system that got us where we are. We should learn from these historical lessons and not throw away the benefit of our heritage.

CHAPTER NINE

THE JUSTICE SYSTEM WORKS WHEN GIVEN THE CHANCE

Studies...... have found that jury verdicts bear a reasonable relationship to the severity of the harm suffered.
2 Kelso & Kelso, *Jury Verdicts in Medical Malpractice Cases and the MICRA Cap*

The current societal and political debate over the justice system, and the role of juries and courts, is not a new debate. That debate was going on from the beginning of our time. For all of the good will that existed after the inception of this nation, there were, even at that time, factions warring over the function of the judiciary. In his unique look at two of our most important early public figures, Professor James Simon of New York Law School details some of the intriguing parts of that story in <u>What Kind of Nation.</u> The subtitle of the book is "Thomas Jefferson, John Marshall and the Epic Struggle to Create a United States." This fascinating book portrays, in very personal and poignant detail, the two very different views these two important men had about how our nation should lay the groundwork for the functioning of our judiciary.

What is always interesting about history is its applicability to the present. Professor Simon's book shows how the struggle of that time "resonates still in debates over the role of the federal government vis-a- vis the states and the authority of the Supreme Court to interpret laws." Jefferson believed that the *Constitution* called for narrow federal authority, was suspicious of the Supreme Court (including Marshall), and even supported the first unsuccessful impeachment attempt of a Supreme Court justice. Marshall understood that a strong and independent judiciary offered the best protection for the *Constitution*, ultimately leading to the opinion in *Marbury v. Madison,* establishing the Supreme Court as the conclusive voice of Constitutional interpretation.

One thing that is so very important about the formative time in our history, and is also so very important about the struggles of today, is that history influences future. That history of Jefferson and Marshall defined the roles of our government institutions to the extent that those definitions determine today's results. To the same extent, today's results will determine those of the future. If we allow the principles formed over two hundred years ago to be eroded by today's politics, we will have to live with the results of our decisions for many generations. We had better get it right now, or our descendants will long live under our rules before history will re-examine them.

Despite the differences on policy between Jefferson and Marshall, there were some points on which their minds met. They had vastly different views on our nation's kinship with the French, and the extent to which we should align ourselves with either side of the 1800 French Revolution; Jefferson thought that a weak federal government with limited powers and more power in the states would help guarantee the people their freedom. Marshall, on the other hand, felt that the federal government should be the repository of most of the power, especially over commerce. Both men knew, however, that a democracy, if it was to work, was required to find the will of the majority, but "always with respect to the rights of the minority." They often differed on what they thought was the right approach to reach that end. The major difference of opinion which they had revolved around the role of the Supreme Court. Jefferson believed that power in the Court would dilute the legislative authority, ultimately detracting from the will of the people. Marshall believed that the courts were "bulwarks of union and protectors of law." Simon, 148.

The famous case, usually the first one discussed in any American History discussion of the function of our Supreme Court, *Marbury v. Madison,* is known for its holding that the Supreme Court has the authority to hold Congressional acts unconstitutional. What is so fascinating about the decision, however, is the winding road that Marshall took to get to this holding. The original suit was brought by William Marbury, who felt aggrieved that he had not gotten what he thought was his rightful appointment as justice of the peace for the District of Columbia, since the commission for that post had not been properly delivered by the Adams administration prior to Jefferson's swearing on March 4, 1801. The Judiciary Act of 1789 stated that cases such as this could be brought in the Supreme Court as the court of original jurisdiction, which is exactly what Marbury's lawyer did. However, the *Constitution* does not provide for the Supreme Court to have original jurisdiction in such cases.

Confronted with what could have been a severe blow to the Court's authority, Marshall could have simply accepted the Act, accepted jurisdiction, and ruled that Mr. Marbury was entitled to his commission. You would have never heard of the case. Marshall, however, knew that our Constitutional government must have one final arbiter of what was Constitutional and what was not. If Congress could determine for itself what was Constitutional, then so could the Executive Branch and the Court. No one would be supreme and chaos would prevail. Marshall asked whether the Court owed its primary allegiance to the fundamental law contained in the *Constitution* or to an ordinary act of legislation. "The *Constitution* is either a superior paramount law, unchangeable by ordinary means, or it is on a level with ordinary legislative acts, and like other acts, is alterable when the legislature shall be pleased to alter it....the legislature [could not] change the rules of governing our constitutional democracy as it pleased. They must, therefore, have intended for the *Constitution* to be supreme." Simons, at 186.

Marshall's opinion, therefore, held that it is emphatically the province and duty of the judicial department to say what the law is. If that were not the case, then Congress, at the will of the majority, could pass any law, no matter how unconstitutional, and the courts would be duty-bound to apply it in their decisions of right and wrong, punishment and liability. Marshall, although he believed and stated in the opinion that Marbury should have a remedy since he was entitled to receive his commission, which was his right, could not have his case filed in the Supreme Court as a case of original jurisdiction, since the *Constitution* did not give the Supreme Court that power.

The genius of Marshall in his decision was this–he greatly enhanced the power of the Court while dodging a decision on the merits of the case. The Court never made a ruling on the question of what should be done about Mr. Marbury's commission. Rather than accepting the power to make the decision on that question, and lose political capital by going against the Jefferson administration, Marshall gained for the Court what has proven to be its greatest influence on this nation by dutifully refusing the power which Congress attempted to give it in the Judiciary Act of 1789. This authority and duty to interpret the *Constitution* has proven to be the Court's great equalizer with the Legislative branch.

Another of Marshall's displays of genius comes in the fact that, before he wrote about the Court's lack of jurisdiction, he wrote in agreement with Marbury's lawyer on the issue of Marbury's right to receive the commission. Had he addressed the jurisdiction point first, and simply ruled that there was no jurisdiction, he never could have written on the merits of the case. By writing first of the fact that the case had merit for discussion, Marshall created the opportunity to chastize the Jefferson administration for not giving Marbury what was duly his. Thus, he was able to seize upon this case as a way to discuss his thoughts on civil liberty, taking the stage from the Republican party that was so opposed to the Federalists (Marshall's former party) views on how to best achieve civil liberty. Marshall stated: "The very essence of civil liberty [is] ...the right of every individual to claim protection of the laws, wherever he receives an injury." Our government, if it is to be a government of laws and not men, must then furnish a remedy for the violation of a vested right. Simon, p. 184.

These two men who both so loved their country, who both served in its highest chambers, who both were lawyers, consummate politicians, libertarians, had vastly different views on politics and how to achieve certain ends. They had so many things in common, yet spent most of their years struggling against one another. Nonetheless, they believed strongly in one common idea–that each person in this country was uniquely entitled to the protection of the laws. The protector was in Jefferson's mind the legislature, deriving its power from the people directly. The protector in Marshall's mind was the *Constitution*, deriving its power from superior law, just as stated in the preamble. As much as I am an admirer of Jefferson, as many times as I have been to stand on the ground at his home in Monticello, outside of Charlottesville, Virginia, and perceived the marvel of his intellect, talent and philosophy, I have seen the wisdom of Marshall. How can a legislature, concerned only with the will of those who elect them and send them back to their legislative halls, not be influenced by considerations destitute of the thoughts of the moral minority? If we are to give our *Constitution* supremacy, how can we not let it stand above all other law?

Marshall's genius has proven to stand the test of time. The Supreme Court's binding, final, supreme and ultimate power to determine law has been what has held this nation together in times of turmoil of historical proportions. In the period of Reconstruction and the passage and interpretation of Constitutional Amendments after the Civil War; in the late eighteenth and early twentieth century when we were trying to balance the nation's growing economic and international prestige with the rights of the people; during the tumultuous 1960's when civil rights and liberty were being re-defined; and in the Watergate era when our government's institutions could have been shaken to their very core.

Watergate–just another third-rate burglary

A great Constitutional crisis makes for wonderful politics, just as we saw in the Jefferson-Marshall struggle. One of those great crises came in the Watergate prosecution of President Nixon. We were past the 1960's by then. We had seen the assassination of one of our most beloved presidents–JFK; the assassination of Martin Luther King, one of the most beloved spiritual, moral, racial equality leaders and teacher of racial equality; the assassination of presidential candidate, Robert F. Kennedy and an attempt on the life of presidential candidate George Wallace, men from two direct opposite ends of the political belief systems. We learned that we could send men to the moon, but we could not prevent one citizen's anger from killing another. We were approaching an end to the Viet Nam era, but not the end of its deep consequences. We had gone through a period when everyone was questioning the ethics of our government, the moral fiber of our leaders, and the direction that our country would take. Spiro Agnew had resigned the Vice-Presidency under a cloud of suspicion of bribery at the hands of the wealthy and well-connected. We needed someone or something to lead us through those times with a sense of purpose, morality, direction. That turned out, again, to be our Supreme Court.

In the Watergate scandal, the showdown between right and wrong came on July 8, 1974. It was on that day that Special Prosecutor Leon Jaworski arrived at the United States Supreme Court to argue his point–that the judicial power to interpret that laws of the land had the authority to subpoena documents from the President, despite the President's claim of executive privilege. The President's lawyers stated that the Court had no right to rule on the case because the matter was a political one, which the Court was not empowered to decide. In other words, the argument was that the President could decide what he wanted to give the special prosecutor, and that the President's decision could not be questioned.

Jaworski, who had subpoenaed tapes of conversations to support his claim that Nixon had been involved in a conspiracy to cover up the burglary, argued that the judiciary is the final arbiter of what the *Constitution* says, not the executive branch. Jaworski argued, "Now the President may be right in the way that he reads the *Constitution*, but he may also be wrong. And if he is wrong, who is there to tell him so?" *"Law, a Treasury of Art and Literature"* , p.339-341, from "The Right and the Power." Jaworski made the point that it is emphatically the province of the judiciary to say what the law is, arguing *Marbury v. Madison.*

From antiquity to modern times

In the very earliest recorded instances of the existence of the jury system, the jury began as an attempt to take the pressure off of the judges who recognized their own prejudices and imperfections. The right to a jury is institutionalized in our *Constitution*, recognizing it among our dearest and most revered liberties. The Seventh Amendment to the *Constitution*, guaranteeing the right to trial by jury in all cases, is one of the least known to most citizens, but the one that is the most important to the branch of our government whose purpose is to be a check on the other two branches. The judiciary could not function without the juries, whose purpose is to give the government its most direct and functioning connection to the people the government is supposed to serve.

It is interesting to note that our society places a premium on the will of the majority in our democracy to elect the representatives that make our laws, yet the ability to vote is granted to people with precisely the same qualifications as those who serve on juries. Why is it, then, that juries are so maligned as being ignorant and illogical? Could it be simply that some decisions of those juries go in a direction that certain members of our society do not like. When was the last time that you heard of a hospital or a doctor that agreed with a jury's decision against them?

The right to a trial by jury must be preserved without the severe limitations that are now sought against it. Without it there is virtually no opportunity for the average citizen to have any direct impact on the rules our society makes. What other place in the workings of the government can twelve people insure that the will of the majority can not be unjustifiably imposed upon a minority? What other place in our society can one person whose wife has been cremated by a Ford Pinto inferno demonstrate the fact that the Ford Motor Company knew the inferno would occur, but did nothing to stop it, all in the name of profit? If our society can allow a jury to impose a sentence of death in a criminal case, then why should a jury not be trusted with issues of just compensation in a civil case? The only reason is because the large corporations and insurance companies have convinced the public that the right to jury should be relinquished. But how will that sit when the CEO of that insurance company is himself the victim of medical negligence? Will he think that he should be given a jury to understand his plight?

Anyone who wants to determine for himself the benefits of the jury system should begin by looking at our legal, political and religious history. The Mosaic Code, designed to safeguard a national entity, permitted the emergence of a form of democratic government that lasted over 800 years. This Code laid down the first principles of separation of church and state, as well as the first foundation that is "indispensable to any democracy–an independent judiciary." Dimont, M., *Jews, God and Country,* "On Mosaic Law" (1962). These laws of Old Testament times, written by the man who led the ancient Jews out of bondage and into their promised land, were the first to state that the law should derive from a covenant that people had with a superior being.

The Magna Carta, signed by King John of England in 1215, was the result of a bargain struck between the King and rebels, to gain a return to fealty and homage. The liberties granted therein were many, and it has been said that the document is not so much a legal document as it is a symbol of sentimentality. Nonetheless, it was the turning point in the English history of self-government, which has become our history of self-government. How we were able to manage to boil the liberties down from the sixty-three chapters of the Magna Carta to our ten in the Bill of Rights may only demonstrate our superior thriftiness with words. It may, however, demonstrate our ability to focus only on what was and is important to us. We felt the importance of the trial by jury. We have not since then felt such an extreme importance of anything else, except the abolition of slavery, voting rights for women and all races, due process, an income tax, and a few other procedural matters pertaining to elections.

Alexander Hamilton and James Madison wrote their part of the *Federalist Papers* to explain to the people of the new Republic how the democratic institutions would work. Madison favored a system leaning more toward power vested in the states, whereas Hamilton wanted more power in a centralized government. These two lawyers, along with another lawyer, John Jay, wrote the *Federalist Papers* to help with the battle for the passage of the *Constitution*. That battle was won, in part, on the strength of the analysis provided by these papers and the public discourse on the bold experiment called the *Constitution*. The liberties which have been preserved by that experiment over the past two hundred and fifteen years are now threatened by the calls for severe limitations on the right to trial by jury. A reading of the body of work of these three statesmen demonstrates the regard they all had for the institution of the jury. Even when there was a monumental battle between the "centralists" and "decentralists" over the nature of our new federation, there was no disagreement among these three, or even among those in society or the other writers of the day, over the role that the jury was to play in our democracy. Hamilton, who was not near the "democrat" as Madison, stated that the independence of the judiciary operates as an "essential safeguard against the effects of occasional ill humors in the society....[and] as a check upon the legislative body in passing [the laws].

Classic legal struggles over the past two centuries have been fought over the underlying meaning, intent and application of the *Constitution*.

Thomas Jefferson and John Marshall fought each other for much of their lives to balance the powers of the government against the rights of the people. Abraham Lincoln fought the Confederacy so that the Union could prevail under the power of the government to preserve the *Constitution*. Clarence Darrow fought William Jennings Bryan, in a highly charged and emotional case, to preserve the right of freedom of speech-- the individual to be free from the government's authority over what man says. Louis Brandeis, called "the people's attorney," fought for the little guys against corporate monopolistic power. All of these legal battles have occurred as a result of the rights declared under the *Constitution*, the fact that our judicial system is the ultimate declarant of the meaning of the *Constitution*, and the belief of these lawyers that the rights secured under the *Constitution* could not be taken away by a legislative body. Although it might be popular to take away that judicial power (by legislating away rights in medical malpractice cases), such legislation would be the wrecking of our Constitutional right to trial by jury granted in the Seventh Amendment.

The "People's Attorney"

About every fifty years there comes along a lawyer who has such immense talents that those who witness his work put him above all others in his class. One such lawyer, in my estimation, is Louis Brandeis, born on November 13, 1856, a little more than 100 years after Thomas Jefferson and about 50 years after Abraham Lincoln. Brandeis, whose father had come to the United States about eight years earlier to escape what was becoming the beginning signs of anti-Semitism in middle and Eastern Europe, grew up in Lousville Kentucky, working in his father's grocery store. Unlike Lincoln, he had formal schooling, and was able to attend Harvard University to obtain his law degree. Like Lincoln, however, he had the ability to draw people to work with him and to capture their faith in his ability to achieve. He was tireless in his efforts and his patience to achieve things that he believed to be important to society and the proper functioning of democracy.

The biography of Louis Brandeis, written by Louis J. Paper in 1983, entitled simply Brandeis, succinctly details the most significant accomplishments of one of America's truly great Supreme Court justices. I have chosen to call attention to Brandeis for a couple of reasons that I believe are important. First, his accomplishments are not widely known to many people other than those who regularly study Constitutional law and lawyers. Second, he is probably best known for his deep conviction of what he called True Americanism. Because our country was populated by immigrants from so many different lands, one did not become a part of this country until he learned to share the American ideals, the foremost of which is "the development of the individual for his own and the common good." Louis D. Brandeis, "True Americanism," in *Business–A Profession,* pp. 365-368.

No more compelling demonstration of belief in this ideal can be given than by showing the number of different ways in which Brandeis chose to work for the individual and the common good, against what he perceived to be the corrupting influence of "bigness" and corporate greed. He began his public advocacy in 1887, at the age of 31, when he began to work with others to fight the entrenched Boston Catholic interests, who were constantly seeking and receiving public expenditures to benefit their own private interests. It did not matter that the powerful lawyers for private interests would be offended. His public reaction to the oppression of workers at the hands of large steel manufacturers brought his convictions more into the public eye. In the fall of 1893, after reading that Carnagie Steel had hired security guards who opened fire on striking workers and killing many people, Brandeis began to realize that "the common law, built up under simpler conditions of living, gave an inadequate basis for the adjustment of complex relations of the modern factory system." Paper, *Brandeis*, p. 39.

Brandeis' skill as a trial lawyer was admired by many. He became famous for assembling more facts about the problems and issues in the case than even the clients could master. When it came to presenting a case to the jury, he was comforted because of what he called the common sense of the people when compared to the uncommon sense of judges. *Brandeis*, p. 49. But although he could fight with the best of the lawyers in front of the jury, he was often at his best when engaged on behalf of the public against what he considered a large evil of a conglomerate interest. In 1897, he took on the owners of the Elevated, the railway system of Boston, who wanted to take control of all of the public transportation and remain in charge of the rates that they could charge for their services. The battle began at the local level through Brandeis' assembling public interest groups and writing letters to the papers and meeting with public figures. For four years he assembled the best group of public support against the most powerful lawyers, lobbyists and business owners that the corporate railway could muster. In the final analysis, for no pay (he even ended up paying money from is own pocket for the time he missed working for the firm's regular clients), he worked tirelessly on behalf of the public and secured for them ownership of the railway system, which would guarantee that the corporate entity could not have its own way with the public.

Brandeis did not back down from taking on the five largest life insurance companies in the country when life insurance premiums were being eaten up by the company "expenses," leaving nothing for beneficiaries when the insureds passed away. In 1905, a group of policyholders of Equitable Life Insurance, the largest in the country, approached Brandeis. He studied the economics of the situation and determined that life insurance companies expenses, per dollar invested, were seventeen times greater than the expenses of banks and other savings institutions. This he determined was due to the lack of regulation of the insurance industry. Rather than create a federal bureau to take control of the problem, a remedy advocated by many at that time, Brandeis gave a speech on the problems associated with the accumulation of a large amount of money and power in the hands of a few, as was the case in the insurance industry, and distributed 25,000 copies of the speech across the country, in an effort to obtain a groundswell of support at the state legislative level to create savings banks that would allow the salaried workers to reap much more benefit from their invested dollars than they could through life insurance. He also enlisted the support of every major newspaper in the state, and fought in hearings at the legislative level. Finally, in May of 1907, the bill passed and was signed into law, allowing workers who invested 75 cents a week from the age of 21 until the age of 61, to have a benefit of $2,300, rather than $830, which would have been the amount earned in the insurance plan without Brandeis' efforts.

His accomplishments and tirelessness as a private lawyer were excelled only by those of his as a Supreme Court Justice. Beginning from the time of his approval in the first Senate subcommittee to vote for him ("the real crime of which this man is guilty," said one senator,"is that he has exposed the inequities of men in high places in our financial system. He has not stood in awe of the majesty of wealth."), to the date of his retirement in 1939, he was dedicated to the same propositions. His last great accomplishment as a Supreme Court Justice was the fashioning of a 5-4 majority to write the opinion in Erie v.

Tompkins, which required the federal courts to apply state common law to cases before them, giving state law a stature that it had not theretofore held. That feat of Brandeis required great ingenuity and resources, as well as the reversal of 100-year old precedent which had clogged the federal courts and given federal judges difficulties for years. He did it by examining the *Constitution*, finding that Congress had not been there given the power to create a federal common law. This was consistent with his view that democracy worked best when controlled by those at the lowest levels near to the problem. The same should hold true for us now.

Lawyers as instruments of public philosophy

Lawyers are not supposed to be meager voices of the government, chosen to do the work of administering what the powers would like. We are to use our minds, our hearts, our skills, our knowledge of humanity and our spirits to secure to others the rights that we would like to have secured to ourselves. When Hitler shaped the legal profession in the Third Reich, he "cleansed" the legal profession. The entire German Bar was reorganized and centralized twice during the Third Reich, and a new National Lawyer's Code was enacted, aimed at completely controlling professional activities and insuring its adherence to the legal doctrines of Hitler. The new member of the Bar was free to practice his profession as long as he exercised his legal skills in complete harmony with the demands of Nazi legal theory. Willig, "The Bar in the Third Reich." The Nazis had an aversion to independent lawyers, much like the corporations of the day (other than, of course, their own lawyers), because they appeared to represent an ideology alien to their own.

Yet, our society disapproves of such warped roles of lawyers. We disapprove of such roles so vehemently that we provided to the very perpetrators of the "cleansing" our very own theories of law and justice. When the Third Reich failed, and it came time to place history's judgment upon those men, we did not give them a trial at Nuremberg with lawyers chosen for the outcome that we could legitimately have desired in our hearts and emotions. We gave them our Supreme Court Justice Robert Jackson as the prosecutor, who gave his summation of the charges against the accused. He said "The United States has no interest which would be advanced by the conviction of any defendant if we have not proved him guilty on at least one of the counts charged against him in the indictment. Any result that the calm and critical judgment of posterity would pronounce unjust would not be a victory for any of the countries associated in this prosecution." The Nazis were given the "kind of trial, in the days of their pomp and power, they never gave to any man." Jackson, Robert H., "Summation of the Prosecution at Nuremberg"(1947)

After the worst of all crimes against humankind, after being viciously attacked and invaded by our enemy, after losing tens of thousands of our young countrymen of what has been called "the greatest generation," we gave OUR ENEMY the kind of trial which our countrymen now wish to rob from our most seriously injured victims. What has happened in barely one-half of a century? Have we become so callous to the injuries to our fellow man that we can not see the injustice of the proposals floating about?

Tort reform journalism

When one of our major publications takes on the jury system, as did *Newsweek* in one of its cover stories last year, some citizens who have been forced to turn to that system have felt compelled to respond to the assault. Since Linda McDougal was one of those people who chose to resort to the civil justice system guaranteed to her under the Seventh Amendment, according to "Lawsuit Hell," *Newsweek's* cover story on our civil justice system, she was just another freeloader looking to hit the jackpot. Ms. McDougal said that she would take offense to such articles-being maimed by someone else's negligence isn't winning the lottery--except that she is used to these articles. She wrote to *Newsweek*, after the article:

> "They all use the same words to discredit the system and people who get some justice from it. Don't get mad, get even, someone once said. I'm a wife, the mother of three sons and an accountant for a small company

in Wisconsin, so I'm busy. But I've also
made appearances around the country over
the past year, reminding people that our jury
system is the only hope an ordinary citizen
like me has when she's been wronged. The
system isn't perfect——what is? I
assumesome lawsuits really are "frivolous,"
but our system has a lot of safeguards
against abuse.

"Just as I don't judge the medical profession on
the basis of the people whose errors changed
my life forever, I don't judge the justice
system on the basis of a few bad cases. I
judge it on the thousands of people
throughout American history who have
gotten some measure of justice from a judge
or a jury that they would never have gotten
from an insurance company, an HMO or
some vast conglomerate. I've read the
experts who say we need all kinds of
limitations on injured people and juries
because insurance companies and
corporations need "predictability" about
their potential liability. They want
predictability? What about me? What
happened to me was unpredictable. I'm
tough, I have a wonderful family, so don't
feel sorry for me--but don't ask me to feel
sorry for those companies, either.

"Sometimes, the malpractice is egregious,"
NEWSWEEK admits. But who's in the best
position to determine if a case is egregious
or frivolous? The choices seem to be a panel
of experts of some sort, or a panel of

ordinary citizens--a jury. I don't apologize for trusting ordinary citizens--our friends, neighbors and coworkers. The story mentions a case in Kentucky in which "a mother sued her daughter's school after the girl had performed oral sex on a boy during a schoolbus ride... The woman blamed poor adult supervision, saying her daughter had been forced.

When the subject is tort "reform," I've learned to pay close attention, because most of the cases that make the rounds on the Internet and talk shows are urban legends, either misleading or flat-out false. A simple Internet search told me that the board of education had determined that the girl had been the victim of a sexual assault. Prior to this conclusion, the principal had suspended her for 10 days. After this conclusion, she was suspended again, this time for not reporting the assault. This was the last straw for the mother, and why she filed her lawsuit. Among her demands: that the board set up training for its employees on dealing with sexual assaults. Ask any parent whether this was a reasonable response to what happened.

NEWSWEEK says people sue ministers for failing to prevent suicides, but I believe that every state court that has considered the question of clergy malpractice has rejected the claims. You say volunteers of all sorts are supposedly worried about lawsuits, but I know that both federal and state laws prohibit suits against volunteers. I think journalism's obligation is to set the record straight, not spread misinformation.

"Naturally I'm drawn to the case mentioned in the cover story about the couple's lawsuit against a hospital for failing to prevent their child from becoming disabled by a rare birth condition. I haven't been able to find details, but I'll bet that one sentence cannot do justice to the facts here——or to the tragedy.

"You see, I know how tort-reform journalism works. I know how these stories get written, and who writes them. I also know whose interests are served. Not mine in Wisconsin. Not that girl's and that mother's in Kentucky. Not that California family's. I also know that if all those who want to restrict the legal rights of ordinary citizens have their way, I wouldn't have waited seven months for an apology from the doctors, which I got only after my story became public. I would have waited forever. I Trust Juries——and Americans Like You Taking away our legal rights isn't reform. In cases like mine, the civil-justice system is our only hope." Signed, Linda McDougal.

One of the favorite tricks of the tort reformers is to quote a line from Shakespeare– "Let's Kill All of the Lawyers." This quote is given in an attempt to make the listener believe that, ever since ancient times, society has wanted to get rid of lawyers to make things more livable. Most of those people who raise Shakespeare's name to the debate fail to recognize that the quote was one made by a villain in the town square as he advocated anarchy and the overthrow of an orderly society. In other words, "if we get rid of the lawyers we can have our way."

Sound like anyone you know? In the next Chapter, we will learn some things about how the insurance companies have brought upon themselves their own problems, and are now trying to punish others for their problems.

Was Antiquity better than modern times?

The tactics of the cases of old were much different. Some cases today turn on how good lawyers are at keeping things from the other side, not what the evidence is. One of the most popular approaches in the defense of medical malpractice cases is to claim that even if a doctor did not do what he should have done, he did not make the patient any worse than he already was. This approach is the one that the defendants took in Dixon Klein's cases. This is known as the "causation" defense. It often works, because a doctor's negligence can not create liability for him unless his actions led to some injury to the patient. In other words, the doctor's actions or failure must have caused some independent harm to the patient, other than the harm that the patient already would have had. For example, if a cancer patient is not diagnosed timely, then the doctor is not responsible for the damages caused by the cancer, he is only responsible for the consequences of the delay in diagnosis.

Often times it is difficult to prove that the plaintiff is any worse off as a result of the negligence of the doctor, especially if the disease of the patient is one that is difficult to treat. In Dixon's case, the defense was that Dixon's glaucoma was going to cause him to go blind, even if Dr. Lye had found it to begin with. That placed the burden on Dixon's lawyers to prove a negative–that Dixon's disease was not far enough along at the time of his visit to Dr. Lye that he would have been blind.

The causation defense is one that is a wonderful tool for the defense for a variety of reasons. First, it requires the plaintiff to prove a negative–that the patient was not going to be the way he now is. Even more important for the defense is the fact that the causation defense requires the plaintiff to spend a lot of money. In order to overcome the defense, the plaintiff has to get experts to state that based upon the condition of the plaintiff and the normal disease process, the plaintiff would otherwise be disease free. In order to do that, all of the plaintiff's medical records for many prior years, and all of the records from the date of the claimed negligent treatment afterward, have to be reviewed by some expert in the field of plaintiff's injury. Taking the example of the patient who claims that the defendant failed to diagnose a tumor in the lung, the defense will claim that the cancer would have killed the plaintiff even if the tumor had been diagnosed timely. Then the plaintiff will have to hire an oncologist, and probably a pulmonologist, to testify that plaintiff, with proper treatment, could have been salvaged and would have been cancer free.

You can imagine the difficulty and expense in that proposition, especially when it costs anywhere between $500 and $1,000 per hour for these experts to work. By the time they have reviewed all of the plaintiff's pre and post- incident records, given a written report to the lawyer and court (which they are required to do in most states), prepare for and give a pre-trial deposition, and prepare for and testify at trial, they have often charged tens of thousands of dollars per expert to give their opinions in support of the case. In addition, it is often difficult to find expert witnesses who are willing to testify against their peers in their own states, the lawyers are required to travel out of state to meetings with and depositions of the experts. When depositions are taken, court reporters are required to be present taking down all of the testimony, at a cost of several thousand dollars per deposition.

A word of fact about frivolous cases. One of the propositions that the doctors and their insurance companies want you believe is that many frivolous cases are brought just so that the plaintiff can recover some windfall. In order for that to make sense, one first must believe that frivolous cases are ever victorious, and second that a lawyer would want to take a chance on one.

Almost every case against a doctor or

hospital that goes to trial will take at least hundreds of hours of lawyer's time, and at least tens of thousands of dollars in expert witness fees, travel expenses and court costs. In Dixon's case, it was necessary to hire an expert witness who was renowned for his work in the glaucoma area. That was something that Dixon's lawyers were able to do, since it just happened that one of the foremost experts in glaucoma was a professor at the University of Texas Southwestern Medical School in Dallas, just 30 miles away from the courthouse. Fortunately for Dixon and his lawyers, that expert gave testimony that if Dr. Lye had done the tonometer test, it would, more likely than not, been abnormal, leading to a referral to a glaucoma specialist. That expert also testified that, since it was apparent that Dixon's visual fields had started constricting within the six months after Dr. Lye's visit, the glaucoma would have been treatable if the test had been done. With that testimony, there was sufficient evidence for Dixon's lawyers to take his case to the jury.

So, now that the elements of proof had stacked up in Dixon's favor, the case should be pretty much ready to be resolved, right? Dixon had shown that the blank was not filled in, and that the test, more likely than not, was not performed. He could show that Dr. Lye's office was lying about the records. He could show that he would likely be blind, or nearly blind, and that his condition would never have been so bad if Dr. Lye had simply done the test. Smooth sailing to the courthouse!! Not so fast. More on that delay later.

CHAPTER TEN

JURIES ARE NOT THE PROBLEM WITH THE JUSTICE SYSTEM

Harvard researchers found that only one in 7.6 instances of medical negligence committed in hospitals results in a malpractice claim. Harvard Medical Practice StudyGroup, *Patients, Doctors and Lawyers: Medical Injury, Malpractice Litigation,and Patient Compensation in New York*, 1990.

For most people who saw the movie "Ten, " with Dudley Moore and Bo Derek, the line remembered by most is not the one that I think is most applicable to life. There was a scene where Dudley Moore's character went to the home of the priest who was to perform Derek's wedding ceremony, in order to find out how to locate her. In that scene, the priest's elderly housekeeper shuffled away after serving tea to Moore and the priest. While the camera was on her, a "breaking wind" sound came over the theater speakers. The cameras then turned to the priest's dog, whimpering, cowering and huddled in the corner. Moore, with a quizzical look, turned to the priest, who, without breaking a smile, said "Every time Mrs. Kissle breaks wind, we beat the dog."

Every time I hear the politicians cry that juries are to blame, it reminds me of the cowering dog, man's best friend, innocent and unable to speak, hovering in the corner while the offender walks away untouched. The insurance companies leave their offensive gas behind them, while there is no voice for the juries or the victims, sitting in the corner whimpering and cowering. Let's just not hurt the insurance company's feelings, so we can continue to receive our afternoon tea. If the dog could speak, things would be different.

Nation's Largest Medical Malpractice Insurer Declares Caps on Damages Don't Work

The jury system works. Many states have experimented successfully with measures to protect doctors from frivolous lawsuits and "runaway" jury awards. The states are far better equipped to handle these problems than the federal government. It seems strange that the very people that are the supporters of federal tort reform, seeking to take away rights of average Americans, are the same people that we often hear crying that the federal government should leave us alone, and leave the capitalistic society, or the states themselves, to deal with any other problem in society.

Should decisions of life or death be easier to make than decisions where an insurance company's pocketbook is concerned? People say that jurors should not be allowed to spend insurance company's money by awarding it to injured citizens, but jurors spend hundreds of thousand of citizens' dollars by putting them to be state supported in prisons for the rest of their lives. So, as it turns out, the government allows jurors every day all across the country to spend millions of dollars on prison accommodations, all in the name of betterment of society, but a person who has been injured by negligence of a doctor should not be allowed to collect money awarded by a jury, because we can not trust jurors to do that!! Rather incongruous, isn't it?

Doctors' medical malpractice premiums are at an all-time high because of several factors. Those rates can be made more fair by the states controlling the rate that doctors may be charged for malpractice insurance. Doctors who have had a good record should be rewarded for their records, and bad doctors should not be allowed to influence the rates for all. If the states will enact real measures that will require the doctors and hospitals to police themselves, and will punish those who attempt to hide their mistakes, the people will be protected from bad doctors who repeatedly err and negatively influence the price of insurance for the good doctors.

If the states will put the medical malpractice insurance companies to the task of justifying the reason for increases in their rates, like all other insurance companies, then there would be a real awakening as to the TRUE reasons why doctors are crying for a reduction in those rates. If the federal government would stop protecting the insurance companies from the freedom from regulation under the antitrust laws, then the insurance companies could compete in the same market that all other businesses compete in–the free capitalistic economic system, rather than an unregulated monopoly.

The so-called "solution" to high health care costs proposed by the tort reformers, capping non-economic damages at $250,000, doesn't address the root of the problem of skyrocketing insurance costs. The real culprit is the insurance industry, which controls virtually every aspect of America's health care system and is forcing doctors to pay for its recent investment losses. The insurance lobby, one of President Bush and the Congressional leadership's biggest campaign contributors, operates with a free hand because it is exempt from anti-trust laws.

President Bush blamed high medical malpractice insurance premiums on "lousy juries."

Americans express their patriotism through military service, voting and serving on citizen juries. It is disappointing not only that the President would recommend shortchanging people like Linda McDougal, but also that he does not trust patriotic Americans---our friends, neighbors, and co-workers---who serve on juries. This compassionate conservative simply wants to help his corporate friends in the insurance industry.

Americans are deeply concerned about protecting their families and rising health care costs add to these worries. The federally imposed one-size-fits-all cap on state malpractice compensation claims proposed by the tort reformers at the behest of the insurance lobbyists, doesn't solve the health care problem. This cap won't bring down insurance premiums for doctors, which are rising fast even in states that have their own caps. Until Congress reforms the insurance laws, doctors' livelihoods and patients' lives will continue to be threatened by corporate interests that put profits over people.

It is disappointing to see the attacks on our legal system, the place of last resort for Americans who need to be heard. It appears that the politicians in Washington and the state capitals only trust themselves — not American juries — to decide what is fair compensation for a young woman who never can bear children, a retiree who loses his eyesight, or a family whose toddler dies due to preventable medical malpractice.

Closing the courthouse doors to victims of serious medical malpractice is especially hypocritical on the part of President Bush, who did not hesitate to file a lawsuit over his daughter's minor fender bender. The *New York Daily News* reported that President Bush sued Enterprise Rent-A-Car over a minor 1998 auto accident in which no one was hurt. A car driven by an Enterprise customer with a suspended driver's license hit Bush's 1995 Jeep Cherokee, driven by daughter Jenna Bush. The accident was so minor that police weren't even called to the scene. The case settled for $2000--Source: "Bush turned litigious, targeted rental car firm over fender bender," *New York Daily News*, 8/26/2000 If she had lost a limb or become paralyzed, would $250,000 be enough for her? It seems the President trusts the justice system when he wants it to protect his interests, but doesn't think that Americans whose lives have been devastated by medical malpractice deserve the same rights as his family.

It also is ironic that President Bush unleashed one of his biggest rounds of jury bashing in Pennsylvania, the home of Senator Rick Santorum, another Washington political leader who doesn't practice what he preaches when his own family's interests are at stake. The same year he voted against letting patients sue their HMOs (in the Patients' Bill of Rights), Senator Santorum took the stand in a $500,000 medical malpractice lawsuit against his wife's chiropractor, saying her injuries were hurting his re-election chances.

When Florida passed caps and other restrictions on patients in the mid-1980s, Aetna and St. Paul studied their own medical malpractice claims history. Their internal memos conclude that caps do not save doctors money on medical malpractice premiums. Caps don't solve problems; they create new ones. If the insurance company won't pay for the care and loss of patients critically injured by medical malpractice, who will? Taxpayers. If you want to fix the problem, take away the insurance companies' antitrust exemption to keep them from colluding and price-fixing; require prior rate approval; and make them demonstrate the need for a rate increase in a public hearing. The answer is insurance reform, not tort reform.

President Bush visited a Pennsylvania hospital chain a few days after it agreed to pay $7 million and apologized publicly for killing a 72-year-old patient. If he cares about patients, why didn't the President support the victim's family instead? Frank Thornton died after doctors misplaced a breathing tube in his esophagus instead of his windpipe, depriving him of oxygen for almost 10 minutes. Mercy Hospital failed to tell his widow about the error and fought the lawsuit brought by his family until the trial began, then agreed to settle for $7 million and a public apology. Mercy Chief Executive Officer James May apologized at a news conference and admitted that the lawsuit was NOT frivolous. "Widow's Reward is Answers in Death," *Wilkes-Barre Times Leader*, 1/14/2003.

When U.S. Sen. Rick Santorum of Pennsylvania testified in his wife's medical malpractice case (after voting to protect HMOs against patient lawsuits), he said her injuries hurt his re-election campaign. Karen Santorum sought $500,000 in the lawsuit, although there were only a total of $18,000 in medical costs, and no lost wages, since Ms. Santorum did not work outside the home. That's a request of $482,000 for non-economic damages, nearly twice the cap that Senator Santorum and his congressional colleagues now believe is best for the rest of the victims of malpractice. Why does Senator Santorum think his family deserve more legal rights than the rest of us? "Judge Strikes Down Award in Santorum Case," *Roll Call*, 1/10/2000.

The final report of the interim Select Committee on Insurance Availability and Medical Malpractice Insurance, which studied the issue for a year, concluded that "any limitations placed on the judicial system will have no immediate effect on the cost of liability insurance for health care providers." That's what happened last year in Nevada, where insurance companies refused to lower doctors' malpractice rates after enactment of a cap supported by the insurance industry. In Missouri, another state that caps damages, malpractice premiums are skyrocketing although the number of malpractice claims and the cost per claim have been declining. Another study by Americans for Insurance Reform (www.insurancereform.org), a coalition of 100 consumer groups, found malpractice insurance premiums in West Virginia and elsewhere track economic cycles, not pay-outs in malpractice cases, which have remained flat for the last decade. During economic downturns, insurers raise rates to make up for investment losses, the group found.

Still, the California Medical Association, where a $250,000 cap has been in place for nearly 30 years, is getting an increasing number of calls from physicians who have been notified of large increases in professional liability insurance premiums and from others who have been dropped by their carriers. In some cases, the physicians say they have had no settlements or suits filed against them.

Most of the public does not know that insurance companies profits from what they call "lines of business" in medical malpractice, personal injury and product liability insurance, is not regulated or limited in any way by the states or the federal government. An act known as the McCarren-Ferguson Act leaves the regulation of insurance solely to the state governments. The state governments have passed statutes and regulations which limit the amounts that insurance companies can charge for both homeowners' and automobile insurance. That is why we often read in our local newspapers, or hear on our local news, that the state boards of insurance have ruled on the insurance companies requests for rate insurance in homeowners' or auto insurance. There is no such regulation of the other lines, such as product liability or medical malpractice.

Risk Management: Honesty May Be the Best Policy

It would be interesting to know how the system would work if health care providers would simply acknowledge mistakes and try to deal with the consequences in an honest and forthright manner, rather than covering facts and hiding the ball. The *Annals of Internal Medicine,* established by the American College of Physicians, is a journal that has been in publication since 1927. An article appeared in that journal on December 21, 1999, written by Steve S. Kraman, MD; and Ginny Hamm, JD, one a doctor and another a lawyer. See, Ann. Int. Med 131:12; pp. 963-967. It reports of an experiment in honesty by the Veterans Affairs Medical Center in Lexington, Kentucky. The experiment was called a "humanistic risk management policy that includes early injury review, steadfast maintenance of the relationship between the hospital and the patient, proactive full disclosure to patients who have been injured because of accidents or medical negligence, and fair compensation for injuries." The results were favorable, and the authors state that another such experiment resulted in "encouragingly moderate liability payments."

Here's how the experiment went: In 1987, after losing two malpractice judgments totaling more than $1.5 million (partly because of inadequately prepared defenses), the management of the Lexington center decided to use a more proactive policy in cases that could result in litigation. This new policy was intended to better prepare the risk management committee to defend malpractice claims by identifying and investigating apparent accidents and incidents of medical negligence. However, when investigation identified an incident of negligence of which the patient or next of kin was apparently unaware, ethical issues arose. The committee members decided that in such cases, the facility had a duty to remain in the role of caregiver and notify the patient of the committee's findings. This practice continues to be followed because administration and staff believe that it is the right thing to do and because it has resulted in *unanticipated financial benefits to the medical center.*

Since this policy has been in place, many settlements have been made. Five settlements involved incidents that caused permanent injury or death but would probably never have resulted in a claim without voluntary disclosure to patients or families. Many other settlements involved patients who had expressed dissatisfaction with an outcome; after investigation, the committee agreed with the patient and initiated a settlement. All cases were negotiated on the basis of reasonable calculations of actual loss. Thorough, timely case reviews allowed the committee to defend against nuisance claims——claims without merit that institutions sometimes settle without contest only to avoid the cost and work of a lawsuit.

During the 7-year period examined in detail (1990 through 1996), the Lexington facility had 88 malpractice claims and paid out an average of $190,113 per year (a total of $1,330,790 for 7 years). The average payment per claim was $15,622. Seven claims proceeded to federal court and were dismissed before trial. One claim proceeded to trial and was won by the government.

The authors concluded that, despite following a policy that seems to be designed to maximize malpractice claims, the Lexington facility's liability payments have been moderate and are comparable to those of similar facilities. They stated that plaintiffs' attorneys, after first confirming the accuracy of the clinical information volunteered by the facility, are willing to negotiate a settlement on the basis of calculable monetary losses rather than on the potential for large judgments that contain a punitive element. This can benefit a facility by limiting settlement costs to reasonable amounts. It also fairly compensates patients who have been injured because of accident or error. This is important because such compensation is deserved but is infrequently offered. The hidden expenses of litigation are also substantial. The authors estimated that it costs the government $250,000 for a single malpractice case (from initiation through an appeal, including costs of medical experts, travel, and other incidental expenses). A local settlement, however, involves only an attorney, a paralegal specialist, and a few other hospital employees.

The experience of the Lexington facility suggests the financial superiority of a full disclosure policy, and we hope that this report will spur a more detailed examination of the issue. The Veterans Affairs medical system is the largest integrated health care system in the country, and current policy mandates a risk management process similar to that used in the Lexington facility. If this type of process is implemented and followed, more convincing data on this question may become available within the next few years.

The author's final conclusion? **"We conclude that an honest and forthright risk management policy that puts the patient's interests first may be relatively inexpensive** because it allows avoidance of lawsuit preparation, litigation, court judgments, and settlements at trial. Although goodwill and the maintenance of the caregiver role are less tangible benefits, they are also important advantages of such a policy." **Let's see if we can summarize what is actually said in this Journal— published by doctors for doctors:**

Plaintiffs lawyers are not greedy or looking for a windfall;

Malpractice victims are not out for a huge

verdict; they just want the truth;

The hospital is better off financially just paying the legitimate claims;

Where there is no merit to a case, the jury finds against the plaintiff.

In current systems of practice, patient compensation is frequently owed, but rarely offered

The authors of this article could have written the book you are currently reading.!! Each of the above five propositions are the exact opposite of what the insurance companies wish for you to believe. Each of these five propositions are nearly verbatim the arguments of the American Trial Lawyers Association, the organization of that supposedly corrupt group of trial lawyers. This is the only article that I could find describing such an experiment. I wonder if the insurance companies would tell their doctors, and the hospitals would tell their nurses, to follow this policy, would insurance rates go down? Has any other system of health care providers thought of this approach? This article was published by the American College of Physicians, not just some small potato. One of the widest-read publications in the medical world, on an experiment conducted by the largest healthcare system in the country. I wonder why we have not heard more about it. Is there some incentive in not allowing hospitals and doctors to be honest?

Look closely at the wording of the article, it says that the liability payments (amounts paid to injured victims) were about the same as those of similar facilities. The biggest benefit is this–according to the article, the **government saved around $250,000 in litigation expenses for each claim filed**. There were a total of 88 claims made during the seven-year period in which the experiment was conducted. The average **liability payment per claim was $15,622.** Doesn't that tell you that hospitals and doctors spend more money defending cases that they could easily and inexpensively settle, and still get the non-meritorious claims dismissed or win them?

Maybe businesses really know the truth, too!

Even some business publications have realized that some of the arguments of the tort reformers are without merit. For example, the March 3, 2004 issue of *Business Week* argued forcefully that jury awards are not the cause of the rise in the cost of malpractice premiums. In a Commentary entitled "A Second Opinion on the Malpractice Plague," *Business Week* cited conclusive evidence that state courts are not clogged with an explosion of malpractice claims, and that premium costs have not risen more slowly in states that have enacted damage caps. They concluded that, on these matters "and many other key points, proponents of caps simply aren't coming up with the facts to make their case."

Denver Post medical reporters Arther Kane and Allison Sherry, in a editorial series published in March of 2004, during the middle of the Colorado medical malpractice debate, discussed the effect that secrecy has on doctors malpractice. The maxim that "the public's business ought to be conducted in public" should be especially true of the Colorado Board of Medical Examiners, which investigates allegations of substandard medical care. Patients who entrust their lives to Colorado's 16,000 doctors have a right to know if their doctor has been disciplined.

In their exhaustive investigative series, "Buried Mistakes," *Post* reporters Arthur Kane and Allison Sherry spotlighted several egregious cases resulting in death or permanent disability for patients. According to their findings, only a minuscule percentage of doctors are disciplined every year, so there seems to be no epidemic of malpractice. But the board's secretive modus operandi (despite multiple red flags about bungling physicians) has failed to adequately warn the public. Acknowledging that a doctor's reputation is precious, some secrecy, especially in the early stages of probing a complaint, may be warranted, say the authors. But in many of the cases examined by Kane and Sherry, doctors who made inexcusable mistakes received only secret warning letters. It's also troubling that during the six years reviewed, the number of doctors allowed to surrender their licenses or retire was three times the total whose licenses were revoked. Revocation is a rarity in Colorado - no medical license was revoked in 2003.

Of 35 doctors disciplined after patients died between 1998 and early 2003, only one lost a license.

The board dismisses about 80 percent of the complaints it gets. Of 835 complaints in 2003, 732 didn't result in public discipline, and most were dismissed outright, Kane and Sherry discovered. Part of the problem may be that the workload could be too heavy for the board, which has only 11 full-time employees and 15 investigators (paid out of license fees) whom it must share with 27 other boards within the Department of Regulatory Agencies. Sharing investigators may be OK for passenger tramways or surveyors, but not for the medical board. Also, state law on medical mistakes is murky, and the public is left to trust the board's interpretations because hearings are closed to the public.

Improvements in medical technology needed

One of the things that everyone should agree upon, regardless of their positions on the other issues in this book, is the following proposition: Improvements in medical technology systems and medical information systems can help health care providers save lives. Just reading any major general periodical in the United States will highlight the amounts of work necessary to make improvements in these systems. What if we could find a way to make doctors and lawyers clasp hands, rather than bash heads, in an effort to work together to find ways to help your children and grandchildren?

One of the most common complaints that doctors and insurance companies have is that punitive damages (remember these are not the damages to compensate the victims, but serve to punish the reckless wrongdoers) are too frequent, too high and too useless. While there is obviously significant disagreement over that position, no one could dispute that a large measure of good could come from a system that provided for a portion of the punitive damages being utilized for scientific studies for improvement of medicine. The federal government spends billions of dollars every month on health care for our citizens. That money comes from your taxes.

Wouldn't it be nice, if every time a punitive damage award was paid by the insurance company for a reckless hospital or doctor, one of two things happened. Either (1) your tax dollars would be supplemented by money already paid by insurance premiums, or (2) additional money would go to a fund to study a cure for Alzheimer's, Lou Gehrig's disease, child leukemia, or mental health. Prescription drugs costs make up about 11% of all health costs - the second largest portion after hospital spending - and are projected by the Centers for Medicare and Medicaid Services to reach 14% in 2010. Despite these facts, the administration backed a Medicare bill that prevented the Medicare administrator from negotiating lower prescription drug costs. If punitive damages are awarded so often, wouldn't it have been better to support a bill that would divert some of these punitive damage funds to the public benefit?

One of the philosophical issues that is perplexing in the overall debate is the extent to which the federal government should inject itself into the medico-legal debate. Generally, conservative politicians and their constituents believe that the federal government should leave most of the legal system issues to the states. The outcry for federal tort reform is a major exception. There is no arguing the fact, though, that the federal government is already heavily involved in medicine. Medicare, funding for disease study, the National Institute of Health, and the National Center for Disease Control are all federally funded programs and entities. Punitive damage money deferral to one of these programs would not require neither new red tape nor new bureaucratic entity. Oversight and enforcement would be easy. Any payor defendant or insurance company would have every incentive to see that the appropriate amount of money went to the appropriate entity, rather than to the plaintiff or attorney that whipped their tail at the courthouse. Their conscious could even allow them to sleep better, since they contributed to medical research and information systems technology!!

<u>Malpractice premiums– a needle in the haystack of dollar bills</u>

How much of a doctor's revenue goes to malpractice insurance? A March 2002 government report by MedPAC, a congressional advisory commission, says doctors, on average, were expected to spend 3.2% of their revenue on malpractice insurance last year. That compares with 12.4% for staff salaries, 11.6% for office expenses and 1.9% for medical equipment. Calculations based on two surveys published by *Medical Economics* magazine - widely read by physicians–last year show that OB-GYN doctors paid the most for malpractice insurance, as a percentage of their revenue, 6.7%, and cardiologists paid the least, 1.5%.

Doctors and insurers say the lure of the big win prompts many to file frivolous suits. But a 1990 Harvard University study suggested that only one in eight victims of medical negligence ever files a claim. When they do, it's an uphill fight: Lawyers sometimes have trouble finding a local doctor who will testify to a colleague's mistakes, attorneys say, and jurors often are inclined to give a physician the benefit of the doubt. "If it clearly is not a meritorious case, I would have to be a blithering idiot to take that case on," says Dan Hodes, a Newport Beach, Calif., personal-injury lawyer. Plaintiffs' attorneys often must spend tens of thousands of dollars to prepare a suit, and they risk losing it all if the case fails and they get no contingency fee.

This is the third time the controversy over medical malpractice insurance has peaked in three decades. In the 1970's, federal wage-and-price controls limited how much insurers could raise rates. At the same time, inflation was high and the stock market was troubled. Carriers cut back on policy-writing or abandoned the market. The biggest problem for doctors is that the health care market has changed since the 1980s, making it much more difficult to pass higher insurance costs along to patients. That's because managed care insurers, Medicare and Medicaid all limit reimbursements.

At the same time, the congressional study reported that caps on pain and suffering awards would translate into very small savings - 0.4% - on overall health insurance premiums for the general public. That's not much, given that consumer health-insurance premiums are rising by about 15% a year. So, even if everyone has a damage cap of $250,000, your health insurance costs will not go down, they will continue to rise at the same rate that they have in the past.

Why should we tell juries what they are allowed to do, just so that we can assure that doctors can earn the type of living they would like to earn. James Foreman, a managing director at Towers Perrin, an employee benefits consulting firm, who sees every type of benefit in every market, says, "I have sympathy, but all of us are seeing increases in insurance, whether malpractice, health or homeowners'. Doctors are jumping on the bandwagon. Yet most are seeing an increase in their bottom-line pay. How many other businesses can say that today?" *Seattle–Post Intelligence,* March 22, 2004.

Caps on Damages do not work

The nation's largest malpractice insurance carrier, GE Medical Protective, was the biggest proponent of damage caps in the legislative session in Texas in 2003. During that debate, they continued to insist on the beneficial effect that would be seen on doctor's premiums if the cap was placed on non-economic damage. GE Medical Protective (yes, the same GE that is run by Jack Welch–they decided several years ago the medical malpractice insurance business would be profitable, but apparently it was not profitable enough), very shortly after the cap went into effect, filed for a rate hike. They told the Texas Department of Insurance that, "Non-economic damages are a small percentage of total losses paid. Capping non-economic damages will show loss savings of 1.0%." Medical Protective and other supporters of medical malpractice caps had repeatedly argued that damage awards were the primary reason for skyrocketing medical malpractice premiums. For example, in a March 2004 report, GE Medical Protective, one of the nation's largest malpractice carriers, claimed that capping economic damages is a "critical element [of reform] because in recent years we have seen noneconomic damages spiraling out of control."'"[from Health Care Crisis: Causes and Solutions].

Apparently the "out-of-control" they were referring to was about one percent of premiums collected. The Texas rate increase and the actuarial data submitted by the company contradicting the oft-stated importance of caps should lead policymakers to look to insurance regulation, rather than malpractice caps, as a solution to high premiums. GE Medical Protective also sought a 29.2% rate hike in California. However, because of California's system of insurance regulation, the hike was challenged, resulting in the company reducing its rate proposed increase by 60%. Unlike California's system, the Texas Insurance Commissioner, who disputed the need for Medical Protective's increase in that state, does not have the regulatory authority to block inappropriate rate requests. The way to reduce insurance rates is not caps on damages in lawsuits.

The right of patients to sue doctors, hospitals and HMO's for negligence does not raise insurance rates. Caps on damages were touted by the insurance industry and medical industry as a model "tort reform" for the nation. Doctors were told that the skyrocketing premiums they must pay to purchase malpractice insurance coverage would be reduced if such laws were enacted. Studies conducted during and after the 1980s "crisis" told a different story. The U.S. General Accounting Office, published a study of six states that had enacted many different forms of tort law restrictions during the "crisis" of the mid-1970s, including caps on compensation. The GAO report showed that the price of medical malpractice liability insurance in California had increased dramatically since the passage of MICRA. In fact, "premiums for physicians increased from 16 to 337 percent in southern California ... between 1980 and 1986."

A later, comprehensive review of insurance industry date spanning the period for 1976, when the California law took effect, through 1991, demonstrated that its restrictions did nothing to ease the cost of malpractice premiums. The average premium was higher than the national average in most years after passage of the cap. The total cost of malpractice insurance premiums paid as a percentage of total healthcare costs was higher in California than in the nation. There was no improvement in insurance premiums until the passage of Proposition 103. The report concluded that the chief effect of the caps was to enrich the insurance industry. See, U. S. General Accounting Office, Medical Malpractice: Six State Case Studies Show Claims and Insurance Costs Still Rise Despite Reforms. (Washington, D. C. ; U. S. Government Printing Office, 1986); National Insurance Consumer Organization, Medical Malpractice Insurance: 1985-1991 Calender Year Experience (Alexandria, Va; National Insurance Consumer Organization, March 1993, Exhibit 3, Sheet 1.

If the premiums will be lowered by caps on non-economic damages, then why have the states where the caps have been imposed not seen decreases in premiums for malpractice coverage? If insurance companies believe what they say, then why won't they open up their books and let people look at them so that we can see where the money goes?

If malpractice awards are the problem that the insurance companies say they are, why is it that the statistics show an entirely different picture? The only ones for whom large verdicts are really a problem are the repeating offenders of the medical world, who have not been weeded out because there are no teeth in the system that grants them the right to work on your body. Look at the experience of all of the states where caps have been placed. You see no benefit!!

Look at those doctors who have been repeat offenders. Why are they even able to get malpractice insurance? Look at Mr. Romero, at Kingwood Medical Center, in Houston, who was severely brain damaged when he nearly bled to death under the care of the nomadic drug addict. Why was this surgeon even allowed to change a bed pan, much less cut open a man's body and fiddle around with his spinal cord? When the case was over and the dust had settled, Mr. Romero was left with nothing left from his ordeal and a six-year long litigation trail. He had some of the finest, most well-respected lawyers, who have the respect of all who know them, and Mr. Romero's trip to the courthouse left him with that ruling that the hospital, who knew all of the sordid past of the surgeon, was, nonetheless, not responsible for his injury. NOT A DIME!!! Yet, the medical community has no shame in saying that people get too much money from the system!! That is rubbish, hypocrisy, and lies without any remorse. Yet, as you will see in the next Chapter, it is the trial lawyers that society loves to hate. What a propaganda machine the insurance companies have!

CHAPTER ELEVEN

PLAINTIFF'S LAWYERS -- YOU LOVE TO HATE THEM

It appears that malpractice defendants—rather than plaintiffs—may be somewhat too inclined to resist settlement and push cases to trial." 11 Merritt and Barry, "Is the Tort System in Crisis? New Empirical Evidence," 60 Ohio St. L. J. 315 (1999).

We no longer live in the time when small town lawyers deal with small-time issues, and everyone in town was everyone else's friend. That does not mean that real people with real issues can not be civil to one another, and treat each other with the respect that we each deserve. Lawyering has become commercialized, just like medicine, and lawyers tend to lose sight of the fact that our clients and the public do expect, and should expect, more personal service from us than what they get from an on-line catalog or the giant department store.

I would argue that lawyers, more than any other profession, owe the public, the courts and even their adversaries, a duty of care. That duty of care is to refrain from frivolous claims and frivolous defenses. That duty should include the obligation to investigate the merits of the claims and defenses that are made, so that everyone in the system can rely on the fact that both sides are acting in good faith.

There is a very ironic aspect of this argument. The trial lawyers who argue that the medical profession should be held to a duty of care to their patients, should also be held to a duty of care. That duty is the same whether the lawyer is working on behalf of the injured victim or on behalf of the health care provider. The duty of care encompasses, if you represent a plaintiff, making every effort possible to verify the allegations made in their charges against the defendant. It also encompasses, if you represent a defendant, making every effort possible to verify that the facts stated in the defense are accurate, and that true facts alleged by plaintiff be stipulated to and not challenged.

It would be inconsistent, hypocritical, and self-ridiculing for a plaintiff's lawyer to assert violations of duties by a doctor, if the lawyer has not performed a thorough investigation of the facts and medical issues.

Does Atticus Finch live any more?

There is a wonderful book written by a lawyer whom I have never met, but it is my goal that in my travels I will meet him soon. His name is Mike Pappatino, and he has written a book entitled In Search of Atticus. The main thesis of the book is that the lawyers of today have lost a great deal of their professionalism, their goodness, their sense of obligation to society and to their clients. Any person who has read Harper Lee's novel To Kill a Mockingbird has met the type of lawyer who has that professionalism, goodness and sense of obligation.

We can not turn back the hands of time. However, we can all be mindful that we sometimes overcompensate for the stress of modern-day law practice by exhibiting aggressiveness and rudeness to our clients and our adversaries. It is hard to be otherwise with all of the increasing pressures, but our continued reluctance to change may result in the loss of our clients' right and our own livelihood. Much of the current day rhetoric that results in tort reform is made possible by the fact that society holds lawyers in low esteem. In order to change that we all need to grasp hold of a higher self image that will promote better behavior; we need to make our personal lives and law practices more gratifying in some way other than our ability to make money; and we need to take time to let others know that good things that we attempt to do every day when we go to the office or the courthouse.

In his book, lawyer Mike Pappatino wrote of the results of a survey that he conducted, where he found that over three-fourths of the lawyers surveyed believed that they need to take more time to improve the quality of their lives. Over half of the respondents said that they had become less of a legal scholar and more of a businessman, and nearly fifty percent stated that they are much more suspicious of people than they were when they first started practicing. Even worse, with the stresses of such job dissatisfaction, distrust and frustration, how do we cope to try to keep ourselves functioning? A recent study of the American Bar Association says that 79% of us get anxious, 52% become more critical of ourselves, 65% of us do not exercise, and 88% do not practice any relaxation techniques. With such results, how can we expect the public to perceive us as anything more than a group of businessmen who look for nothing other than the bottom line, and do not care how it is we make that bottom line as good as it can be.

If we are dissatisfied, distrustful, cynical and frustrated, and most of us take no action to remedy those feelings, isn't it apparent that we create for ourselves a very negative image. Instead of choosing to interact with others with humility, grace and dignity, we feel forced to bring out the macho, Rambo tactics because we feel that is the only way to win, and winning is what it is all about. So again, what does the public see? It sees sees our profession selling itself for the bottom dollar to those who have been injured, and us bragging about our successes, rather than informing the public about how we serve society or our communities.

The art of peacemaking is outdated and becoming obsolete. Many courts now have practice of requiring either mediation or arbitration to try to resolve litigation. There is nothing wrong with either mediation or arbitration, since those devices do resolve a substantial number of the cases in the system, freeing judicial resources for other matters. However, it was not until the late 1980's that mediation and arbitration began to become widespread. Prior to that, the lawyers and their clients would find a way to come together and settle their cases, sometimes even on the "courthouse steps" on the way into trial. But nearly every substantial case in large metropolitan areas goes to some form of dispute resolution, because of the understood fact that the parties and their lawyers are incapable of discussing and analyzing their cases dispassionately and objectively.

       For the past three years, after I hung up my trial lawyer shoes, I began serving as a mediator for medical malpractice cases. I still do a fair amount of that work. What is often astonishing is the trivial matters that lawyers on both sides of the case can not find a way to agree upon. Mediation is supposed to be used as a tool to help the parties communicate and come to a fair resolution of the case. Often I find that a large part of the mediation session is wasted with the lawyers wrangling on minute procedural matters or semantic details, all in an effort to somehow get the upper hand or create a face for the other side. All of this is supposedly in the name of obtaining the best result for the client.

       Lawyer to client—"I may be a jerk, but I am your jerk!!"

       This expression is a selling point of some trial lawyers. Is it said facetiously? Perhaps. Is it meant to convey the impression that they are helping their clients by being difficult to get along with? Probably. Does it convey the public image that lawyers should want to convey? Absolutely not. Without being judgmental about whether such an expression should be used, it is clear that many clients have come to expect that if their lawyer is to do the best job that he or she can for the client, that lawyer must act like a sociopath.

There is not sufficient space in this book to discuss all of the reasons that society got where it is on the point of its attitudes toward lawyers in general and trial lawyers in particular. The event that I believe took the first bid step on that road is the case of Bates v. State Bar of Arizona,,434 U.S. 881, 98 S.Ct. 242, 54 L.Ed.2d 164 (1977), where the United States Supreme Court said that it is a violation of the freedom of speech to prohibit lawyer advertising. Until that decision in 1974, if a lawyer got recognition, it came from the value of his work, the recommendations of his peers, the satisfaction of his clients, and the goodwill that he established. All of a sudden, a lawyer could spend money to directly appeal to his chosen segment of desired clients. Thirty years later, we have TV ads for the "tough, smart lawyer," the "Texas hammer," and the lawyers "With the biggest verdict in the county."

I do not here express any opinion on the constitutional merit of the Supreme Court's decision in *Bates*. I am not a constitutional lawyer. I do not express an opinion on whether any or all of the lawyers who advertise heavily are or are not qualified, dignified, caring, or ethical. I believe that the ill wrought by the *Bates* decision is that the decision itself, and the industry that it begat, have given the public the perception that the practice of law is not different from any other profession. The public perception of lawyers went down precipitously in an extremely short period of time, historically speaking. That perception began a snowballing effect. The perception led to the reality. Once the public no longer set lawyers apart, then there was much less incentive for lawyers to set themselves apart. If the public believes that we are just like any other business, we might as well act like any other business and at least get the rewards of acting that way.

People (including some trial lawyers) do not understand medical malpractice cases

One of the things that I always believed when I was a practicing plaintiff's medical malpractice lawyer was that lawyers who did such work were as careful as I was about the cases that I accepted for prosecution. I have learned that is not always the case, even though most lawyers are very careful about having a sufficient basis for their claims. When I began to build my practice, I hired a full-time nurse to review every case that came in the door. That nurse had twenty years of experience in working in the medico-legal field. Her initial job on every case was to make a full investigation of the facts to determine whether it was a case in which the client really was hurt by negligence, as opposed to some acceptable judgment call made by the physician. If the nurse, through a complete evaluation of the medical literature on the subject, believed that the case had merit, we would next consult with a doctor whose credentials in the applicable area of medicine were unquestionable. If his opinion was that the proposed defendant did not commit a negligent act, we would not take the case.

This is what makes the system work. If there is no case, there is no case. There was a point in time years ago where a plaintiff's lawyer did not need to do anything more than get a client and then file the case. That is no longer the rule in most states. Most states now require that there be some showing of a consultation with a qualified physician who practices in the relevant area of medicine. Such requirements are good, but even if there is not such a requirement, the lawyer should always seek initial medical opinions. The reason? Lawyers are not doctors, and can not make medical judgments, any more than doctors can make legal judgments.

There are some lawyers, usually inexperienced and perhaps unethical, who will file a case without ascertaining that the client was really a victim of medical malpractice. That is a very rare occurrence, but it does happen, and when it does it can cause serious harm, both professional, emotional and financial.

Some of the cases for which I have served as a mediator were cases that should never have been brought. Other cases for which I served as a mediator were cases that the doctor or hospital had no meritorious defense. A problem always arises in both types of cases. A plaintiff's lawyer who really has no case, and a defense lawyer who really has no defense, is usually hard-pressed to admit the serious weaknesses in his case. It is a sad thing that any of these cases has to go beyond the first stage. Every moment of time of both parties, every night of sleeplessness, every day of worry, every minute of lawyer time, every minute of judge and court personnel time, and every ounce of energy spent on the case, is wasted.

If we could gather, bundle up and utilize, for some worthy purpose, all of the money, energy and emotion spent on cases with no merit or with no meritorious defense, society would have a great and useful tool at its disposal. All of those lawyers, making all of the spirited arguments, all wasting their time and their clients emotions. *It happens on both sides of the docket. No one has a monopoly on frivolity.* These cases are the ones that bring on the bad thoughts and comments about lawyers. These are the cases where a lawyer on at least one side of the case has not done his client a service.

A case is not necessarily frivolous just because it is not won by the plaintiff. How many doctors say their defense was frivolous just because the jury said the doctor was negligent? A judgment that the plaintiff has not proven his case does not mean that there was no basis for the suit. If there were no basis for the suit, the judge would have dismissed it long before it ever saw the courtroom with a jury in the box. There are numerous procedural remedies available to the defense that will take a frivolous case out of the system without a jury ever making a finding.

The vast majority of cases that are filed are the cases where the lawyers have done their work, in a system designed for such work to be done. These are the cases where there are good lawyers working on both sides of the case, doing the things that their clients and society charge them to do. They are trying to investigate and discover the facts, frame the legal and medical arguments, present the evidence to the jurors best suited to the task, before a judge qualified to adjudicate the process. These are the cases where the juries are doing their job in this country day in and day out, without any fanfare, without sufficient praise, and certainly without adequate monetary compensation.

Additional measures should be taken to promote legal efficiency, deter unwarranted conduct, and prevent the waste of precious resources. Every dollar spent to defend frivolous claims and every dollar spent to assert a frivolous defense is a dollar that could be spent on new medical technology, training for nurses, or double-checking to see that policies and procedures are followed. Many of the dollars that are spent on lawyer advertising is a dollar that could be spent on representation of the poor or on educating the public about the benefits of the legal system. The lawyers who go to the courtroom only so that they can claim that they got the biggest verdict are the lawyers that should be spending more of their dollars on a new law library for their law school.

What most people do not know is that many lawyers do give vast amounts of money and time on behalf of the poor, on legal education, and in pro bono work. What lawyers do not do is boast about those activities. Some of them boast, instead, about how good they are in the courtroom or what a great time they had chewing on an adverse expert witness. We have all been guilty of it, and it is not only unbecoming to us, but also detrimental to our clients in the long run.

No skid marks

You have probably heard the joke about the difference between the dead dog and the dead lawyer on the side of the road–there are no skid marks next to the lawyer. It is funny, but sad at the same time. What if you substituted for "lawyer" a member of a certain race, religion, sex or person of certain sexual preference? The question that I always ask when I hear a new lawyer joke is, "why and when did we get there?" My dad was a lawyer and his father was a lawyer (as well as Attorney General and Lieutenant Governor of Florida). My mother's grandfather and his brother were lawyers. My middle name, Townes, is the name of the building that houses the University of Texas School of Law–it was named after my great-great uncle. I have a long and proud history of lawyers in the family. Did my ancestor lawyers even know what lawyer jokes were? My dad told me he heard his first one a couple of years before he died in 1985.

We know that trial lawyers are one

of society's biggest stereotypes. Uncaring, money-grubbing, rich, immoral, and without any spiritual essence. The good Lord knows that I have been uncaring at times, I have been immoral on a few occasions, and I have been money-grubbing as well. Those are not the times that I have been most proud of myself. I would like to know how many people who read this book, or, just as an example, how many doctors, have never been any of those things. The basic religious tenets of most of the world's religions tell us that we have all sinned and come short of the glory of our own supreme being. Does that mean that we have no redeeming personal, spiritual, or social value? Does that mean that we have so little value that it's ok that we are killed without society shedding a tear for our souls? It seems strange and sad that it is ok to make these jokes. But what bothers me more is that I somehow feel that I am not allowed to come to the defense of my own profession without everyone saying that I am overly sensitive, and that it is "only a joke."

Not too long ago I was at a nice backyard barbecue (these are big in Texas) hosted by one of our local judges. In attendance were lawyers and non-lawyers. I sat at a table with one of my favorite court reporters and his date, along with some other gentlemen whom I did not know. The ballot provision which would impose caps on damages in medical malpractice cases was to be up for a vote in a few short weeks. While making casual conversation with one of the gentlemen I did not know, I was asked by him what I thought about the ballot provision. I gathered from his question, and some other conversation that I had overheard from him, that he was very much for the caps. I first confessed my sin of being a lawyer, then I told him very generally, briefly and gingerly how I felt about caps on damages. His reply was, "I'll tell you what–if I had to choose between killing my doctor and killing my lawyer I would kill my lawyer. In fact, I would rather save my plumber than my lawyer." I did not know what I had said to bring on such a comment. For the next several days, the hate in his tone, which I accepted as being truly sincere, continued to ring in my mind. I still wish I knew exactly where that hatred came from. Trouble is, some people hate you even though they never have met you, and you can not change that, if you are a lawyer. I could never pretend that I could even come close to feeling as the African Americans felt in the south of the 1950's and 1960's, but I decided that I would try to make something positive from the backyard barbecue experience–I would try to use it to help me understand how persecuted people must feel when bigotry shows its ugly face.

There are, obviously, countless differences, both in number and intensity, between the prejudice against lawyers and that prejudice that has so stained other periods of our history. One thing that is vastly different is this–lawyers have, to an extent, brought some of the venom and vitriol upon ourselves. We are, by comparison to many others, very fortunate in our economic situation, and in our capability to help other people. Many of us have not used these capabilities as we should have for the benefit of others, either in *pro bono* work, in reduced fee work for the underprivileged, or in giving of our financial resources to worthy causes. Ironically, though, this lack of motivation is not most prevalent among trial lawyers, who have given countless hours, money and free work to underprivileged. My local trial lawyers association has, for some fifteen years, had more volunteers at the Habitat for Humanity housing projects than any other organization in town. I haven't seen many banking, real estate, corporate or securities lawyers working there.

As we discussed in Chapter One, any system of laws must generate from its people's knowledge of morality and right, regardless of how the public perceives lawyers. That knowledge gives legitimacy to the laws, creating not only the incentive to abide by them, but the spirit to understand them, and the humanity to apply them in given situations. In Chapter Twelve, we will talk about some things that will help us achieve that legitimacy; in Chapter Thirteen, we will see the value of those morals, and their place in this important debate.

CHAPTER TWELVE

CAPS ON DAMAGES WILL NOT HELP ACCESS TO THE HEALTH CARE SYSTEM

53 percent of the 15 states with the worst access to primary care impose medical malpractice damage caps; 60 percent of the 15 states with the best access to primary care do not have medical malpractice damage caps.
Health Professional Shortage Area database maintained by the
Bureau of Primary Health Care,
U.S. Department of Health and Human Services

      We have been discussing the causes of the complaints about the civil justice system. Any improvements in the system must be aimed at the problem. As you can see from prior chapters, I believe that the changes should start with the insurance companies. But, let's talk about the jury first, just to analyze what could be done from that end. Any system of jurisprudence that has a jury as the primary fact-finder must, obviously, rest upon the integrity of that jury.

In order to be able to depend upon the integrity of the jury, we must be able to take two propositions as given. First, that each juror is unbiased in its perception of the facts and resolution of the issues. That is, that each juror is subject to intense and unlimited questioning into his motives, biases, prejudices, predisposition and attitudes. I have previously mentioned the book, <u>To Kill a Mockingbird.</u> Anyone familiar with the storied trial of Tom Robinson, a poor, black man on trial for the alleged rape of a southern white woman in the early twentieth century, understands the importance of a system that allows unlimited challenges to jurors whose predisposition is for one side of a case over the other.

The second proposition that should be given in the makeup of a juror, and indeed in the composite jury, is that there should be the capacity to understand the factual issues that are in dispute in the case. That is the proposition, I believe, one of the matters that is the most difficult for us to achieve in our system as it is currently designed. That is because jurors are now simply called upon to make decisions that are far more complex than many that they made in earlier days. We all know that stop signs are to be heeded, and thus a juror knows that it is negligent to run a stop sign. We all know that a speed limit is posted on a highway because it sets the standard for the behavior of the motorists traversing that highway. Thus, when a jury is asked to judge whether a motorist was negligent in the operation of his automobile on that highway, a jury is well within its capability to render an answer to that question.

If we put a juror's mind to different, and more complex tasks, however, we go a step beyond what is within the ordinary capability of a lot of people. That is not to say that jurors are not smart people. I believe that they are and that we can not function without them. But, what they are asked to do in medical malpractice cases is to carry a heavier load than what they carry in a car wreck case.

Take, as an example, a case where the question is whether a neurosurgeon was negligent in causing a microscopic tear in the lining of the spinal canal during the course of a lengthy surgery to repair a ruptured disc in a patient's spine. Or take the example of a jury decision over whether a pediatric cardiovascular surgeon used the wrong approach to reach the constricted portion of the descending aorta, and thus did not appropriately suture the vessel together at the conclusion of the surgery. I have handled each of those cases. When those cases are prosecuted, the plaintiffs will undoubtedly have an expert witness to testify that the allegedly offending surgeons were negligent in the manner in which they undertook to accomplish the tasks they assumed. Then, each of the defendants in these two cases, the neurosurgeon and the pediatric cardiovascular surgeon, will also undoubtedly have their own expert witnesses to express the contrary opinions.

How is the average lay juror to answer this question? Answer it, he must, however, under the system in place in all jurisdictions in our nation. So, what tools does that juror utilize to assist in the exercise? What procedural safeguards are there to assure that he is properly equipped to answer the question? What substantive rules of law exist to enhance the probability that the input given to the juror will be pure, unbiased, logical, accurate and complete?

These are the questions that the lawmakers should be asking. We should be finding the best ways for the jurors to work in their tasks toward the ultimate goal. We should be looking for the laws that will go the farthest toward assuring the best process by which the juror receives information, assesses that information, and comes to his final conclusion for the right verdict.

Let us first ask the threshold question that serves as the basis for the whole controversy. Is there anything wrong with the current jury system when it comes to the adjudication of disputes over the quality of healthcare? Looking back at the first three chapters of this book, you can see that the system is not nearly as broken as some would have you believe. However, because we know that there are abuses in the system, and because we know that there is a large amount of mistrust of juries and lawyers by those in the medical profession, we know at the least that some changes should be considered in order to put some degree of trust back into the system that is often thrust upon the unwilling participant, for at least two reasons.

First, and most directly, if doctors do not trust the jury system, they will necessarily engage in what is commonly called "defensive medicine," which means that they will undertake many unnecessary tests and procedures, at an unnecessarily large cost, in order to avoid subsequent criticism that they did not do all that they could have done to detect certain disease processes or deter some unwanted condition. Some might argue that defensive medicine is not necessarily a bad thing, because it could be said that we want to encourage all testing, since even a slight risk of remote harm warrants additional testing, no matter what the cost. However, many physicians will tell you that they have at least a subconscious fear, or perhaps a predisposition, that they should do some things that are unwarranted or unnecessary based upon the risk/reward balance, in order to avoid potential liability. If good doctors are to have the ability to use their professional judgment to determine what tests should be done (unfettered by HMO's or other corporate interference), then the arbitrary watchful eye of a subsequent, inquisitive and retrospective jury should not be allowed to affect that judgment.

The second benefit of all parties having trust in the system is much more indirect, yet altogether, I believe, real and pervasive. One of the outrageous and unnecessary costs of the process of adjudication of healthcare disputes is what I will call the frivolous defensive litigation cost. The cost that I attribute to the lawyers for the healthcare providers leaving no stone unturned in the scorched earth litigation practice. Law firms that defend healthcare providers, without exception, base their fees solely on the amount of time that they take to defend the plaintiff's claims. The more tools of defense they utilize, the more money they make. What this often turns out to be is a lawyer, or often a large team of lawyers, writing themselves a blank check at the time that they open their litigation file at the beginning of the case, knowing that the doctor, who almost always takes the position that nothing was done wrong, will want the toughest defense he can possibly obtain. This is even more the case in lawsuits against healthcare providers because these cases, as a general rule, involve more serious injuries than other, non-medical malpractice cases.

In smaller cases, the cost of defense is more apt to be kept under control, because an ultimate loss will result in a smaller payment being made by the insurance company. But in large injury cases, with the potential for a large jury verdict, the defense is ultimately willing to spend whatever is necessary to try to make the plaintiff take the wrong course, or to create opportunities for the plaintiff to trip up.

One interesting phenomenon is the extent to which a large defense expenditure is justified solely on the mistrust of the system itself. After all, if the litigants do not trust the jury to be fair, or they believe that somehow an unfair result will obtain at the conclusion of the case, then there is additional incentive to spend whatever is necessary to deter the opposition. When there is no impetus for respecting the system at all, and thus no incentive to rely on the system to achieve a just result, one will do more to bring about a result that will take the jury out of the case. When you think that the system is somehow cheating you, then you believe that you need to cheat first, in order to lessen the effects of the cheating system.

Just in human terms, without regard for the jury system, if you think that I am going to do everything I can to see that you lose everything that you have, then you will do all that you can to see that I get the opposite result. The quest becomes a game in itself, with the process taking a back seat to the needs and desires of the participants. This is not what judicial process should be, at all.

The judicial process should be there to benefit the adjudication of the dispute and promote a just outcome. It is not there to be used as a game to see who can manipulate it to their best advantage. Who can say where it all started, and who can say when it will end? I truly believe that, unless we are able to get some trust and respect back for the process itself, and the results that it achieves, then we will ultimately have nothing left to strive for, and the question of what type of system we have to help the injured and protect the innocent will no longer be the question. The question will then be who can make the best political use of the public attitude toward the process, in order to legislate the largest benefit for themselves.

I believe that we should not be looking, as the insurance companies tell us, for ways to lessen the monetary awards, to lower the cost of doing business for doctors and hospitals, or to assure that insurance companies are able to make a profit in their investments. We should be looking for ways to maximize the integrity of the jury process and thus maximize the potential for the right result.

How does one define "the right result?" Each side always believes that it is right. The only way to define "right" in this system of jurisprudence is the result that is the most predictable and just in a broad range of circumstances. The only real way to measure "right" in any given case would be to take fifty experts in the subject matter, give them all of the facts without any fluff, advocacy, or hyperbole, and have them answer the question given the jury, with the outcome being the answer given by the large majority of those fifty experts. That manner of decision is, obviously, unavailable in our justice system.

There are many decisions that are

made by juries in cases where the subject matter at issue is not one upon which there are as many as fifty experts in the entire country, and even if there were, no one would pay all of them to come and give their testimony.

So, do we simply say that because it is difficult to come up with a right answer to the negligence question, we will simply do away entirely with the jury system? Do we simply say that the jury's answer is so unpredictable that we will just declare that they are going to be limited to a certain pre-assigned sum of money, regardless of the seriousness of the injury and its effects on the human? Do we simply outlaw anyone making claims for damages for medical malpractice, only because the issues in medical malpractice cases are more cumbersome and complex than those in claims for damages occurring in automobile collisions?

These can not be the answers to the problem, whether the problem be one of crisis proportions or not. Medicine is infinitely more complex than it was just thirty years ago. Why else would there be as many specialists and sub-specialists as there are? As society becomes more complex, so do its rules of engagement, otherwise known as laws. As I stated in the preface to this book, changes in society are necessarily mirrored in its laws and their application. Do we give up on having laws just because the task is more difficult than it was in the past? Should we have a rule that says that, because the adjudication of disputes in a court of law is becoming more complex, we are not going to allow access to the courts for adjudication of those disputes any longer? Should we have a declaration that, because we want to keep doctors from leaving practice, we are going to look the other way when our citizens are maimed by healthcare that does not meet a reasonable standard of quality? Who and what are we protecting? Should we, in order to avoid inconvenience to good doctors, protect those who render poor quality healthcare, at the expense of those who are wrongfully injured?

These are the answers that are being pushed upon the public, and the public now seems to be more and more willing to accept those answers. But what about when you or your loved one is the victim of the doctor who cuts off the wrong leg, removes the healthy instead of the cancerous lung, or gives your child a life in a wheelchair? Will you then wish that you, and the lawmakers chosen by you and for you, made an effort to find the better answers to the problem. Isn't that what lawmakers are for? Aren't we supposed to find the answers to the problem, rather than just pretend that the problem does not exist? Or worse yet, should we implement a policy devastating to the most severely injured, when that policy is not anywhere near the answer to the problem?

We know that we have a health care system that has errors occurring at an rate much higher than we desire, at a cost of hundreds of thousands of human lives, but most of us choose to ignore that fact because they have not yet suffered as a result of it.

One way to keep HMO's from making decisions that should really be made by doctors is to require them to make their treatment guidelines public. Although that will not make them legally responsible for making the wrong decisions, it will at least allow doctors and their patients to know what it is they are fighting against. One case, again obviously brought by a dreaded trial lawyer, was for that very purpose. In California, according to a January 24, 2003 article in the *New York Times*, Kaiser Permanente, the US' largest nonprofit HMO, will publish guidelines used by its doctors for treatment of hundreds of diseases. This is a result of 2 lawsuits filed by consumer groups over patient care.

<u>Whose remedy should we use?</u>

We know from the earlier chapters in this book that doctors fail to police their own; that insurance companies try to skew the facts on their profits and costs; and that they fabricate stories of frivolous lawsuits. What can we do to help people have affordable, high-quality health care, as well as the ability to obtain some justice when they have been negligently harmed by the care of their physician or hospital?

First, we need to make everyone aware of the extent of the problem. Remember the study of the National Institutes of Health finding that nearly 100,000 patients were killed each year by hospital error, along with significant injuries of much more substantial proportions? There is now a study of what doctors and the public believe about those findings. Vol.347:24; pp.1933-1940; (December 12, 2002) of the *Journal of the Department of Health Policy and Management*, Harvard School of Public Health, Boston.. In the national survey of 831 practicing physicians, who responded to mailed questionnaires, and 1207 members of the public, who were interviewed by telephone after selection with the use of random-digit dialing, respondents were asked about the problem of preventable medical errors. Thirty-five percent of the physicians and forty-two percent of the public reported errors in their own or a family member's care, but neither group viewed medical errors as one of the most important problems in health care today. A majority of both groups believed that the number of in-hospital deaths due to preventable errors is lower than that reported by the Institute of Medicine. The public and many physicians supported the use of sanctions against individual health professionals perceived as responsible for serious errors.

One conclusion that can be drawn from this survey is that most people do not believe that they really could get hurt by error. If they do not believe that they can get hurt, then why would they even believe that we need to have the doctors and hospitals making efforts to reduce error. Secondly, if no one perceives the extent of medical error that has been proven, no one is going to be emotionally charged to believe that their right to sue over injury should be preserved. People do not want to have even the subconscious belief that medical error could ruin their lives. But, it does ruin lives. When it hurts one person, it often ruins the lives of multiple people, and ultimately harms the public in the form of cost of medical care and loss of contributions to society.

The public also needs to know that the issue is being raised again and again by the supporters of tort reform. They are not going to go away. Republicans vowed to highlight the issue again later in the year the last time it was defeated in the U. S. Senate. The backers of the measure, which would curb jury awards in medical liability cases against obstetricians and gynecologists, fell only twelve votes short of the 60 necessary to have the bill considered by the Senate. The final vote, 48 to 45, fell mostly along party lines. "We're going to keep going until we succeed," said Senator Elizabeth Dole, Republican of North Carolina, at a news conference before the vote. Senator/Doctor Bill Frist of Tennessee, the majority leader, said after the vote, "I want to keep the issue out there, because I think patients are being hurt." How right he is about that!!

With doctors around the country complaining bitterly that the rise in liability insurance premiums is forcing them out of business, Republicans, including President Bush, have made a revision of malpractice law a central part of their tort law agenda. But the effort, which has met with success in the House, is gaining less traction in the Senate. "Our medical litigation system is failing the American public," Dr. Frist, a surgeon, said in introducing the bill. He added, "The ultimate victims are the patients who see that their access to care is being threatened, and in some cases their access to care is disappearing." If you choose to agree with Dr. Frist, do so only because you have researched and understood his claims, and have considered thoroughly all of the potential causes of the situation, the effects of the situation, and the effects of the changes sought.

There are those who know that the bill would strip patients of their right to legal recourse, and they said that the supporters, in bringing the measure up for consideration without a committee hearing, were simply playing politics. "Here is a bill that would take a chain saw to the legal rights of the American people," said Senator Patrick J. Leahy of Vermont, the senior Democrat on the Senate Judiciary Committee. He added, "It is an election year and their lobbyists came up and said we really want this bill, so here it is." The lobbying on both sides has been intense, with doctors and business groups, a traditional constituency of Republicans, pushing hard for the legislation, and consumer advocates and trial lawyers, who traditionally back Democrats, fighting hard against. In an interview, Senator Orrin G. Hatch, Republican of Utah and chairman of the Senate Judiciary Committee, acknowledged that in forcing a vote, Republicans were trying to highlight what they regard as the influence trial lawyers have on Senate Democrats. Saying it was impossible to overcome the trial lawyers' lobby, Mr. Hatch said, "The only way we're going to get that done is to have them vote time after time after time."

A fix for frivolity

Yes–there is a problem in that some people think of a lawsuit as the first answer when they believe that they have been wronged. Any one person thinking that is one person too many. After all–the lady who "spilled coffee in her own lap" was made a millionaire!! (We now know the fallacy of the McDonald's argument). Reading only the headlines, it seems that everyone else around us is being compensated, or as some would put it, rewarded, for unfortunate events or circumstances.

There are those plaintiffs that rationalize that we see the federal government handing out trillions of dollars to welfare recipients, so each of us should get some money, and a lawsuit sounds like a good way. Why not file a suit to get our own turn at society's trough, when we read in the paper that the officers of large corporations fraudulently made off with billions of dollars of others' retirement funds, but are yet to be brought to trial? Let's just swing our bats for the fences--look to the "lawsuit lottery," and society will be none the worse for it. That is, in fact, the mentality of some who came to me in my private practice as a plaintiff's trial lawyer.

Unfortunately and undeniably, there

are those who think that way and there are those lawyers who take advantage of that mentality. Should the answer, therefore, be that we just punish everyone who thinks about filing a lawsuit and we can do away with the problem; or should it be that we advance and enact rules of law that will punish and deter such thinking and such actions, while preserving the rights of the vast majority of moral and right-thinking people whose lives have been disrupted and destroyed by errant, negligent, or reckless wrongdoing?

As a trial lawyer and businessman, the money that was the hardest for me to part with was the money that I paid, prior to accepting a case for prosecution, to obtain an opinion from an expert on the merits of the case. But, that money was the most important money that I could spend. Why? Because it did not behoove me to accept a case that was not meritorious. Looking again at the statistics showing such low chances of success in medical malpractice cases, I knew that I must refuse cases without merit. No client could change my mind, no matter how much he was looking for the "lottery," and no matter how just he thought his cause. Just like doctors, lawyers can not be compelled to represent people they do not want to represent, and the vast majority of trial lawyers do not take cases unless they believe they have at least a real chance of legitimate success.

Despite the hostility of some toward our federal judiciary, our United States Supreme Court has rendered some decisions (binding on state courts) which place severe restrictions on the types of opinions that expert witnesses can express. If a court is not convinced that the opinion is reliable, based upon sound science and proven facts, that court must refuse to allow that testimony. Since the outcome of every medical malpractice case depends upon expert witness testimony, there is already built-in protection from baseless claims.

There is no reason why each of the states, if there is a problem with frivolous cases in that state, cannot be flexible, innovative, creative and fair in interpretation and application of the rules pertaining to expert testimony. Judges are well-equipped to listen to expert testimony and perform the role of "gatekeeper" to decide whether a witness's opinion is one that is supported by science, reason and facts. If it is not, then the non-meritorious case never makes its way to a jury decision.

Wouldn't it be better, rather than having a rule that inhumanely limits the recovery of even the most horrendously injured malpractice victim, to rely upon our state court judges, the vast majority of whom are right-minded, and currently a large number of whom are conservative? They can and do keep frivolous cases from hurting the system or its participants. Wouldn't it be better, rather than giving the same treatment to all cases, when we know that each case is different, to give individual treatment to each person seeking justice, whether plaintiff or defendant?

Let's look at two hypothetical cases. Case # 1–A plaintiff is injured because he tried to get out of bed in the hospital, in violation of the doctors orders. That plaintiff has to spend an additional $2,000 on medical care, losing two months of work, and then getting completely back to normal. The plaintiff's lawyer hires an expert witness who says the right thing for the plaintiff-- this expert testifies, and the jury hears, that the plaintiff's injury was caused by hospital error. Assuming that this jury is one of those rarities that the tort reformers loathe–a jury less than capable, that somehow wants to punish hospitals. That jury awards $250,000 to the plaintiff–far above the amount reasonable to compensate that plaintiff. That verdict will stand, even with caps on damages, if no judge will change the result.

Case #2–A different plaintiff is injured in the same hospital because a nurse forgot to set up an oxygen monitor. That plaintiff, a 42-year old homemaker, is brain damaged when the oxygen delivery system fails and she is not properly oxygenized for twelve minutes. The experts on both sides agree that it was negligent for the nurse to fail to set up the oxygen monitor, and that the injury was caused by this error. Her maximum recovery, under the tort reformers proposals, is $250,000. In fact, because of all of the required expert testimony costs of this suit, and lawyer's fees, she will probably be left with less than $100,000.

These two cases cover the wide

spectrum of possible cases, both in the types of negligence and the resulting injuries. It is obvious from the juxtaposition of the two cases, that the tort reformers rule is unfair to the brain-damaged homemaker. It is equally obvious that the result in Case #1 is not fair to the hospital. Shouldn't we try to frame a rule that maximizes the opportunity for the judge in Case #1 to deter the injustice to the hospital, and maximizes the opportunity for the judge (perhaps even the same judge) in Case #2 to deter injustice to the brain-damaged homemaker? That rule would not be a cap of $250,000 on non-economic damages. That rule should be one giving the judge the power, and in fact the obligation, to refuse to allow the expert in Case #1 to testify, or to limit the amount of recovery. More can be done with this power and obligation than any other, to disrupt and deter the possibility of the injustice of frivolous lawsuits.

Assuming that most would agree that we should attempt to enact the laws appropriate to the task of preserving the rights and punishing wrongdoing, how do we best accomplish that? First, we need to understand and differentiate between fact and fiction. We learned in Chapters Two, Three Four and Five that all lawsuits are not frivolous, that healthcare providers do, in fact, kill or maim hundreds of thousands of people every year, and that medical malpractice lawsuits have some rules that are different from those rules in other cases. We also learned that there is a small minority of doctors and hospitals that have the most severe and largest number of malpractice claims. Those are the facts. It is fiction that "insurance carriers are going broke from having to pay too many claims," or that "good doctors are closing their doors because they can't afford to pay for malpractice premiums."

Shouldn't we preserve a place for meritorious claims against negligent healthcare providers, leaving open the possibility that special rules and consideration be implemented and placed to assure the most fair, reliable and just outcome? If that is the way we go about promoting fair results, then we must find the rules that will promote that end.

Virtually all of the claims of medical malpractice are litigated in the state courts, since there are no federal statutes whose interpretation is involved and these disputes are almost exclusively between residents of the same state (and thus there is no federal court jurisdiction that would enable the case to be brought in federal courts). So it is the state legislatures that must create the experiments that will determine what we can do to best effectuate just outcomes in these cases. One of the cornerstones of our *Constitution* is that state legislatures are given the latitude to try their own approaches, within certain constitutional constraints, to solving the problems that their citizens face.

We can take a look at the experience of the state of California in the 1970's and see that placing ceilings on damages does not bring down the insurance premiums, which is the only real crisis of which most people speak currently. But if we are to try to make a system that will be respected more by all, and thus lend itself to less defensive medicine and defensive litigation practices, we should try to create a system that is efficient for both sides, while still leading to the best chance for the result which could be achieved if submitted to those fifty unknown and anonymous experts.

Along with the criticism of the juries, a pervasive theme of the tort reformers is that the expert witnesses who are called upon in the trial of these cases will say anything in order to receive their expert witness fees. As one judge put it in a notorious case, the notion is that an expert, for the right amount of money, will testify to such things as "the moon is made of green cheese." So, one area for potential review and reform is the way in which experts are utilized, and the effect that they have on the jury and its ability to render decisions. But the tort reformers want only one rule–limit the amount a jury can award, no matter how serious the injury. They do not want, however, brain-damaged victims, supported by scientifically sound expert testimony from learned and honest witnesses, to be given the right to have even a modest amount of money to try to put their lives or the lives of their loved ones, back together.

Real and powerful sanctions for real and powerful results

There is a remedy that judges have that is not used nearly as often as it should be used. It is the imposition of some penalties or punishment for actions of lawyers that are done with disruptive intent. These remedies are known as sanctions. They can be imposed against lawyers or parties, and can be in the form of money or contempt actions (resulting in jail time or other retribution such as community service). The range of conduct that can result in sanctions is vast. The range of willingness of judges to impose sanctions is also vast, and many would say that judges are far too reluctant to impose sanctions. I believe that removing such reluctance would go a long way toward reducing frivolous claims, frivolous defenses, and frivolous procedural actions.

The types of conduct for which judges should impose sanctions differs from state to state, but it is generally conduct that serves no useful purpose toward finding or presenting the truth, and is only done to harass, intimidate, or badger the opponent. One good example of such conduct occurred in Dixon Klein's case–once Dr. Lye's lawyers figured out that the evidence was getting worse and worse for them, they apparently determined that they should become as much trouble for the plaintiff as they possibly could. One of the ways that they could do that was to file as much paper as possible, requiring Dixon's lawyers respond. This is often a good way defense lawyers have of trying to force the plaintiff and plaintiff's lawyer to give up, or to settle the case for less than they should.

One of the techniques that the defense used in Dixon's case was to file what is known as "Requests for Admission." This tool was at the time a tool under the Texas Rules of Civil Procedure that was intended to give the parties a way to limit the issues to those that are genuinely in controversy, so that the parties will not waste time obtaining proof of things that will not be disputed. However, they are not intended to be a tool to waste the time of the other side. When the defense filed a fifty-three page document containing one hundred and seventy-two requests, most of which were related to things in no way pertinent to the issues in the case, I picked up the phone, offered to answer the relevant requests and asked them to withdraw those requests that were burdensome and irrelevant.

The defense lawyer refused, necessitating another hearing, wasting the court's and lawyer's time. On that occasion, I filed a "Motion for Sanctions," which asked that the court fine the lawyers for defense for the harassing use of discovery tools. That motion was the only time in my career that I had ever had to file such a motion, but the conduct of the defense lawyers was such that I could not ignore it. It was not until the hearing on the motion for sanctions that the requests for admission were withdrawn by the defense lawyers.

One of the tools that courts often use

to help expedite the litigation process is called "Alternate Dispute Resolution." Alternate Dispute Resolution comes in different forms, but the most common one is called Mediation. Mediation is a process where all the parties to a lawsuit, and their lawyers, appear together for a conference before a mediator. The mediator servers as a communication facilitator, to determine if there is a way that the parties can agree on a resolution of their case. The mediator does not have the authority to make any decisions, or to require the parties to do anything. He only tries to make all of the parties see all of the good and bad to all sides of the case, so that they can try to agree on a settlement.

A mediation session was held in the Dixon Klein case. In fact, there were two separate mediation sessions held. On both occasions, it was the defendant that requested that there be a mediation session. Each of those sessions lasted one full day. Each session required that the parties pay a mediator, costing $2,000 per session. Each session required the attendance of all of the lawyers and the parties for a full day. Dixon took off work, as did his wife who was now working to eventually try to help replace the stream of income that Dixon was losing. However, after two full days of mediation, with all of the expense and time required, the defendants never made an offer of even one dollar to settle the cases, even though they were the ones who requested that mediation be scheduled. So all of the time and money for lawyers and the mediator were wasted. Nothing was accomplished.

I later found out that the reason nothing was offered in settlement is that the two defendants were arguing about which one should offer more than the other one. You see, Dr. Lye was a defendant because he is the one that did not do the test, and the owner of the clinic was a defendant because he owned the clinic and did not require that a tonometer test be done. So, it was not the plaintiff that was causing all of the expense in the case, it was the defendants who could not see eye about how to settle the case. A ridiculous waste of time, money, and resources. This type of bad faith conduct should be considered as a basis for sanctions, but because of the fact that I knew the Court would not grant a motion for sanctions, I saw no reason to file one.

I would like to say that this conduct could be described as "unbecoming a lawyer," but unfortunately it is becoming far too like some lawyers. I previously mentioned a book by Ralph Nader, entitled *No Contest*. Nader does an excellent, thorough and factually detailed analysis of some of the problems of our legal system that he believes are brought about as a result of the behavior of powerful corporations and their powerful law firms.

In a section entitled "ABC's of Discovery Abuse," Nader describes the plight of two people who were unfortunate enough to have their case delayed for ten years as a result of abusive tactics of the defense team. Michele Shephard and LaRue Graves, graphic artists in the Washington,

D.C. bureau of ABC news, both African-American, participated one day in a meeting of several employees, the purpose of which was to discuss minority grievances. These types of meetings are protected under federal law. The meeting was held with the knowledge of ABC executives and notices of the meeting were posted in the bureau's office hallways. The meeting was to be private. Soon thereafter Graves was fired, and Shepherd claimed that her supervisor refused to relieve her from an overly demanding work schedule.

They both filed suit, claiming that ABC retaliated against them for participating in the minority meeting. D.C.'s 230-lawyer firm, Wilmer, Cutler and Pickering, one of the most powerful in town, represented ABC. That firm is headed by William Cutler, former White House Counsel to both Presidents Carter and Clinton. After three and one-half years of discovery and delay, the plaintiff's lawyer filed a motion for sanctions, alleging that Wilmer, Cutler had altered a document produced in discovery and had harassed two potential witnesses.

The trial judge, United States District Judge Royce C. Lamberth, held a hearing lasting four days, hearing testimony regarding the allegations of the motion for sanctions. The evidence produced was that ABC management induced an employee from the personnel department to attend the minority meeting and report back to management. The evidence at the hearing showed that the employee reported to his supervisor, who wrote a memo to her superiors. When that memo was produced to the plaintiff's lawyer, it made no reference to either of the plaintiffs being at the meeting. However, the secretary who typed the memo recalled that it did mention the presence of at least Plaintiff Shepherd.

The plaintiffs also presented evidence that a Wilmer, Cutler attorney, partner Stephen Hut, had approached a potential witness in the case, another employee in the graphics department. Although the woman had told other lawyers for BC that she did not want to talk about the case, Hut came to her office at lunchtime, with her co-workers around her, asked for a meeting with her, and used words and demeanor that she perceived as harassing.

The plaintiffs waited three years for the judge's ruling, which turned out to be a blistering attack, finding "flagrant misconduct" by ABC and its lawyers, which mandated "imposition of the most severe sanctions for abuse of the judicial process." That did not deter ABC and its lawyer. They added another firm to their arsenal: Miller, Cassidy, Larocca &Lewin, with a reputation for being able to get a client out of a tight jam. As if that was not enough legal firepower to fight off the allegations of two workers and their one lawyer, two ABC management officials who were named in the suit hired the 115-lawyer firm of Williams & Connolly, whose $645,000 per annum of profits per partner tops the D.C. list.

The ABC lawyers were gearing up for a fight. They appealed Judge Lamberth's decision to the D.C. Circuit Court of Appeals. On August 25, 1995, two months shy of the meeting leading to the dispute, that Court overruled Judge Lamberth, in an opinion written by Judge David Tatel, who was appointed to the Court one year earlier, while Lloyd Cutler (ABC's lead lawyer) was White House Counsel, advising President Clinton on judicial appointments. In other words, the Judge deciding ABC's lead counsel's ethics was recommended for his job by that very lawyer. Judge Tatel had been a partner at the 327-lawyer Hogan and Hartson, the city's largest firm.

Nader points out an interesting contrast in the case tactics of ABC. Only four days before their victory in the discrimination suit, ABC had settled defamation lawsuits brought against it by tobacco companies R.J. Reynolds and Phillip Morris, by paying the tobacco companies attorney's fees of $15 million, and issuing an apology. The allegedly defamatory story was produced by Pulitzer Prize winner Walt Bogdanich, who insisted that his reporting (claiming that the tobacco companies "spiked" their cigarettes extra nicotine from outside sources) was accurate. Even First Amendment experts have stated that ABC was bullied into apologizing for a true story. As Nader points out:

> "It was worth trying to wear down two former employees and their solo practicing lawyer, even after a federal judge had found egregious conduct on ABC's part. But it was

not worth fighting another tenacious corporate opponent, even when ABC's position was solid and a grave matter of public health was at issue. So Phillip Morris got an apology, while Shepherd and Graves got a fight."

It seemed to me that it was worth spending over two pages on some of the details of this case, in order to point out how the system is full of opportunities for abusive, delaying, obstructionist, and verging-on-corrupt conduct. Each state has different rules in place for appointment or election of judges, for dealing with abusive and harassing conduct, and for imposing sanctions on offending lawyers.

While we often hear of the "wealthy" trial lawyers who are alleged to control the system, the public is not told about the 300-member firms of the big cities, or even the 50lawyer firms of the medium-sized cities, whose lawyers are at least as pervasive at the receptions for judicial candidates or appointees. Judges are not easily corrupted, but they are human, as are the lawyers who appear before them; they often find it difficult to impose sanctions on the lawyers who help them get or keep their benches, or who play golf at the same country club.

Why are insurance carriers the only unregulated business?

Doctors' medical malpractice premiums are at an all-time high because of several factors. Those rates can be made more fair by the states controlling the rate that doctors may be charged for malpractice insurance. Doctors who have had a good record should be rewarded for their records, and bad doctors should not be allowed to influence the rates for all. If the states will enact real measures that will require the doctors and hospitals to police themselves, and will punish those who attempt to hide their mistakes, the people will be protected from bad doctors who repeatedly err and negatively influence the price of insurance for the good doctors.

If the states will put the medical malpractice insurance companies to the task of justifying the reason for increases in their rates, like all other insurance companies, then there would be a real awakening as to the real reasons why doctors are crying for a reduction in those rates. If the federal government would stop protecting the insurance companies from the freedom from regulation under the antitrust laws, then the insurance companies could compete in the same market that all other businesses compete in–the free capitalistic economic system, rather than an unregulated monopoly.

Money, Politics and the Good old boy network

Pat Robertson claimed, on May 1, 2005, on national television that the judges in the federal judiciary were more dangerous than "a few bearded terrorists" who fly planes into buildings. No one in this country could figure out why he said that, but he is expressing a view about the members of the federal bench that is held by many. What Pat Robertson has not explored is the Federalist Papers, the compilation of pamphlets written by James Madison, Alexander Hamilton, and John Jay, three of the country's most stellar Constitutional scholars of their day. These writings taught our ancestors, in part, that democracy works best when the judicial system is allowed to do its job. People such as Pat Robertson who now take out their hate on lawyers and the courts, criticizing the very people and institutions who are there to preserve a system to protect our liberties and lives, will ultimately need the help of the courts and lawyers.

The corporations have been successful in bringing about the perception that we need to do away with trial lawyers, and do away with courts and do away with juries. They have done that so that they can overwhelm the public's ability to take care of itself and leave the corporations unchecked in their ability to create wealth at the expense of the public.

The problem is not that courts, trial lawyers and juries hurt the average person. The problem is that corporate lawyers, some judges who find it difficult to stand up to the corporate lawyers, and the insurance companies who love to use both of them, have pummeled the average little guy down to being a second-class citizen. The only thing we have left that can stand toe-to-toe with the big guys is a group of twelve good and true, listening to proven facts that can not be squelched by abusive behavior, and making decisions that can not be influenced by the need for re-election, by campaign funds, or by a fancy meal, trip or country club.

Judges should not be elected officials. They should not be required to ask for money for their re-election campaigns from the people that appear before them for adjudication of disputes. The jurors who serve in courtrooms around the country should be entitled to base their decisions on facts that have just as great an opportunity to be brought to the light of day by either side of the case. Why should one side of a suit be able to harass witnesses, change documents, or fabricate testimony, all without retribution or consequences. Expert witnesses should be required to base their conclusions upon factual matters that are equally available to both sides and upon scientific bases that have been tested and seen the light of day.

We have special Social Security judges, special family law judges, special criminal judges, special bankruptcy judges, special juvenile judges. Why couldn't we have special medical malpractice judges, with sufficient expertise to make the tough and close decisions on scientific matters? Wouldn't this give both sides the confidence necessary to engender trust in the system? Why not have some consistent, universally-applied rules about screening suits for merit at an early stage of the litigation, preceded by required thorough and complete disclosure of information necessary to perform such screening? Wouldn't this work better than the game-playing of hiding the ball, squelching the facts, sometimes even trying to change the facts, and trying to manipulate witnesses into saying what one lawyer wants them to say?

In Texas, there has been some support for a change in the judicial election system. In a December 23, 2002 article, Bruce Davidson of the San Antonio Express News, reported that the legislature might soon consider revising the process under which all judges in the state are elected. The ultimate goal would be to sever relationship between special interest contribution and judgeship. This type of reform receives support from the American Bar Association, which advocates merit selection and public finance. No matter how sincere, honest and full of integrity a trial judge may be, it is difficult for anyone to not think about the next election, when those elections have become more and more expensive as each election cycle comes and goes. None of these judges wishes to have to solicit campaign contributions. They all deem it unprofessional, but they have no choice.

An independent, knowledgeable, courageous, impeccable judiciary, armed with adequate procedural methods with teeth, will go a long way toward helping the justice system.

438

Legislative oversight of insurance pricing policies, state medical licensing boards with power and willingness to deter negligent conduct, and hospitals and insurers with a desire to keep bad doctors away from innocent patients will go a long way toward reducing error and insurance premiums. Putting all of these together, while preserving the right to a fair, impartial and full presentation of pertinent facts to a jury, will give everyone more confidence in the results of our medico-legal adjudications.

Last, but not least, why shouldn't we consider a system of truthfulness, like the experiment the Kentucky Veterans Hospital, chronicled in the Annals of Internal Medicine? When there was an experiment of fessing up to errors, trying to be fair with payments, and sharing information needed to get to the truth, the process saved everyone money and everyone was well-served. Truthfulness–now there's a thought!!

We need to get the word out that our democracy was put together for a reason. We need to let people know what is behind the claims of all sides and what is the reason for the falsities that we hear. There is nothing wrong with the jury system. Most things are right with the jury system. There is no reason why the courts can not be able to serve the function that they have always been called upon to serve. What it takes is a public willing to put in their service, and lawyers who are dedicated to making it work.

A government that runs with the influence of

large monied interests will always work for the benefit of the large monied interests. But the government is to be run not just for their benefit, but the benefit of all of us. Yes–the corporations are "people" under the law, too. And in fact if corporations are happy, many people are employed and many people will be helped. But the fact of the matter is that the influence of the large corporate interests may increase to the point that people allow them to surreptitiously and systematically fritter away our personal rights, which are the cornerstone of this democracy.

The *Constitution* was created by people, all of whom thought that the right to a trial by jury was at least as important as the freedom of speech and freedom of religion. Nothing should be able to detract from the importance of that right, and nothing should be important enough to take it away or lessen its influence.

<u>Black robes do not despots make.</u>

The judicial branch takes the brunt of criticism, as we hear the terms "liberal judges," and words from Tom Delay about how the judges in the Schaivo case "will pay," and other pejoratives such as these. There are two issues that are brought up by such sentiments. First, are the judges wrongly usurping the will of the someone in this country? Second, if so, whose will are they usurping?

Different states have different ways

of choosing people for judicial posts. Unfortunately for the lawyer-haters, almost all judicial posts require the appointee to be a lawyer, with minor exceptions in courts with very limited jurisdiction and power. In the federal court system, which decides cases on only two types of cases (cases of at least $75,000 in controversy between residents of different states; and cases involving federal law or regulation), all of the judges are appointed for life. These courts do not often get involved in cases between patients and health care providers, since the federal courts rarely have jurisdiction of these cases. Unlike federal judges, the vast majority of state systems provide for the selection or retention of judges through some form of popular election. "Eight states select judges through partisan elections. Thirteen do so through nonpartisan elections. Of the remaining twenty-nine states, initial appointments are made by the governor or legislature in six states, and by some form of merit selection commission in twenty-three states, but in seventeen of those twenty-nine, the judges stand for reelection or retention election. In total, then, state judges are subject to election, reelection or retention election in thirty-eight states."An Independent Judiciary; Report of the ABA [American Bar Association]Commission on Separation of Powers and Judicial Independence. (1997).

In an effort to gather more information concerning state judicial independence, the Commission circulated a list of six questions to state and local bar presidents and executive directors in all states and territories. A total of 245 bar leaders were contacted. Ninety three responded and supplied the following information:

> Over two-thirds of those responding perceived a major or a minor threat to decision-making independence in their state; Those who perceived such a threat thought that four factors, in descending order of importance, contributed to that threat: 1) judicial confidence is being eroded by excessive criticism of judges; 2) judicial reelection is too politicized; 3) judicial selection is too politicized; and 4) judges are too dependent on campaign contributions. Almost two-thirds perceived a major or a minor threat to institutional independence in their state. For those perceiving such a threat, the primary contributing factor was that the judiciary has insufficient control over the size of its budget. A majority of those responding to our inquiry believed that judges were sufficiently accountable in their state, although a significant minority thought the judiciary was not accountable enough. The two most important factors contributing to the assessment of those who thought the judiciary was insufficiently accountable were 1) the available means of judicial discipline are ineffective; and 2) there is no effective means to hold judges accountable for decision-making delay.

The respondents in this study are NOT all trial lawyers. These are the leaders of the local bar associations, coming from the ranks of all lawyers. One would have to ask, if the means of judicial discipline are ineffective, and if judicial election is too politicized, then who has the power in the judicial election process? Could it possibly be those that put the money into the judicial elections? Consider the case of Justice Priscilla Owen, now a federal judge who was one of President Bush's controversial nominees to the federal judiciary, and formerly a Texas judge (where all judges are elected in partisan elections) for over ten years. When she first decided to run for the Texas Supreme Court, the highest court in Texas, Carl Rove, then living in Texas and helping Governor Bush determine who he should support as new judges, helped raise more than $926,000 for her campaign, almost half from lawyers and others who had business before the court, according to Texans for Public Justice, a group in Austin that tracks Texas campaign donations. Mr. Rove's firm was paid some $247,000 in fees to assist her. Her experience up to then largely involved obscure legal cases involving pipelines and federal energy regulations.

Justice Owen, along with Justice Janice Rogers Brown of the California Supreme Court, at the time that this book is going to print, came to the center of the partisan battle in the Senate over changing the filibuster rules. Senator Bill Frist of Tennessee, the Republican leader, said that the two state justices, whose confirmations had been blocked by Democrats, would be brought to

the Senate floor as part of the fight over changing
the rules. Even on the conservative, all-Republican
bench that the State Supreme Court had become,
Justice Owen occasionally stood out among her
colleagues. Alberto Gonzales (formerly White
House Counsel under Bush and now Attorney
General) was a Texas Supreme Court justice at the
time, and wrote on one occasion of Justice Owen,
that the position she took on an issue was "an
unconscionable act of judicial activism" because it
would create certain requirements in a statute that
he Legislature did not enact.

The case of Justice Owen is not
alone. I am sure that there are many situations
where Judges are, at least in the eyes of one or
another party to any side of an issue, not as
independent as we would like. That is certainly true
in the minds of liberals, conservatives, Republicans,
Democrats, and people on every side of every issue.
We should, therefore, do everything that we can to
take politics out of judicial selection. That is what
the framers of our *Constitution* did when they
provided for life tenure, except by impeachment
pursuant to the terms of the *Constitution*. That is
also what they did when they provided that the
judges of the federal judiciary should not be elected,
but appointed by the President, with the advice and
consent of the Senate. That is the role the other two
branches of the government get to play in the
federal judicial branch. That is how majority will is
implemented, with the limitation that the minority
has a voice, through the Senate selection process.

These men and women who interpret the laws all over this country should then be on their own, unfettered by politics, favoritism, money, or anything other than the law, except for such conduct as requires their removal according to law. Only then can we come close to the ideal.

CHAPTER THIRTEEN

A WORD ABOUT MORAL VALUES

"the most profound loss of all will be to the fairness and equality of our civil justice system, as the effects of cap laws send the message that women, the elderly, and theparents of dead children should not bother to apply."Lucinda M. Finley, "The Hidden Victims of Tort Reform: Women, Children and the Elderly," paper delivered toThrower Symposium, Emory Law School, February 19, 2004.

Moral--those who do the damage should be the ones to pay for that damage. Immoral–secrecy and manipulation prevails over openness and honesty. Who could argue? The conclusion to Dixon's case did not come until the Friday before it was to go to trial on the following Monday. After the two mediation sessions where the defendants offered nothing to settle the case, even knowing that Dixon was going blind as a result of the failure of the defendant to do the tonometer test, no settlement discussions occurred for several months. We set the case for trial, knowing that unless we got the case to the courthouse that we would never get anything for Dixon's suffering and loss. It was not until the week before trial that the defense lawyers called me and invited further settlement discussions. Because of the fact that we had already made demands for settlement, I told the defense lawyers to make an offer. They did, albeit a lowball offer. It was, however, enough impetus to get the ball rolling and to, after several discussions, lead to a settlement of the case. Why did this not happen earlier? At every stage of the case, Dixon's case seemed to be getting better.

The amount of the settlement is confidential, at the request of the defendants. You see, defendants never want anyone to know how much they paid, because it can come back to haunt them later. All I can tell you is that the amount of the settlement was even more than Dixon would have been happy to receive at the beginning of the case. The reason is that the more the case went on the more the defendants lied and the angrier he became. When defendants lie and get caught, the settlement value of the case goes up, because lying makes the jury angry. Often juries make very large awards when they see that the defendant is not being truthful with them. That is the most common reason why you see awards that are very large. So, if they can lie and get away with it, they save money. When they can lie and get caught, they pay more!! Besides the anger, there had been tens of thousands of dollars spent on expert witness fee, and litigation expenses, as a result of the defenses put forth frivolously. It became necessary to receive more in settlement to put an equal amount of money in Dixon's pocket.

After all of the paperwork and the dismissal of the case, I went on with my life and other cases. I heard nothing from anyone connected with the case for three years. One day, three years after the conclusion of Dixon's case, I got a call from one of the insurance companies, and I learned that there was still a case going on. One of the doctor's insurance companies had sued the insurance company for the other doctor, claiming that it should be reimbursed part of what it paid to settle Dixon's case. The call came to me, asking me to testify about how the evidence came about and how that impacted the settlement. So, now that the case had been over for three years, and the insurance companies had to pay more because of their clients lies, they still were litigating over those lies for an additional three years. Yet they say it is the plaintiffs who drive up the costs. Does it figure?

The Blind Intersection

When we speak of politics today we must not overlook the importance of talking in terms of the moral values inherent in any position. We should look at the arguments that are made by those who would like to see certain reforms or certain actions taken by the courts or the legislative bodies. If we look at the moral value of the different positions that may be taken on the issue of the civil justice system pertaining to healthcare delivery, we can see a number of different arguments that have been made and could be made.

In an effort to determine where the moral value scale ends up, we should first take a look at the various positions taken by the two sides of the debate. The first side is the side that wishes either to do away with or substantially limit recoveries in cases against health care providers. The position that they take is allegedly supported by claims about the people that bring such lawsuits as parties, and the lawyers who represent them. First, we have heard that the parties who would bring such lawsuits against healthcare providers are out to take advantage of a "lawsuit lottery" that would give them a windfall that they do not deserve. A look at the statistics on verdicts in health care cases (discussed in chapters two and three) shows differently.

For the sake of argument, if we assume that there are some people who sue their doctors or hospitals only to win a sum of money to which they are not entitled, then we can obviously count that as a moral value deficiency. Then we face the argument of those who malign the trial lawyers, since a trial lawyer is necessary to bring such a case. Therefore, the lawyer who would go along with their plan to extract a sum of money to which the client is not entitled, is one who is lacking a moral value. In order to believe that the system promotes such immorality, we have to also believe that the system allows lawyers to do this and "get away with" their immoral actions. We now know from the true statistics that the system is not inclined that way. So, in support of limiting what juries can award, the reformers claim three things–amoral parties, amoral lawyers and an amoral system. We have seen now that the realities and statistics prove none of those work.

On the other side, we have the people who want to allow juries to continue to decide the cases on their merits, and not put an arbitrary limitation on the amount of damages awarded to the plaintiffs in cases against health care providers. These people do not claim that changes need to be made to stop some immoral actions of another group. No, they only claim that the current system should be kept, allowing the juries to decide issues of fact that a judge submits to them to determine the liability of the parties in the case. I have not heard anyone on the side of the jury system saying that the system needs to change to better compensate the victims, or to further punish the offending doctors or hospitals. The ONLY moral value advanced by the proponents of the jury system is that those who do the damage should be the ones to pay for the damage they have done, according to what a jury of their peers decides. Isn't that morally justifiable? Shouldn't that be the very definition of morality? We can look at anyone's definition of morality, whether it comes from the bible, mythology, or nursery rhymes. "Do unto others;" "An eye for an eye;" "You reap what you sow," or the story of the Little Red Hen. The civil justice system is based on one premise, and one premise alone–that unbiased people gather together under rules known to all, looking at all available untainted evidence, with all sides having equal opportunity to be heard, in order to determine right or wrong, and to duly compensate those who have been harmed by wrongdoing.

The definition of negligent wrongdoing has been the same for centuries under our common law–"failing to act in a way that a reasonably person should act under the same circumstances." Sounds vaguely like "failing to do unto others as you would have them do unto you," doesn't it?

Because of the fact that the advocates of reform have chosen to draw such a bright and definite line in the sand, there is no compromise that will be acceptable to them. They have, for over twenty years, been after the civil justice system, wanting more and more limitations on your rights, and chipping away at the justice system. They have often succeeded in inflicting the public with tunnel vision, slowly eroding the public's field of vision as to the true facts. Since they will not stop until they have removed the jury as the voice of their victims, the only thing that can stop them is your understanding of what is going on.

Unless the public figures out what is happening, there will one day be a huge crash of the justice system, with nothing left but the pieces to be picked up. It is a blind intersection, where no one can see that there will be a horrendous impact around the corner. The street that the reformers are traveling is one they know well, since they built it, brick by brick, from the ground up. The justice system is traveling its road, minding its own business, keeping its eyes out for the people that it is supposed to be protecting. You, the victim, walking quietly along the sidewalk, can not see what is coming around the corner. You won't know it until the impact. That is the way the reformers built the intersection. They have put their tank of destruction on its path, caring not that you will be the one hurt when that impact comes.

What is it that is wrong with that system that has worked for so many centuries for so many people of all stations and walks of life? The biggest wrong is that the system, as it currently operates, allows the insurance companies to keep their profits shrouded in secrecy, while those companies argue that the high cost of settlements and verdicts is running them out of business. Isn't openness and honesty a moral value, or should we reward secrecy and manipulation?

The framers of our *Constitution*, stating their intents and purposes said:

We the people of the United States, in order to form a more perfect Union, establish Justice, insure domestic Tranquility, provide for the common defence [sic],promote the general Welfare, and secure the Blessings of Liberty to ourselves and our posterity, do hereby ordain and establish this Constitution for the United States of America.

One of the provisions that they made to accomplish the purposes was the following:

"In Suits at common law, where the value in controversy shall exceed twenty dollars, the right of trial by jury shall be preserved, and no fact tried by a jury, shall be otherwise reexamined in any Court of the United States, than according to the rules of the common law." Seventh Amendment to the *Unites States Constitution*.

Our courts and legislatures have followed that provision of our *Constitution* for 215 years. There is not one solitary legitimate or factually supportable reason why we should not continue to follow that rule. There is a reason why the *Constitution* is supreme. It was expressed by the authors of the *Federalist Papers*, as they communicated with the country. We have a supreme law of the land. Our legal scholars from 1800 to the present, Thomas Jefferson, Justice John Marshall, Abraham Lincoln, Justice Louis Brandeis, Leon Jaworski, and Clarence Darrow all recognized the reason for our *Constitution* and the government that it created. Our founders knew what tyranny looked like, as they had seen it firsthand and had escaped its chains. If tyranny is now bound to exist, it is created by the concentration of wealth, power, and influence in a segment of society whose rules are either non-existent or so confused and esoteric that they never see the light of public scrutiny. Are tyranny's chains those forged by people like you and me who learn and study the facts? Or do you see those chains forming in closed boardrooms, secret meetings, political halls, and private societies whose members protect each other, while manipulating the system to preserve their profits? Our democracy has always known the way to unbind the chains. Read the *Constitution*.

454

For a complete subject and word index, please visit www.AmericasTunnelVision.com, and you will find a link to the index. Due to the size of the book and printing constraints, and the fact that many people do not care for an index, we decided to make the index separate.

We appreciate your purchasing *America's Tunnel Vision.* We have forthcoming titles:

America's Tunnel Morality: Law and Morals in a Changing Society. Why do our politicians and government officials believe that they have the capacity to know our moral values? How is it that some politicians, who claim to run on "family values ," believe that they have the corner on that market? Aren't the values of human dignity, freedom, spirit and liberty equally as important as protecting corporate welfare?

America's Tunnel Mind: Expanding Your View of Political Values. A book about the way that we can enable all of our citizens to understand the importance of living in a society where everyone's rights are preserved by the government, rather than being jeapordized by the government. That ideal that our forefathers envisioned, talked about, wrote about, and tried to embody in the *Constitution,* is now endangered by the monied and, in many cases, corrupt political system that runs our country.

For Corporate, Group or Association discounts, please contact:

Editor@HoratioPress.com or
Horatio Press
New York, New York
646-290-6258

One in three women will die from heart disease, but only one in five will be timely diagnosed by her doctor...

Insurance companies are not regulated by the federal government, but you are regulated by the federal government in everything you do......

Health care costs have gone up in states where caps have been placed on jury awards.....

as many as 98,000 people in this country die each year from hospital error. Hospital error kills more people than any form of cancer except lung cancer. Insurance plays a vital role in compensating those who lose life or limb.

Note to the reader from the author:

I hope you can see, after reading this book, that it is not about doctor-bashing. It is about how doctors are human beings, like all of us, and are subject to error. When they are hurried, pressured by the constraints of time, and pressured by insurance companies to see too many patients, the care of the patient will suffer.

Like all groups of human beings, the group of doctors contains some bad apples, just like the group of lawyers contains some bad apples. We can not let the bad apples in either group spoil the system for those who are hurt by it. The answer comes only from knowing the facts, giving each person his or her own dignity and worth, and requiring those at fault to answer for their failures. I hope this book is a step in that direction.

Michael Townes Watson

458

HP

Horatio Press

95 Horatio St. #209;
New York, N.Y. 10014
Phone 646.290.6258
www.HoratioPress.com
www.AmericasTunnelVision.com

America's Tunnel Vision–How Insurance Companies' Propaganda Is Corrupting Medicine and Law, may be purchased for associations, consumer groups, or other groups at a discount of 30% off the retail price in quantities of twenty or more. For ordering information---

1. Please contact:

editor@HoratioPress.com   or

2. Go to:

www.AmericasTunnelVision.com, and click on the "order" link, where you can obtain the group discount

460

Horatio Press has devoted itself to an honest discussion of how we as a nation stay true to the principles of liberty, justice, equality and dignity for every citizen.

If you are an author or contributor to such a discussion, we are interested in hearing from you, and welcome your input. Please go to the website, www.AmericasTunnelVision.com, and fill out the contact form, or visit our weblog link at that site.